Teenage Parenthood: What's the Problem?

the Tufnell Press,

London,
United Kingdom

www.tufnellpress.co.uk

email contact@tufnellpress.co.uk

British Library Cataloguing-in-Publication Data
A catalogue record for this book is
available from the British Library

| paperback ISBN | 1872767087 |
| ISBN-13 | 978-1-872767-08-6 |

Printed in England and U.S.A. by Lightning Source

Teenage Parenthood:
What's the Problem?

edited by
Simon Duncan, Rosalind Edwards and Claire Alexander

iv

Contents

Chapter 1

What's the problem with teenage parents?

Simon Duncan, Claire Alexander, Rosalind Edwards

1. Introduction: demonising teenage parenthood

On 13th February 2009, the front page of *the Sun* newspaper carried the headline, 'Dad at 13'.[1] Alongside a full-page photograph of 'Baby-faced father' Alfie Patten, with his new born daughter, Maisie, the story told of the baby's birth to Alfie, aged thirteen, and Chantelle, aged fifteen, 'after just one night of unprotected sex'. The paper quoted Chantelle: 'We know we made a mistake but I wouldn't change it now. We will be good loving parents ... I'll be a great mum and Alfie will be a great dad'. Sun columnist Jane Moore was more sceptical, dismissing their aspirations as 'heartbreakingly naïve', blaming both the failure of sex education in schools and the declining moral values of society—'the thin end of a wedge that will break the existing cracks in society so wide open that there'll be no hope of repair'. Over the following weekend, a storm of moral condemnation and outrage grew throughout the print and TV media and from politicians across the political spectrum. In the press, the focus—and the blame—settled squarely on the 'underclass' family background of the young parents, with the *Daily Express* commenting:

> You only have to take a look at their parents to see where it all went wrong. Imagine everyone's surprise that Chantelle's parents live on benefits and, despite her dad being jobless, have six children. Alfie, meanwhile, is the son of a single mother and a father who's fathered no fewer than nine children ... a world of broken homes and benefits, where irresponsibility and fecklessness reign supreme.   (*Daily Express* 15th February 2009)

The Sunday Times similarly saw the event as a symbol of a Britain in moral decline and symptomatic of the growth of an underclass living parasitically on

---

1. After a DNA test Alfie was later found not to be the father, which reportedly left him 'extremely distressed' (the Times Online. May 19 2009).

the welfare system—something, they argued that the country could ill-afford in a time of recession:

> Britain is doing low-life better than almost all other developed countries. A growing segment, which Charles Murray ... called the underclass, is devoid of the values and morality of a civilised society which foolishly provides the financial incentives to behave badly ... As each generation moves further away from family stability, we lumber ourselves with the enormous cost of propping up failed families and living with the social consequences. It is a grim prospect, especially as the country moves into deeper recession.   (*The Sunday Times*, 15th February 2009)[2]

Responses to the news from politicians, left or right, followed this agenda. Labour's children's secretary, Ed Balls, was quoted as saying 'It's not right—it looks so terrible ... I want us to do everything we can as a society to make sure we keep teenage pregnancies down' (*The Sunday Times*, 15th February 2009). The Conservative Party went further in making teenage parents a symbol for wider breakdown. For example former party leader Iain Duncan Smith, responsible for the Party's report on *Family Breakdown* (Social Justice Policy Group, 2007) argued that 'The case exemplifies the breakdown in British society. The problem of family breakdown has sadly become deeply intergenerational'. Teenage parents, he went on, were linked to other social 'problems' such as youth crime and drug addiction, criticising 'ineffective remedial policies, whether they take the form of more prisons, drug rehabilitation or supporting longer and more costly lifetimes on benefits' (*The Sunday Times*, 15th February 2009). David Laws, the Liberal Democrat spokesperson for children, schools and families, resisted these broader societal implications but pointed to the social marginalisation and individual pathologisation of young parents, claiming 'It's clearly not the case that all of Britain is broken ... (but) ... Because of their poor backgrounds we have a significant segment brought up in chaotic and unloving situations. Unsurprisingly, they often become chaotic and unloving themselves' (ibid).

This is hardly a new story. Periodically tabloid frenzies erupt when atypical cases of young mothers or fathers are seized upon and luridly sensationalised (Selman 2003). For example in May 2005 a furore erupted over three teenage pregnancies in one Derby family (Bunting 2005). This can directly influence

---

2.   The article even went so far as to compare Alfie and Chantelle to Karen Matthews, who in 2009 drugged and imprisoned her daughter to get money from the public and the media

policy, thus media reports in September 1999 of a fourteen-year-old boy who got his twelve-year-old girlfriend pregnant (Freely, 1999) stimulated the Child Support Agency to 'vigorously' pursue young fathers, so as to make them recognise their responsibilities through financial payments (SEU, 1999, 11.2). All this lends credence to extreme 'solutions', like Fay Weldon's idea (apparently following government propositions) that all girls at twelve should be implanted with long term contraception, and so 'effectively sterilising girls for a long period of time' (Daily Mail 15.2.08). Journalists do try to put a different view on occasions—thus in the *Guardian* articles quoted above Madeleine Bunting claims that it is not babies, but social disadvantage, that 'ruins young mothers' lives', and Maureen Freely asks just why we should assume that a fourteen-year-old boy cannot be a good father. Nonetheless, the majority—according to a 2008 Ipsos MORI poll—believe that the country is in the grip of a socially catastrophic 'teen pregnancy epidemic'.

The reaction to the story of Alfie and Chantelle, like these earlier stories, points to a broader set of discourses around teenage parenting that consistently mark out the media and political responses to this issue. First, there is the taking of what are extreme and untypical cases as representative, and as a lens through which the broader social issue of teenage parenting might be understood. Second, there is the construction of teenage mothering as a uniformly negative experience for the mothers themselves, their children and for society as a whole. Third, there is the linking of teenage parenting with moral and cultural breakdown, placing children, parents and extended families beyond the pale of 'civilised society' (*The Sunday Times*, 15th February 2009). In this way teenage parents are positioned in some assumed 'underclass' where teenage mothers are commonly portrayed as ignorant and irresponsible, or even immoral, and young fathers are pictured as feckless. Both may be criminal. In this way the public discourse about teenage parenting has become conflated with a wider social threat discourse about the decline of marriage, single parenting, and teenage sexuality. Finally, there is the conflation of social problems with economic costs, most particularly around the supposed 'benefits culture' that 'encourages' young women to get pregnant at the expense of the rest of society. Tony Kerridge, of Marie Stopes International, was thus quoted:

> We have got the social aspect of young girls in the UK seeing having a baby as a route to getting their own place. These sorts of lifestyle choices can be dealt with on an educational level if teenage girls realise what

they are contemplating is a route into social deprivation and being in the benefits culture for the rest of their lives.

(*The Guardian* 14th February 2009)

Indeed, the idea of 'cost'—moral, social and economic—appears to stand at the heart of the issue of teenage parenting, and points to the prevailing concern, in the media, politics and policy, with an overwhelmingly individualistic and economistic model of the good mother/father, the good family, and the good citizen. In this view the ability to work, to earn and to pay are assumed as the primary prerequisites of social participation and recognition. Caring for others in families and communities is downplayed and under-valued. What seems axiomatic in this discourse is that teenage parents are necessarily and incontrovertibly *bad people, bad parents* and *bad citizens*, condemned to a lifetime of poverty, social handouts and economic apathy, and destined to repeat these failures across the generations. In this way the issue of teenage parenting, as presented publicly, combines a potent fusion of moral and economic crisis, of cultural and social dysfunction, wrapped in the virtuous certainties of impending disaster.

There is a severe problem with this 'public', axiomatic, view of teenage parenting, however—the evidence does not support it. As the chapters in this book show, there is little evidence that lack of knowledge 'causes' pregnancy, or that increased knowledge prevents it. Teenage birth rates are much lower than in the 1960s and 1970s, and overall are continuing to decline, while few teenage mothers are under sixteen. Age at which pregnancy occurs seems to have little effect on future social outcomes (like employment and income in later life), or on current levels of disadvantage for either parents or their children. Many young mothers and fathers themselves express positive attitudes to parenthood, and mothers usually describe how motherhood makes them feel stronger, more competent, more connected, and more responsible. Many fathers seek to remain connected to their children, and provide for their new family. For many young mothers and fathers parenting seems to provide the impetus to change direction, or build on existing resources, so as to take up education, training and employment. Teenage parenting may be more of an opportunity than a catastrophe.

It is the task of this book to present a range of research evidence about the real nature and experience of teenage parenting in Britain. Fulfilling this aim throws up another problem—for, like all axioms, the public myths around teenage parenting have proved strongly resistant to any evidence to the contrary.

This presents us with a follow-up question—why is there such an invested need in presenting an unremittingly negative image of young parents, and what does this say about the values placed on family and the role of paid work in twenty-first century Britain? How—and why—have policy makers and news makers got the story about teenage parents so wrong?

2. New Labour and teenage parenting: an economic or moral agenda?

2010 marks the year by which New Labour pledged to halve the number of pregnancies for under-eighteen year-olds in the UK. The government's ten year Teenage Pregnancy Strategy was launched in 1999 in a report from the Social Exclusion Unit (SEU), then at the heart of government in Cabinet Office and itself resulting from a putative 'underclass unit' set up by Peter Mandelson, then Minister without Portfolio, in 1997. The report, which has set the framework for government policy since then, saw teenage pregnancy as a major social and economic problem, where Britain did much worse than other west European countries (SEU 1999). Or as Tony Blair, then Prime Minister, put it, in his forward to the Social Exclusion Unit report:

> Some of these teenagers, and some of their children, live happy and fulfilled lives. But far too many do not. Teenage mothers are less likely to finish their education, less likely to find a good job, and more likely to end up both as single parents and bringing up their children in poverty. The children themselves run a much greater risk of poor health, and have a much higher chance of becoming teenage mothers themselves. Our failure to tackle this problem has cost the teenagers, their children and the country dear. (SEU, 1999, 4)

The SEU report identified the causes of this problem as low expectations and ignorance among teenagers, and mixed messages from the media. While the SEU report made clear a strong relationship between teenage pregnancy and social disadvantage, this association was downplayed either as cause or remedy, rather young parenting was seen to strongly reinforce disadvantage. And the way out was through a dual goal of prevention and direction—to reduce the number of under-eighteen pregnancies by half, and increase the number of teenage parents entering education, training or employment to sixty per cent (ibid).

The heady political symbolism and mobilisation created by the media's moral panic reinforced the need for government to be seen to tackle what was already identified as a problem for 'teenagers, their children and the country'. All this was underlined by contrasting national teenage birth rates or, as Tony Blair put it in his foreward to the SEU's 1999 document, Britain's 'shameful record' (p. 4). British rates remained among the highest in the 28 OECD developed countries (30 per 1000 in 1998, compared to 10 or less in Germany, France, Scandinavia and the Netherlands). Only the USA at 52.1, and more marginally Canada and New Zealand, had higher rates (UNICEF, 2003). This comparative failure has an important policy impact, as suggested by the highlighting of international comparisons in most government and policy reports. For while the UK seemed to be 'stuck', as the SEU put it (1999, 7), the experience of western Europe implied that teenage pregnancy and parenting, perceived as a difficult social problem, was nonetheless amenable to policy solution. Underlying this comparison is an issue around economic, as well as social, competition—how can Britain compete with an inadequate workforce, where teenage pregnancy supposedly restricts educational achievement and employment participation.

This international comparative lesson was emphasised by the appreciation that local rates also vary widely across Britain; it is not just young women who are poorer that are more likely to become pregnant, and least likely to use abortion to resolve pregnancy—they also live in poorer areas. In contrast, some richer areas in Britain have teenage abortion and pregnancy rates more like supposed European exemplars such as The Netherlands (SEU 1999, Lee et al. 2004). The 'problem' of teenage pregnancy was ripe for intervention by a reforming new government.

Hence the New Labour government rolled out its teenage pregnancy strategy from 1999 onwards, originally under the direction of a Ministerial Task Force, and co-ordinated by the Teenage Pregnancy Unit (TPU). Starting in 2001, each top tier local authority had an agreed teenage pregnancy strategy to reach local 2010 targets around the desired national average. Each local strategy was led by a Teenage Pregnancy Coordinator, working with a Teenage Pregnancy Partnership Board, and supported by a Local Implementation Grant. These local Strategies were supported and performance managed by a Regional Teenage Pregnancy Coordinator, based in the regional government office. Local indicators, such as levels of conceptions in targeted age groups, availability and use of services, and health outcomes, were devised to help monitor progress towards achieving these targets (see TPU 2000). In line with government objectives for 'joined-up' approaches to service and policy development, work locally was intended to proceed in conjunction with other national government initiatives such as Sure Start, Sure Start Plus and the Children's Fund, and other national government departments were expected actively to support the strategy. In this way the TPU would hopefully reach the two main targets, as set by the Social Exclusion Unit—to halve the under-eighteen teenage conception rate by 2010 and to substantially increase the participation of teenage parents in education, training or employment

This is an impressive machinery. But the 'low expectations' explanation—which points towards tackling social disadvantage—seems to have been neglected. Rather, policy in practice focused on the 'ignorance' explanation (Arai 2003 a, b)—British youth were seen as deficient in their sexual health knowledge, poor users of contraception, shy about sex, and wary about accessing services. Perhaps this focus was the more appealing when current policy thinking tends to stress individual behaviour and motivations, rather than structural influences on behaviour, like social disadvantage. Certainly on a relatively low budget (the initial TPU budget was only £60 million) it might have been here that the policy implementers hoped for 'quick wins', when taking on social disadvantage would cost a lot more and take a lot longer. Policy then ended up pathologising teenage pregnancy and childrearing, when it was seen to arise from 'inappropriate motivations, ignorance and sexual embarrassment' (Arai 2003a, 203), rather than supporting the positive features of parenting.

How has this approach endured the experience of implementation? The Department for Communities, Schools and Families report *Teenage Parents: the next steps* (2007) was to give new guidance to local authorities and primary care trusts given the previous eight years experience. The report recognises failures in reaching the desired targets—the reduction rate in teenage births was only 11.8% over the period, rather than approaching the desired 50% by 2010; similarly only about 30% of teenage mothers were in employment, education and training (EET), rather than 60%. Hence the need for a 'refreshed strategy' as the report's introduction puts it (p. 6). There was also a whole battery of research produced since the SEU's original 1999 report, which as a whole pointed to a substantial gap between policy and experience, indicating both that the outcomes for teenage parents were not as dire as assumed and that young parenting encapsulated many positive features as well as problems. This includes research reviewed, or directly commissioned, by the TPU itself (TPU 2004, Teenage Pregnancy Evaluation Team 2005). But despite recognition of 'What teenage mothers and young fathers say' in the new 2007 report (in its chapter four), the existing two-track approach remained. Teenage parenting was as a problem in and of itself and should be cut, and the further need was to integrate remaining young parents into a productive workforce. 'Refreshed' was more about changing the implementation channels from specialised services into mainstream midwifery and health visiting services, Children's Centres, and Youth Support Services.

The report bases the essential continuation of the two-track approach on its enumeration of the disadvantaged characteristics of teenage mothers, and the poor outcomes they—and their children—experience, using a whole range of social and economic indicators (in chapters two and three). There are a number of key features that can be identified in this policy portrait of teenage parenthood, and that echo the media and political representations discussed above. First there is the clear gendering of this discourse, with the focus being primarily on young mothers, while young fathers play a very secondary role. This links into an assumed conflation between young motherhood (where many will live with partners or grandparents, and others will have 'live apart together' relationships') and single motherhood. Second, there is the insistence on the negative consequences of teenage pregnancy on both the mother and child, in which health, emotional and economic 'wellbeing' are taken as the key problem areas (and largely seen as interchangeable). Third, there is the emphasis on prevention of pregnancy rather than support for teenage parents—and in the 2007 report, rather chilling, concern to prevent further pregnancies for young mothers (for some young mothers, especially those with partners, would like to reach a desired family size). Fourth, is the conflation of socio-economic deprivation with teenage pregnancy, the implication being that teenage pregnancy is a cause of poverty. The report asserts that these poor outcomes are partially independent of wider factors of social deprivation and rather points to 'the lifestyles and behaviour of teenage mothers' (p. 13) as contributory factors. Fifth there is the 'classing' of the issue, with teenage pregnancy linked to specific socio-economic groupings, and their associated problems, in particular the low levels of labour market participation. Sixth, there is the insistence on education, training and paid employment as the sole legitimate pathway to social inclusion and to ameliorating the negative effects of young parenthood.

Hence Beverley Hughes, then Minister for Children, Young People and Families, wrote in her forward to the 2007 report that:

Children born to teenage mothers are more likely to live in deprived areas, do less well at school, and disengage from learning early—all of which are risk factors for teenage pregnancy and other poor outcomes.

(DCSF 2007: 3)

Equally, one could write that teenage mothers commonly show resilience and motivation, and become more socially connected and purposeful, where pregnancy usually marks a turning point for the better, become more likely to take up education and employment, and do no worse—and often better—than their social peers once pre-existing disadvantage is allowed for. This contrast is the terrain of this book.

3. The myth of the teenage pregnancy epidemic

The perceived social threat from teenage parenting is buttressed by a negative public consensus around teenage conception and pregnancy itself. This consensus assumes that teenage pregnancy is increasing rapidly, that this increase is particularly marked among younger teenagers, that all teenage pregnancies are unplanned, that all these unplanned conceptions are unwanted, and that new teenage mothers are inevitably also single mothers without stable relationships with partners. All these assumptions are unfounded, but all serve to bolster the negative evaluation of subsequent teenage parenting, and hence the nature of the policy response.

Newspaper headlines frequently announce 'soaring' teenage birth rates, creating an 'epidemic' of births to teenagers. Indeed as many as 81% of respondents to a 2008 Ipsos MORI poll thought that teenage pregnancy was increasing, while about a quarter of the 16-24 age group thought that 40% of 15-17 year-old girls became parents each year. In fact there have been substantial declines in both birth rates and absolute numbers of births to teenagers since the 1960s and early 1970s (see Table 1). By 2007 only 11.4% of conceptions were to women aged under 20, with an even smaller share of births—6.4%. In addition few teenage mothers are under 16, only around 6% in 2006, accounting for just 0.9% of all births in Britain by 2007, while around 80% of teenage mothers were 18 or 19 years-old. Overall, teenage birth rates are now at around the same level as in the 1950s, that supposed 'golden age' of family.

Table 1 Live births and birth rates for women under 20, 1951-2008

	Numbers of live births	*Birth Rate per 1000 women aged 15-19*
1951	29,111	21.3
1956	37,938	27.3
1961	59,786	37.3
1966	66,746	47.9
1971	82,641	50.6
1976	54,500	29.8
1981	60,800	30.9
1986	57,406	30.1
1991	52,396	33.1
1996	44,667	30.0
2001	44,189	28.0
2004	45,028	26.9
2005	44,830	26.3
2006	45,509	26.6
2007	44,805	26.0
2008	44,683	see note

Sources: ONS Birth Statistics, Health Statistics Quarterly
Note, 2008 birth rate not available at time of press

What *is* different is that in the 1950s and 1960s the majority of teenage parents married—although many seem to have been hastily enforced 'shotgun marriages', notorious for high rates of dysfunctionality and breakdown (Coombes and Zumeta 1970, Thornes and Collard 1979). In addition probably around 20% of the children were adopted shortly after birth. In contrast, by the 2001 census only 9% of teenage parents were married; although around 30% cohabited; in addition around another quarter jointly registered the birth with the father at another address—which suggests some continuing parental relationship on the 'living apart together' (or LAT) model (Selman 1996, 2003). There are now very few adoptions of teenage mothers' children. These trends away from marriage, and towards unmarried cohabitation and 'living apart together' reflect those for the population as a whole, especially among younger age groups (Barlow et al. 2005, Haskey, 2005). Thus in 2006, around 0.5% of all 18-24 year-olds in Britain were married, with 12% cohabiting, while as many as 35% were in 'living apart together' partner relationships (Duncan and Phillips 2010).

Whatever the level of teenage pregnancy, it is assumed in the public and media discourse that all teenage pregnancies are unplanned, that all unplanned conceptions are unwanted, and that most result from ignorance if not wilful immorality. Certainly the Social Exclusion Unit's framework 1999 report identified 'ignorance'—the 'lack of accurate knowledge about contraception, STIs (sexually transmitted infections), what to expect in relationships and what it means to be a parent' as major cause of teenage pregnancy (SEU, 1999: 7). This is repeated in succeeding policy and guidance documents (see Pam Alldred and Miriam David in chapter two). But there is little support for the assumption that teenage parents are particularly ignorant about sex, contraception and parenting, that low levels of knowledge 'cause' teenage pregnancy, or that increased knowledge reduces pregnancy (Arai, 2003a, b, Graham and McDermott 2005). It is hard to find young mothers who become pregnant due to ignorance about sex and contraception (Phoenix, 1991, Wellings and Kane 1999, Churchill et al. 2000). Similarly, a meta-analysis of preventative strategies focusing on sex education, and improved access to advice and contraceptive services, concluded that this did not reduce unintended pregnancies among young women aged between 11-18 (DiCenso et al. 2002).

Indeed a significant minority of teenage mothers, and fathers, positively plan for pregnancy. Some are hoping for birthing success after an earlier miscarriage, others in this group, especially those with partners, plan for subsequent children so as to complete their desired family size and hence 'build' a family (TPS Evaluation Team 2005). Many other teenage parents are 'positively ambivalent' towards childbirth—that is they do not actually plan it, but would quite like a baby and do not use contraception for that reason (Cater and Coleman 2006). For most teenage parents pregnancy may well be 'unplanned', but then so are many, if not most, pregnancies for all women—the very idea of 'planning pregnancy' is something of a grey area to say the least (Fischer et al. 1999, Barrett and Wellings 2002). Few teenage mothers, it seems, regret early childbirth, as many of the succeeding chapters show. As with other women 'unplanned' pregnancy does not necessarily mean 'unwanted' pregnancy for teenage parents. Or as Germaine Greer put it: 'We have 39,000 unwanted pregnancies a year unwanted by the Government that is. No one is speaking for the mums' (The Times, 11. 3. 08).

This set of policy and public assumptions is the starting point for Pam Alldred and Miriam David (chapter two) in their examination on the role and importance of education in young mothers' lives, and on their gendered expectations regarding parenthood. For their research shows how the values and priorities expressed by young mothers do not fit comfortably within the model presented in the Teenage Pregnancy Strategy (TPS), nor with many of the values assumed in, or explicitly asserted by, the TPS. In particular, the chapter questions the assumptions that early mothering is undesirable or aberrant; that education or training in the child's early years is desirable or even accessible to young mothers; and that either 'parenting' or 'studying' can be assumed to be gender-neutral activities. The logic the authors find at work in the young women's lives in their study seems to reflect the dominant values in their community and this logic questions the link between teenage pregnancy and social exclusion asserted in government policy. Similarly, in chapter three Jan Macvarish and Jenny Billings discuss how the teenage mothers in their study, living in Kent, made moral and thoughtful decisions about contraception, proceeding with their pregnancy, and engagement with health and welfare services. Rather than suffering 'broken' family circumstances, teenage parents were often embedded in networks of support, and were optimistic that parenthood would shift them onto a positive life trajectory.

4. Statistical outcomes—social disadvantage versus teenage mothering

The influential UNICEF report Teenage Births in Rich Nations claims that:

> giving birth as a teenager is believed to be bad for the young mother because the statistics suggest that she is much more likely to drop out of school, to have low or no qualifications, to be unemployed or low paid, to grow up without a father, to become a victim of neglect and abuse, to do less well at school, to become involved in crime, use drugs and alcohol.
>
> (UNICEF 2003, 3)

But in fact the statistics show nothing of the sort—if we deal with the errors committed by statements like these. For the statement does not compare like with like in reaching its 'much more likely' attribution of statistical causation; ascribing causal effects to teenage motherhood is pretty meaningless if we compare teenage mothers with all mothers, rather than those of a similar background. Rather, if we wish to measure the statistical effect of teenage motherhood (and then go on to ascribe a social effect, which is not necessarily the same thing) we need to control for variation in other variables, so that we do compare like with like. In more formal terms, statistical analysis needs to control for 'selection effects'. This is a variant of the correlation problem so beloved in statistical textbooks. Variable X may be highly correlated with 'dependent' variable Y, but this does not mean that X causes Y; rather both may be caused by an unacknowledged variable A. In this case becoming a young mother may not cause the poor outcomes—in terms of education, employment and income—experienced by many teenage mothers; rather both young motherhood, and poor outcomes, may be caused by pre-pregnancy social disadvantage. In this sense social disadvantage may 'select' particular young women, and men, to become teenage parents, and this disadvantage will continue post pregnancy. Teenage parenting may therefore be a part of social disadvantage, rather than its cause. But if statistical studies do not control for these selection effects, then they will not be able to recognise this.

In fact there has been a tradition of statistical studies which do try to take account of these selection effects. Some researchers devised 'natural experiments' where selection effects would be better controlled, such as comparisons between cousins whose mothers were sisters, between sisters, or between twin sisters (only one of whom was a teenage mother), and between teenage mothers and other women who had conceived as a teenager but miscarried (who presumably would have gone on to become mothers). This type of research began in the USA, and found that the social outcome effects of mother's age at birth were very small, or as Saul Hoffman (1998, 237) put it in his systematic review of the US research 'often essentially zero'. Indeed, by their mid/late twenties teenage mothers in the USA did better than miscarrying teenagers with regard to employment and income and this meant, ironically, that government spending would have increased if they had not become young mothers (Geronimus, 1997).

The UK based studies available at the time the 1999 SEU report was produced did not take this 'natural experiment' approach to controlling selection effects, and instead relied on more general statistical controls of social background, like educational level, socio-economic status, housing type and so on (for example Babb, 1994, Botting et al. 1998, Corcoran, 1998; see Graham and McDermott 2005 for review). Although they also concluded that much of the adverse social conditions linked with teenage parenting were associated with pre-pregnancy social disadvantage, this is perhaps why they nevertheless came to more ambivalent conclusions about the social effect of teenage pregnancy in itself. Since the publication of the SEU report, however, a number of British studies have taken up the 'natural experiment' approach, with the same results as in the USA. John Ermisch and David Pevalin (2003a), using the British Cohort Study to assess differences between miscarrying and successful teenage pregnancies, found that teen birth has little impact upon qualifications, employment or earnings by thirty years of age. While teenage mothers' partners were more likely to be poorly qualified or unemployed, and this then impacted on the mothers', and their children's, standard of living, this is also akin to a selection effect. In itself, age of birth has little effect. A complementary study using British Household Panel data to follow teenage mothers over time came to similar conclusions (Ermisch 2003), as does a study by Denise Hawkes (2003) on twins, where only one became a teenage mother. Finally, Karen Robson and Richard Berthoud (2003) used the Labour Force Survey to assess the link between high rates of poverty and high rates of teenage fertility among minority ethnic groups, particularly for the extreme case of Pakistanis and Bangladeshis where both variables are particularly high. They concluded that teen birth has little effect on future poverty, and does not lead to any further disadvantage beyond that experienced by the ethnic group as a whole.

In chapter four, Denise Hawkes follows this work in providing a wide-ranging statistical review of the life experiences and circumstances of teenage mothers and their children in Britain, compared with other mothers, based on the Millennium Cohort Study. She uses three indicative sets of statistical analyses to examine: (1) life course experience for mothers prior to the birth of the first child, (2) the early life circumstances of children at nine-months, and (3) health, cognitive, and behavioural outcomes for children at ages three and five. The first set of analyses, confirming earlier statistical studies, shows that teenage motherhood is really a symptom of a disadvantaged life course rather than the cause of it. The second set shows that those children with teenage mothers are indeed born into families experiencing multiple disadvantages. However, it is not the mother's age at first birth which is the main driver of these disadvantages— rather it is the prior disadvantages experienced by the young mothers during their own childhoods. Again, this finding substantiates earlier research. The final set of statistical analyses takes comparison into a new area, and show that having a teenage mother does not significantly affect the chances of a pre-school child experiencing poor health, and makes little difference to how children score on cognitive tests. There is some difference for a few behavioural indices, but this largely disappears once prior life disadvantage is accounted for.

Hawkes notes that the starting point for most policy interventions around teenage parenthood is that the root of the problem is that the mother is a teenager— but her statistical analyses find that being a teenage mother does not in itself lead to poorer outcomes either for the mothers themselves or their children. Rather teenage motherhood often signals a life of exposure, for both mothers and children, to a range of social and economic disadvantages. She concludes that these results suggest a shift in government policy away from incidence of teenage motherhood itself, and a refocusing on the social and economic causes of teenage motherhood. What is more this sort of policy would be sensible because the factors associated with becoming a teenage mother appear to be the same factors as those influencing the life chances of their children.

Perhaps there can never be an accurate statistical measurement of the 'effect' of teenage motherhood, in the sense of finding some ultimate truth (Wilson and Huntington, 2005). Nonetheless, this statistical research tradition shows that—in these outcome terms—teenage childbearing in itself can be seen as only a minor social problem. It is not the teenage bit which is particularly important in these terms, but rather it is social and economic disadvantage which produce poor outcomes. In so far as teenage mothers are over-represented among the disadvantaged, this is because of their 'selection' through pre-existing disadvantage. A policy focus on being a teenage mother can only approach this wider problem of social disadvantage obliquely. Or as Hoffmann concluded for the USA, this sort of statistical study 'no longer supports the notion that teenage childbearing is a devastating event' and 'casts considerable doubt on the received wisdom about the consequences of teenage childbearing' (1998, 238-9).

5. Qualitative accounts of agency—young parents' values and experiences

What about the mothers and fathers themselves? A tradition of small-scale qualitative research focuses on their actual understandings and experiences of becoming a parent. In this way qualitative research can help explain just why the statistical studies find that age of pregnancy has little effect on social outcomes, and may actually make things better. While Hilary Graham and Elizabeth McDermott (2005) see quantitative and qualitative research as contradictory (the former seeing teenage motherhood as a route to social exclusion, the latter as an act of social inclusion), this contradiction perhaps relates more to the way these results have been framed, interpreted and used within opposing discourses (Wilson and Huntington 2005), rather than to the findings themselves. Instead, we can profitably see quantitative and qualitative studies as complementary in providing, on the one hand, extensive evidence about overall social patterns and, on the other, intensive evidence on the social processes that create these patterns (cf. Sayer 1994).

What these qualitative studies find is that many mothers express positive attitudes to motherhood, and describe how motherhood has made them feel stronger, more competent, more connected to family and society, and more responsible. Resilience in the face of constraints and stigma, based on a belief in the moral worth of being a mother, is one overriding theme. For some, this has given the impetus to change direction, or build on existing resources, so as to take up education, training and employment. There has been less research on young fathers, but what there has been tends to contradict the 'feckless' assumption. Like teenage mothers, most of the fathers are already socially disadvantaged, and it does not appear that fathering will in itself make this any worse. But, also like teen mothers, most express positive feelings about the child and want to be good fathers. Most contributed maintenance in some way, and many were actively involved in childcare (this varies by age, with the youngest least likely to be involved.) And, like teenage mothers, there is some evidence that successful fathering could be a positive turning point in young men's lives (see Duncan 2007 for review). In fact it was an invisibility to professionals, as well as housing problems, which often excluded them from the parenting they desired. Again, like teen mothers, young fathers may be less of a social threat, more of a social possibility.

That teenage motherhood has a positive side is an enduring finding over time in this research tradition. Nearly two decades ago, the study by Ann Phoenix (1991) of teenage mothers in London, in the mid-1980s, found that most of the mothers and their children were faring well. Most (and their male partners) had already done badly in the educational and employment systems, and it did not seem that early motherhood had caused this or that deferring motherhood would have made much difference. Rather, if anything, motherhood was something of a turning point which 'spurred some women on' (ibid, 250) into education and employment. Contributions to this edited collection testify that, two decades later, this more positive picture remains pertinent.

While Phoenix's research prefigures the statistical 'natural experiments', it remains unacknowledged in that tradition, and does not feature in the SEU 1999 framework report. The positive side to research findings about teenage mothering seems to be regularly disregarded in the more official literature, even when government commissions the research. Recent examples include TPU commissioned research on teenage mothers in rural and seaside 'hotspots' (Bell et al. 2004), and on teenage mothers and education (TPS Evaluation Team 2005, Hosie 2007). The former noted how for some young women, motherhood: 'increased their self-esteem and enhanced their lives, providing a sense of security and stability in lives characterised by transience, detachment and low economic aspirations' (op. cit. p. *v*), while the TPU's own evidence showed that having a child provides motivation for young mothers to aspire to new educational and employment goals.

That teenage parenting can have many positive sides is a theme that reappears in most of the chapters in this book. In chapter five Eleanor Formby, Julia Hirst and Jenny Owen provide a compelling illustration across three generational cohorts of teenage parents from Sheffield and Doncaster. Having a baby as a teenager did not necessarily predict adversity, and the problems experienced arose more from the particular social and economic circumstances the mothers and fathers found themselves in, rather than the age at which pregnancy occurred. For mothers, difficulties in accessing appropriate housing was a major problem, while fathers recounted their sense of exclusion or marginalisation from the processes of antenatal care, childbirth, and postnatal care. While the mothers and fathers in the sample had not planned pregnancy, all recounted their pleasure at having a baby and never regretted the decision to continue with the pregnancy. Perents across all generations and social classes spoke of their parenting in positive terms, even if early parenthood for the mothers (but not the fathers) was accompanied by a sense of 'loss' of teenage life. All made explicit references to the positive 'turning-point' offered by pregnancy: the opportunity to make new plans, including the beginnings of a strong family unit or renewed efforts to gain qualifications and secure more certain futures. Despite the pleasure and pride that all participants described, stigma was also a feature of parenting that each generation, but mostly mothers, highlighted. Hence, living in a community where young parents were not unusual was cited as hugely influential, contrasting to the isolation experienced by some older and middle generation mothers who lived in middle-class communities where young parenthood was less visible. This theme is continued in chapter six by Ann McNulty. Exploring three generations of related young mothers down the generations in particular families, in the north-east of England, she challenges ideas about intergenerational transmission of low aspirations, and shows how each generation of young mothers in a family wanted to achieve, and wanted their daughters to achieve, in education and employment. Unmet expectations in relation to career options were more a matter of the (often declining) economic circumstances in their localities, rather than any culture of low aspiration. The chapter also notes the marked shift, over recent decades, towards a negative conceptualisation of young motherhood.

This positive theme is replicated in other national contexts. Lee SmithBattle's research in the USA is paradigmatic (SmithBattle 1995, 2000, SmithBattle and Leonard 1998). She followed a small, diverse group of teenage mothers over 8 years, finding that many described mothering as a powerful catalyst for becoming more mature, and for redirecting their lives in positive ways. Mothering often 'anchors the self, fosters a sense of purpose and meaning, reweaves connections, and provides a new sense of future' (SmithBattle, 2000, 35). Indeed, two of the themes identified in a meta-synthesis of US qualitative studies of teenage mothers undertaken during the 1990s are 'Motherhood as positively transforming' and 'Baby as stabilising influence' (Clemmens 2003).

In this way qualitative research can explain the patterns found by extensive statistical studies; they suggest just why teenage parenting does not produce particularly poor outcomes, and can sometimes make things better for young people. In addition, the qualitative research can go further in explaining the processes involved in teenage parenting just because it allows more attention to context and diversity—usually stripped out by extensive studies in their concentration on average measurement (cf. Sayer 1994). This is not just a qualification to the statistical results, whereby teenage parents' experiences can be shown to vary significantly in different social groups and geographical places. For this also takes us to a vital 'missing link', and a key to understanding the agency of teenage parents—the life worlds in which they live. Becoming a teenage mother, and it seems a father, can make reasonable sense in the particular life worlds inhabited by some groups of young women and men. Recently, Rachel Thomson (2000) has conceptualised this as the 'economy of values' particular to different communities, and earlier Ann Phoenix (1991) found that early motherhood was common, and normally uncensured, in the social networks inhabited by the working-class teenage mothers in her 1980's London sample. BatttleSmith (2000) shows much the same for the USA; early motherhood often made sense in terms of local constitutions of opportunity, constraint, and social practice.

In chapter seven (Alexander et al.) we discuss our own research findings, from a small sample in Bradford, that teenage parents saw themselves unexceptionally as 'just a mother or a father' like any other. They were motivated to achieve well in education and employment so as to provide a stable future for their children, while at the same time they lived in communities where family and parenting was placed centrally as a form of local inclusion and social participation. The case of the two Asian mothers, who were married, is an indicative example. In this way ethnicity, as well as class, shaped expectations around motherhood. The young mothers and fathers in the sample spoke of their positive experience and the ways in which having children had given them a sense of responsibility and adult status. The teenage mothers in the study were little different from many other mothers who morally and socially prioritise motherhood, not employment. It is not that the young mothers rejected education and employment, rather self-esteem and identity are centred round motherhood; paid work was important more as a secondary and supportive part of life. While they faced many struggles, these were often linked to problems of wider social disadvantage, and they themselves strongly challenged the idea that these were related to their position as *young* parents. They resisted being characterised solely as a teenage mother or father and saw themselves as having multiple roles and identities, as individuals, partners, workers, students.

In chapter eight Jenny Owen and colleagues develop this theme with respect to ethnicity. Drawing on a study of teenage mothers in Bradford, Sheffield and three London boroughs, they examine in depth the transition to motherhood by young minority ethnic mothers. This reveals the strengths that these mothers draw on to deal with double-faceted prejudice—based on age and race/ethnicity—and their determination to make something of their own and their children's lives. However, at the same time many of the experiences of these young mothers are 'strikingly unremarkable': like older mothers, they are proud of their children; they aim to put them first; and they encounter familiar dilemmas in reconciling 'care' commitments with making a living and reaching accommodations with partners and other family members. This adds further weight to the general argument that 'teenage parents' should not be described as a homogenous group somehow separate from other mothers.

6. Conclusions: experience v policy?

The evidence substantiated in the chapters which follow shows that teenage childbirth does not often result from ignorance or low expectations, it is rarely a catastrophe for young women, and that teenage parenting does not particularly cause poor outcomes for mothers and their children. Expectations of motherhood can be high and parenting can be a positive experience for many young men and women. Furthermore, becoming a teenage parent can make good sense in the particular life worlds inhabited by some groups of young women and men. Policies about teenage parenting, however, assume the opposite. Unfortunately, this also means that policy will be misdirected in its aims, use inappropriate instruments, and may be unhelpful to many teenage parents

This brings us to the last question posed by the 'problem' of teenage parenting. Why then, is there such a yawning gulf between policy assumptions and the experiences of its subjects? And why does policy seem so resistant to evidence? This is the subject of our concluding chapter nine (Edwards et al.); the way forward, we claim, necessitates a 'smashing' of the policy making mould maintained by the 'epistemic community' existing around teenage parenting. We refer here to a network of professionals and policymakers with a shared set of normative, analytical and causal beliefs, with an agreed, shared and self-reinforcing knowledge base, and a common set of interests. Parameters of preferred policy models and narratives of cause and effect are set, to the exclusion of other ideas and information, even if those other data are more representative of everyday reality. The impetus is to retain these dominant and agreed conceptions in developing (further) policies, protecting them not only from critical scrutiny but even from recognising the existence of challenging alternative scenarios. Researchers working outside of these favoured models, with messages at odds with current policy directions, are unlikely to be heard or, if heard, considered relevant.

In this way a monochrome, negative, stereotype of teenage parents and parenting has become embedded in policy, bolstered by shared assumptions about social participation and the nature of social mobility, and by neo-liberal ideas about individual choice and rationality. Ideas about what is 'rational' are integrally linked to what is held to be socially acceptable, which in turn is regarded as a universal 'common sense' applicable in all contexts, rather than being rooted in the specific perspectives of a particular classed and gendered group of people who have the ability to judge others and place them as outside of rationality. In the case of teenage mothers and fathers, they are envisaged as ignorant, immoral or both because they have deviated from the cost-benefit calculative, future-oriented planned pathway of life. As other chapters show, this thinking is at odds with the complex reality of young mothers' and fathers' understandings and motivations, and yet is unequivocally accepted as an accurate portrayal. And all this, we suggest, is underlain by idealisations of children and childhood, where teenage parents, and mothers especially, are regarded as taking on the 'adult' responsibilities of parenthood before they have undergone the necessary sloughing off of the immaturity of childhood. They are (almost) children who have disrupted the regulation represented by the boundaries of adulthood and childhood, embodying the breakdown of social order and the nation's moral turpitude.

The question remains of how to move on. On the basis of the evidence presented in this book, we suggest there needs to be a refocus on the value of parenthood in itself, both socially and for individuals. For teenage parents, this might focus on the positive experience of becoming a mother and father, and on young parents' own resilience and strengths. Education and employment for young parents should be recognised as a components of parenting (which would also include 'full-time' mothering at home), rather than as a return to individualised rational economic planning where children are seen as an obstacle. Policy may also be better directed at improving employment for young people as a whole in declining labour markets, and regenerating disadvantaged neighbourhoods, rather than targeting teenage parenting in itself. Teenage parenting might then be approached as a way through and out of disadvantage, given its positive potential, rather than a confirmation of it. It could be seen as more opportunity than catastrophe. Certainly stigmatising policies directed at the assumed ignorance and inadequacy of teenagers will be inappropriate.

References

Arai, L. (2003a) 'Low expectations, sexual attitudes and knowledge: explaining teenage pregnancy and fertility in English communities. Insights from qualitative research, *Sociological Review*, 521(2): 199-217.

Arai, L. (2003b) British policy on teenage pregnancy and childbearing, *Critical Social Policy*, 23(1): 89-102.

Babb, P. (1993) Teenage conceptions and fertility in England and Wales, 1971-91, *Population Trends*, 74:12-17.

Barlow, A., Duncan, S., James, G. and Park, A. *Cohabitation, Marriage and the Law: Social Change and Legal Reform in 21ˢᵗ Century Britain* (2005) Oxford: Hart.

Barrett, G., Smith, S. and Wellings, K. (2004) What is a planned pregnancy? Empirical data from a British study, *Social Science Medicine*, 55: 545-57.

Bell, J., Clisby, S., Craig, G., Measor, L., Petrie, S and Stanley, N. (2004) *Living on the Edge: Sexual behaviour and young parenthood in seaside and rural areas*, London: Department of Health.

Berthoud, L. and Robson, K. (2003) Teenage Motherhood in Europe: a multi-country analysis of socioeconomic outcomes, *European Sociological Review*, 19(5): 451-466.

Botting, B. (1998) Teenage mothers and the health of their children, *Population Trends* 93: 19-28.

Bunting, M. (2005) It isn't babies that blights young lives, *The Guardian*, 27 May.

Cater, S. and Coleman, L. (2006) *'Planned' teenage pregnancy: views and experiences of young people from poor and disadvantaged backgrounds* Joseph Rowntree Foundation, Bristol: Policy Press.

Clemmens, D. (2003) Adolescent motherhood: a meta-synthesis of qualitative studies, *American Journal of Maternal/ Child Nursing*, 28(2): 93-9.

Churchill, D., Allen, J., Pringle, M. Hippisley-Cox J., Ebdon, D., Macpherson, M. and Bradley, S. (2000) Consultation patterns and provision of contraception in general practice before teenage pregnancy: case controlled study, *British Medical Journal*, 321: 486-9.

Coombs L. and Zumeta Z. (1970) Correlates of marital dissolution in a prospective fertility study: a research note, *Social Problems*, 18: 92-101

Corcoran, J. (1998) Consequences of adolescent pregnancy/parenting: a review of the literature, *Social Work Health Care*, 27(2): 49-67.

Cunnington, A. (2001) What's so bad about teenage pregnancy?, *Journal of Family Planning and Reproductive Health Care*, 27(1): 36-41.

Department for Children, Schools and Families (DCSF) (2007) *Teenage Parents: the Next Steps* Nottingham, DCSF.

DiCenso, A., Guyatt, G., Willan, A. and Griffith, L. (2002) Interventions to reduce unintended pregnancies among adolescents: systematic review of randomised control trials, *British Medical Journal*, 324: 1426-36

Duncan, S. (2002) Policy discourses in 'reconciling work and life' in the EU, *Social Policy and Society*, 1(4): 305-14.

Duncan, S. and Edwards, R. (1999) *Lone Mothers, Paid Work and Gendered Moral Rationalities*, London: Macmillan.

Duncan S. and Phillips M. (2010) People who live apart together (LATs)—how different are they? Sociological Review, 58(1): 112-134.

Duncan, S., Edwards, R., Alldred P., Reynolds, T. (2003) Motherhood, paid work, and partnering: values and theories, *Work, Employment and Society*, 17(2): 309-30

Ermisch, J. (2003) Does a 'teen-birth' have longer-term impact on the mother? Suggestive evidence from the British Household Panel Study, *Institute for Economic and Social Research, Working Papers*, 2003-32, University of Essex.

Ermisch, J. and Pevalin, D. (2003) Does a 'teen-birth' have longer-term impact on the mother? Evidence from the 1970 British Cohort Study, *Institute for Economic and Social Research, Working Papers*, 2003-32, University of Essex.

Fischer R., Stanford, J., Jameson, P. and DeWitt, J. (1999) Exploring the concepts of intended, planned and wanted pregnancy, *The Journal of Family Practice* 48(2): 117-23.

Freely, M. (1999) He's 14, his 12 year-old girlfriend is pregnant, and he'll be a good dad, *The Guardian*, 8 September.

Geronimus, A. (1997) Teenage childbearing and personal responsibility: an alternative view, *Political Science Quarterly*, 112(3): 405-430.

Graham H. and McDermott, E. (2006) Qualitative research and the evidence base of policy: insights from studies of teenage mothers in the UK, *Journal of Social Policy*, 35(1): 21-37.

Haskey J. (2005) Living arrangements in contemporary Britain: having a partner who lives elsewhere and living apart together (LAT), *Population Trends* 122: 35-45.

Hawkes, D. (2003) The socio-economic consequences of early child-bearing: evidence from a sample of UK female twins, Paper given to British Society for Population

Studies annual conference, Leicester, September, www.lse.ac.uk/collections/BSPS/annualConference/2004/fertility14Sept.htm.

Hoffmann, S (1998) Teenage childbearing is not so bad after all. Or is it? A review of the new literature, *Family Planning Perspectives*, 30(5): 236-243.

Kidger, J. (2004) Including young mothers: limitations to New Labour's strategy for supporting teenage parents, *Critical Social Policy*, 24(3): 291-311.

Lee, E., Clements, S., Ingham, R. and Stone, N. (2004) *A Matter of Choice? Explaining National Variations in Abortion and Motherhood*, York, Joseph Rowntree Foundation.

McMahon, M. (1995) *Engendering Motherhood: Identity and Self-transformation in Women's Lives*, New York, Guilford.

Phoenix, A. (1991) *Young Mothers?* Cambridge, Polity press.

Robson, K. and Berthoud, R. (2003) Early motherhood and disadvantage: a comparison between ethnic groups, *Institute for Economic and Social Research, Working Papers*, 2003-29, University of Essex.

Selman, P. (1996) Teenage motherhood then and now: a comparison of the pattern and outcome of teenage pregnancy in England and Wales in the 1960s and 1980s, in H. Jones and J. Millar (eds) *The Politics of the Family*, Aldershot, Avebury.

Selman, P. (2003) Scapegoating and moral panics: teenage pregnancy in Britain and the United States, in S. Cunnigham-Burley and L. Jamieson (eds.) *Families and the State: Changing Relationships*. London. Palgrave Macmillan.

SEU (Social Exclusion Unit) (1999) *Teenage Pregnancy*. Cm 4342, London, HMSO.

Shields, R (2008) Teen pregnancy epidemic 'a myth', *The Independent* Tuesday, 30 September.

SmithBattle, L. (1995) Teenage mothers' narratives of self: an examination of risking the future, *Advanced Nursing Science*, 17(4): 22-36.

SmithBattle, L. (2000) The vulnerabilities of teenage mothering: challenging prevailing assumptions, *Advanced Nursing Science*, 23(1): 29-40

SmithBattle, L. and Leonard, V (1998) Adolescent mothers four years later: narratives of self and visions of the future, *Advanced Nursing Science*, 20(3): 36-49.

TPU (Teenage Pregnancy Unit) (2000) *Implementation of the Teenage Pregnancy Strategy*, Progress Report. London: Teenage Pregnancy Unit/Department of Health.

TPU (Teenage Pregnancy Unit) (2004) *Teenage Pregnancy: an Overview of the Research Evidence* London: Teenage Pregnancy Unit/Health Development Agency.

Teenage Pregnancy Evaluation Team (2005) *Teenage Pregnancy Strategy Evaluation: Final Report Synthesis* London, London School of Hygiene and Tropical Medicine.

Thomson, R. (2000) Dream on: the logic of sexual practice, *Journal of Youth Studies*, 3 (4): 407-27.

Thornes, B. and Collard, J. (1979) *Who Divorces* London: Routledge.

UNICEF (2003) *Teenage Births in Rich Nations*, Innocenti Report Card No. 3, Paris.

Wellings K. and Kane R. (1999) Trends in teenage pregnancy and motherhood, *Journal of the Royal Society of Medicine*, 92(6): 277-82.

Wilson H. and Huntington, A. (2006) Deviant (m)others: the construction of teenage motherhood in contemporary discourse, *Journal of Social Policy*, 35(1): 59-76.

Chapter 2

'What's important at the end of the day?' Young mothers' values and policy presumptions

Pam Alldred and Miriam David

Introduction

This chapter examines the construction of education within the Teenage Pregnancy Strategy by contrasting it with the views of young mothers about education and the role they thought education or training might play in their lives. The teenage mothers' accounts are drawn from Alldred and David's *Get real about sex: the politics and practice of sex education* published in 2007. This book was based upon a study of one Local Education Authority (LEA) in England, which was, according to Government rhetoric, a teenage pregnancy 'hotspot' in the late 1990s and early 2000s. The Labour government's Teenage Pregnancy Strategy (TPS) sought to use education, and the education system (especially secondary schools) to reduce teenage pregnancies. Our study was funded from money to implement the TPS in schools because it was hoped that improving sexual health education would help bring down the teenage pregnancy rate. It was a two year, ethnographic study that investigated, and also supported, the LEA's efforts to implement the TPS by embedding 'sex and relationship education' (SRE) in all its secondary schools.

We explored the views of teachers, nurses, head teachers, pupils, and young people not in formal schooling within each of the LEA's seventeen schools. We found overwhelming support for sex and relationship education (SRE), but rejection of aspects of the Teenage Pregnancy Strategy. This chapter compares the values and priorities expressed by young mothers with some of the values assumed in, or explicitly asserted by, the TPS. It focuses particularly on the role and importance of education in young mothers' lives and on their gendered expectations regarding parenthood. Our research documents lives that do not fit comfortably within the model presented in the TPS and so highlights the gendered, class-based assumptions therein. In particular, we problematise the assumptions that early mothering is undesirable or aberrant; that education or training in the child's early years is desirable or even accessible to young mothers;

and that either 'parenting' or 'studying' can be assumed to be gender-neutral activities. The logic we find at work in these young women's lives seems to reflect the dominant values in their community and to question the logic that links teenage pregnancy to social exclusion in government policy.

The Teenage Pregnancy Strategy and education

The problematisation of teenage pregnancy under New Labour is plainly evident in the *Teenage Pregnancy* report (SEU, 1999), and most blatantly expressed in then Prime Minister Tony Blair's foreword: 'Our failure to tackle this *problem* has cost the teenagers, their children and the country dear' (p. 4). The role of education is clear in remedying the 'fact' that 'too many teenage mothers—and fathers—simply *fail to understand* the price they, their children and society will pay' (SEU, 1999: 4, our italics). The condemnatory tone of policy pronouncements is explicit: 'As a country, we can't afford to continue to ignore this *shameful* record' (ibid.: 4, our italics). The SEU (1999) report identified 'ignorance' i.e. 'lack of accurate knowledge about contraception, STIs [sexually transmitted infections], what to expect in relationships and what it means to be a parent' (SEU, 1999: 7) as one of the three causal explanations for Britain's much lamented teenage pregnancy rate relative to other West European countries (David, 2003b). This allows education to offer a solution.

Framing the solution to teenage motherhood in terms of education is significant. It reflects the increasing individualism and conditionality of the welfare contract (Levitas, 2005), and an increasing desire to mould citizens rather than tackle the conditions of their lives (Driver and Martell, 2002). Individuals and families are expected to meet needs that were previously framed by the Left as societal or community responsibilities. Rather than understanding young parents' needs through a social welfare model, focusing on the relative poverty of young people, and young parents specifically, intervention is focused on change at the individual level—as prevention of teen pregnancy and 'support' for teenage parents—illustrating a broader shift to individualistic rather than structural solutions (Franklin, 2000; Driver and Martell, 2002). In the case of prevention, it is primarily the procreative behaviour of individuals that is to be changed, or more precisely, their economic behaviour, which is seen as interrupted or limited by childrearing. Reducing teenage pregnancy is part of the strategy for combating 'social exclusion', to meet revised economic and welfare targets that seek to exploit the potential role of education to achieve economic ends (Bullen et al., 2000). Social inclusion rather than equality is the aim and is defined by participation in paid work (or training or education towards this). The individual is the economic unit in neo-liberalism. Individual financial responsibilities form the conditional basis for benefits or social care (Levitas, 2005) and since the individual must be economically self-sufficient irrespective of their parenting responsibilities, even lone parents must seek paid work now. Education becomes a more important tool for trying to change individual behaviour when governments have less ability to control factors affecting their economies in global capitalism. Thus the Government's concern is to inculcate in individuals the desirable personal qualities to facilitate its political project (Driver and Martell, 1999; David, 2003a). In this way, sex education became instrumental to the Government's 2010 teenage pregnancy targets with the specific aim of 'halving the rate of conceptions among under 18s' and 'getting more teenage parents into education, training or employment, to reduce their risk of long-term social exclusion' (SEU 1999: 8).

Values and assumptions of the TPS

Our action research project supported the implementation of the *Guidance on Sex and Relationship Education* (DfEE, 2000) in schools, a document published as one arm of the strategy to reduce teenage pregnancy in the UK. As we argue in Alldred and David (2007), the sexualities education curriculum seemed limited by the narrow focus on reducing pregnancy and sexually transmitted infection (STI) rates. The background described above makes sense of its direct assertion of particular 'family values', and our critique of the *Guidance* explores both its assumptions and the values it explicitly seeks to promote.

The *Guidance* constructs teenage pregnancy and parenthood as deviant and anti-social through explicit value statements that 'teenage parenthood is bad for parents and children' (David, 2003b). Given this, the teenage pregnancy rate is to be reduced by: improving SRE in schools; improving young people's access to sexual health services; and by building consensus around a particular set of values that deem teenage pregnancy undesirable and teenage parenthood unacceptable. This is stated explicitly as a value to be taught, and assumed as if it is a matter of consensus. Thus sex education's two-fold aims are to provide *information* about avoiding pregnancy and STIs, and to influence *values*.

The SRE curriculum is structured by three themes: 'Attitudes and values', 'Personal and social skills', and 'Knowledge and understanding'. This allows *values* to be bought into the foreground and legitimised, contentious statements to be presented as fact, and articulates certain individual qualities as skills to be developed. The final two 'Knowledge and understanding' areas are: 'learning the reasons for delaying sexual activity, and the benefits to be gained from such delay, and the avoidance of unplanned pregnancy.' (DfEE, 2000: 5). This labours the point by stating that 'benefits' are 'gains', and is rather one-sided (not, for instance, reasons to have sex when 'the time'—or relationship—is right). Moreover, these opinion-laden statements are presented as fact.

It is assumed that all teenage pregnancies are unplanned, and that all unplanned conceptions are unwanted. There is no qualification of the assumptions that these pregnancies are not intended, are not to couples and are not supported by family; and no mention is made of communities in which early parenthood (within marriage) is expected and seen as desirable. Whilst none of the young women we interviewed described their pregnancies as planned, recent research shows that it cannot be assumed that young mothers' pregnancies are always wholly unintended (Coleman and Cater, 2006).

The *Guidance* is preoccupied with avoiding conception and STIs and asserts for schools an active role through 'providing information about contraception' and on 'where [young people] can obtain confidential advice, counselling and where necessary, treatment' (2000: 15). Sex education is given a legalistic and health-oriented preoccupation with (hetero)-sexual health, the avoidance of underage (hetero)-sexual activity, underage/unwanted conceptions, STIs, and coitus (Corteen, 2006; Epstein and Johnson, 1994, 1998; Mac An Ghaill, 1994). The *Guidance* is not morally neutral about young people's sexuality: it makes more than eight references to the importance of *delaying* sexual activity, and practical safer sex information is legitimised by reference to pregnancy and infections. Its discussion of sexuality is dominated by the issues of STIs, abuse, 'unwanted' pregnancy, underage sex, criminal or 'promiscuous' sexual activity —what teachers referred to as 'the usual scare tactics of sex education'. Overall the construction of pupils' sexuality as risky, and to be discouraged or made safe(r) reflects a 'damage limitation' model (Corteen, 2000). The emphasis on equipping pupils to avoid physical and emotional harm contributes to the negativity around sex and constructs individuals as personally responsible for preventing harm to themselves.

Young people's sexuality is constructed as dangerous at several levels: threatening undesirable outcomes for themselves, their children and for society. Thus whilst an increasing individualism underlies the condemnation of benefit receipt, the same individualist logic is not applied to 'lifestyle' issues such as (if and) when to have children. Teenage parents are not left to live the consequences of their 'lifestyle choices', but are castigated for their negative effect on society and expected to be mindful of the collective.

Such negativity about teenage pregnancy is a result of the valorisation of paid work. The pressure to be financially self-reliant makes engagement with education or training the responsibility of everyone who is not already in paid work. Education or training is seen as a young person's top priority, and the understanding of education is a narrow and instrumental one—as a means of improving one's earning potential or insurance against being 'welfare dependent'—a problematically negative term, as we have argued elsewhere (Alldred, 1999). Even parents of young children, and lone parents, are 'supported' by the benefits system to seek employment or engage in education or training.

When social exclusion is to be tackled by the skilling-up of those who 'risk' claiming benefits, practitioners—including the Schools Reintegration Officer (SRO), our key contact in the community—are tasked with promoting this pro-work agenda. The 'support' offered teenage parents, including the young mothers in this study, is specifically help in returning to education, training or employment. This policy defines social inclusion in purely economic terms, as critics have argued (Alexiadou, 2002; Kidger, 2004) and is another assumption that these young mothers' accounts call into question.

The ungendered 'parents' of policy

The recent uptake of gender-neutral terms by policy—for instance, reference to 'parents', 'young people', 'employees', etc.—fails to recognise that women's increased participation in paid work has not been matched by men's increased participation in housework or childcare (New and David, 1985; Kiernan, Land and Lewis, 2001; Rees, 2004). Studies of heterosexual couples show that even when both partners work full-time, women tend to do more housework than men, and where there are children, mothers tend to do more and take more responsibility for managing the care of children (David et al., 1994; Van Every, 1995). The discourse of 'parents' can therefore mask inequalities. In this case, the difficulties 'young parents' face in returning to EET are compounded by gender.

There is a continuing gender pay gap, with women earning an average of seventeen per cent less than their male counterparts, and mothers identified as the single most disadvantaged group in the labour market, with mothers of under elevens having the greatest difficulty finding work irrespective of their ethnic or social background (Smith, 2006). Difficulties finding suitable childcare and jobs with flexible hours militate against mothers successfully combining work and parenting.

Male and female workers are not necessarily equivalent once their circumstances are considered. Celebration of the employment opportunities brought by globalisation ignores the need of many women for well-paid work within reach of home and school which effectively 'cuts them off from the networking opportunities of the global firm' (McRobbie, 2000: 109). Valerie Walkerdine (2003) has argued that the expectation of upward social mobility through education that is central to the neo-liberal discourse of education is a masculine ideal. The freedom to be a 'self-directed' self-improving learner is harder to obtain for anyone with family responsibilities. Typically mothering involves a greater clash with working or studying than does being a father (and the verbs 'to mother' and 'to father' do not equate). There are conflicting expectations of young women: to be mothers, with an expanding understanding of what constitutes 'good mothering', and to succeed as workers (Aapola et al., 2005) and an unhelpfully individualistic understanding of 'work-life balance' that implies individual organisation can resolve what we would see as structural problems. As a result, in this ungendered discourse of education-for-social-mobility women are set up to fail—and to take individualised responsibility for failing (Thomson et al., 2003; Walkerdine, 2003). Furthermore, as Walkerdine (2003) notes, as self-determination and individuality becomes a new cultural ideal of femininity, and the labour market disadvantages women in general, working-class girls bear the brunt of the conflicts between these values.

The parent as failed neo-liberal subject

Another factor that disadvantages young mothers is their parental status, since parenthood itself runs contrary to dominant cultural ideals of 'freedom' and 'independence'. As Bunting (2006: 31) puts it 'in a society that values consumption, choice and independence above all, it's a wonder that we have as many babies as we do'. The profound dependency of a baby on its mother and often increased dependency of mothers on their mothers/partners and others (Edwards, 1993), in fact, the very orientation to (an)other(s) that defines parenthood defies the self-absorption required by the self-as-project model of adulthood. The long-term commitment of parenthood jars with the self-reinventing subject of intensifying neo-liberalism. Not only does mainstream culture fail to value motherhood, as feminists have argued, but the qualities parenting requires are antithetical to those we are expected to aspire to. Bunting describes an implicit 'anti-natalist bias' in many of the influences shaping the contemporary self: the problem with motherhood (and to a lesser extent, fatherhood) is that it comes at the cost of failure—or at least compromise—as a consumer or worker, or both. This means that the self our education system is currently concerned to help us develop is little use to a new parent. What use is that independent, assertive, knowing-what-you-want-and-how-to-get-it-type with the emotional labour of helping a child develop self-confidence? (Bunting, 2006).

When Bunting describes motherhood hitting most women 'like a car crash', she refers to the experience of *education-then-motherhood* women around whom a new orthodoxy has emerged. Such women have experienced adult life without ('free from'?) children; thus parenthood, if experienced, is distinct from adulthood. Whilst heterosexual activity and parenthood were almost synonymous pre-contraception, the neo-liberal ideal makes no allowance for parenthood. While a new generation of (mainly middle-class) women may increasingly occupy this privileged, hitherto male mode of self-hood, in which public sphere identities as student or worker are central, if they become mothers they are rudely reminded of their gender, in terms of social expectations, including those they have of themselves, and the necessity of their political analysis. It is this 'crash' that explains why it is said that some women 'get (understand) feminism' when they 'get (have) children'.

Some women achieve this work-oriented mode of adulthood through not becoming mothers, and for some, motherhood marks a later life phase, but young parents are outside this new norm. Not for them the *Sex in the City*-style luxury of several years to explore their sexuality, relationships, living independently, earning and work relationships. Instead, their first experiences of sex, a relationship, parenthood and an intensified pressure for financial self-sufficiency may come closely timed. Young parents, for whom adulthood and parenthood arrive together, are unlikely to have identified 'what they want to be or do' or have had long to work on a project-of-the-self (or even a CV). It therefore seems premature to expect them to have identified their pathway through education or training, even if their circumstances hadn't been changed by the arrival of a baby. Moreover the privilege of choice applied to employment, and the idea of a career seem optimistic from locations such as that of our study group, where unemployment is high and what work exists is largely service sector or casual.

The young mothers in our study

We examined the accounts that ten young mothers gave us about their views and experiences. Eight school-aged mothers, one seventeen-year-old mother and a fifteen-year-old soon-to-be mother (and one father-to-be, her partner) told us about their lives in interviews either individually, in a pair, in a couple, or in a group of three. Five had had their babies at the age of fifteen, two at sixteen and two at fourteen years-old. The seventeen year-old, whilst not technically 'school-aged', was attending the same educational project as two other interviewees and so was invited to participate, and she had been a school-aged mother with her first baby. Four were interviewed at home with their babies present, and two of these, for part of the interview, had their own mother and other family members present. The others were either at a young parents' group in a community college or at a large voluntary organisation's *Parents into education* scheme, sometimes with the project worker present. The pregnant young woman clearly expected that her boyfriend would stay in the room, so we took the chance to ask him his views too, whilst noting this context for her comments.

All of these young people were white and working-class, living in an area of economic deprivation, on large estates with bad reputations, on the outskirts of a northern city. The area had had a blue-collar industry which had lent regional identity and pride, but which had been in decline since the late 1980s. Whilst semi and unskilled men had usually been able to find work locally, the remaining work for the old companies was now mostly part-time and taken by women. The region is predominantly white, but there is a sizeable Asian minority, mostly Muslim, concentrated in a couple of areas. The estates in question were comprised of semidetached, local authority houses with featureless gardens and few local facilities. When asked about sexual health clinics or maternity services that professionals saw as the 'local' clinics, most respondents said they did not know that area or how to get there. This obstacle to accessing services illustrated what local practitioners had told us: that this was an area of low mobility, geographically as well as socially. We describe our participants as working-class, and their families tended to be low income, typically large households living in three-bedroom council houses, at a distance from the formal cultural and political centres of the city. Teachers described the local community as inward-looking and traditional in terms of its values around gender, family and gendered authority in the family. We draw on similar findings from other recent UK studies of young mothers where our themes concur, but the fact that even a small group of mothers' lives do not fit the TPS model reveals the limits of its assumptions.

The young women were from several different schools, although a couple of them had stopped attending school before their pregnancies. We were introduced to them by the LEA's School Reintegration Officer (SRO) who worked with all the city's school-aged mothers to help them identify and access employment, education and training (EET). They were all in regular contact with her, and indeed had good enough relationship with her for her to suggest their participation in our research. Previous contact with her is likely to have shaped values, or at least expressed values, and our introduction through her would shape perceptions of our focus, making any expression of dissent from the pro-work/pro-education values highly significant.

Young mothers' experiences of school: lack of respect?

None of the young mothers were attending school: most had left before the end of their pregnancies and the SRO had helped them find alternative education or support in a crèche-supported young parents' group. All but one of them had bad experiences of school before their pregnancies: three had been bullied, three described getting into fights, one described graffiti at school calling her 'a slag', and most had experiences of being picked on. Moreover they shared a strong sense that they weren't respected at school by either their peers or teachers. Sometimes this was offered as a defensive explanation for their behaviour: 'If they'd have shown me respect, I'd have shown it them'. Sometimes 'respect' was a point of contrast with college, where it was felt staff treated them 'more like a person'. The regimented school environment was significant: 'not being allowed to go to the toilet when you want' when heavily pregnant was physically problematic, but in any case was experienced as controlling and infantilising. It was a deeply unsupportive gesture, indicating that being pregnant would not win any concessions. Feeling disrespected by teachers, not being allowed to go to the toilet at will and unhappiness or disengagement at school were also themes in the YWCA's study of twenty-one young mothers in another large English town (Harris et al., 2005). Several of our interviewees mentioned not feeling physically safe from the rough and tumble or aggression of the playground and in one case still being threatened with fights. One young mother was very touched by her learning support mentor staying in touch and bringing a gift of baby clothes when the baby was born, because otherwise she'd felt completely unnoticed in school:

None of the teachers ever spoke to me. Everyone ignored me 'til I was pregnant, then one or two teachers spoke to me and asked how I was.

Our focus on SRE throws these comments into sharp relief: SRE requires conditions of mutual respect and emotional safety in order to discuss value-based topics. Set within the Personal Social and Health Education framework, the aims of which include raising pupils' self-esteem, the pedagogic relationship might ideally model respectful communication and the trust needed to explore difference. Yet what these young mothers described was feeling unsafe, both emotionally and physically, and a lack of trust, respect or recognition. School was not a site in which their self-esteem was protected, let alone promoted.

The young mothers were highly critical of what little SRE they had received, and described it as boring and too biological. They were all strongly in favour of sex education in schools, and even though they said it had been of little help to them, they saw its potential. Indeed they were vociferous in defending frank and direct 'no nonsense' sex education and the improved availability of condoms, rather than, for instance, abstinence education. They would have welcomed more information, at an earlier age, with an increased emphasis on making them realise the risks they were taking:

They're saying it'll make [young people] have more sex, but at the end of the day, they'll do it anyway and at least they've got protection.

Kids need warning. They are going to experiment and need to know what risks they're taking.

Relationships within school compromised their participation in SRE: they did not want to learn from or disclose anything to teachers since they were not trusted not to be judgmental or to gossip with other teachers. They wanted their questions answering by nurses or sexual health experts—people *external* to the school. Many felt that they would be stigmatised even for participating in classroom discussions, although two young women described actively taking part in SRE lessons and were critical of their peers for being self-conscious and 'immature' about the topic.

Our participants all supported the immediate goals of the TPS to improve SRE, however they did not share the TPS's rationale for this, as we shall see. The idea that better SRE will necessarily reduce the teenage pregnancy rate is undermined by the fact that more complex factors lay behind their parental status, including access to sexual health services, and their own values and aspirations, which we explore next.

Family norms and community values

Our participants described the norm as early childbearing, large families, childrearing in three generation or extended family households, financial support from and often complete dependence on parents, and reliance on mothers especially for childcare. All but one said that having babies young was not unusual in their families. One fourteen-year-old said that she was the youngest mother in her family but that sixteen had been common beforehand, and another described motherhood at the age of seventeen as the norm 'round there' and for her family. Several of their own mothers had had their first baby at sixteen or seventeen. Most interviewees had several siblings, and one young woman who had five siblings and was pregnant with her third child said she wasn't keen on 'big families' and wasn't planning a large family herself. Siblings had had babies young too; at least three of the girls' parents were already grandparents. One had a sixteen-year-old sister who was pregnant at the same time, another's brother had had his first child at sixteen and had since had another three (with the same partner). The mother of one interviewee had shared her daughter's experience of an unplanned pregnancy discovered late (too late for an abortion, her initial plan) just a year earlier. This young woman was already involved in raising one small child when she realised she was pregnant.

None of their first pregnancies were planned, and, when asked, most would ideally have waited another year or two, but all but two said they planned to have another child. Only one expressed anti-abortion views, but two were talked out of an abortion and three were put off by an extreme anti-abortion video unaccountably shown in RE. More significant in ruling out the possibility of abortion was the fact that all had concealed pregnancies, typically confirmed at five months or later. In retrospect, a couple admitted suspecting they were pregnant but being 'in denial'. As the youngest participant put it: 'I was thirteen, I really didn't want to know'. But on whether she had felt pressured to have sex, one of them exclaimed:

Lots of my mates already had *babies* by the time I had sex!

This young mother said that seventeen was a common age to have a child in her community and her own family. Her own baby was born when she was seventeen, after a year at college, and was not seen as problematically early by her family. We see the values expressed in these accounts as probably reflecting the values of the local community, and therefore mothers of all ages within it, rather than being specific to *young* mothers. Lee et al. (2004) found a strong correlation between the proportions of under-eighteen and adult pregnancies ending in abortion in different communities and concluded that young women's perceptions of motherhood were shaped by community and family views, including the extent to which having children relatively early was accepted and the importance placed on goals that are not easily compatible with early motherhood, and hence 'local, familial and/or gendered cultural processes' were important in young women's decisions about pregnancy (Lee et al., 2004: 3).

An example of what we are describing as locally inflected values would be the notion of responsibility. Different interpretations of being responsible relate to context and seem to map onto class cultures: Harden and Osgood (1999) found that teenagers having abortions often experienced unplanned pregnancy as a sign of their 'irresponsibility', whereas young mothers we interviewed and those in Tabberer's (2000) study associated motherhood with responsibility: despite fearing parental reactions, going ahead with the pregnancy was framed as taking responsibility, and adapting to new responsibilities was a positive thing, even perhaps a marker of growing up as Thomson et al. (2003) describe. It was a spur to achievement for our most educationally engaged interviewee: who although very able, said that becoming a mother had given her a reason to seek qualifications, when before she had had none.

However, we do not wish to overstate the 'local values' argument. Like Lee et al. we do not wish to see teenage motherhood as simply 'passed down' through the generations (sometimes they 'don't want to make the same mistake my mum did'), but as indicating particular sets of meanings and values that inform decision-making. Firstly, in areas of high teenage pregnancy rates, abortion carries more stigma than does early motherhood, according to Tabberer et al. (2000) and Lee et al. (2004). Secondly, young women's decision-making is affected by their expectations about what can be achieved through education and success in the world of work: 'those who continued their pregnancies could perceive motherhood in a more positive light, since it did not appear to interfere with plans for the immediate future' (Lee, 2004: 4). Thirdly, in our study, as in Tabberer et al.'s, mothering is constructed as immensely rewarding, rather than associated with lack or loss: the chance to develop close personal relationships with a child and perhaps a partner and to take up a position of responsibility. We will discuss the importance of education and of mothering shortly.

Whilst early sexual activity was presented as the norm, pregnancy was generally seen as a matter of being 'caught out' rather than of planning. News of a 'surprise' baby to a celebrity middle-class mother confirmed their view that 'most babies aren't planned anyway' and they noted the injustice of warm media reactions to such pregnancies compared with teenage mothers'. Despite the presentation of early motherhood as commonplace, some of these young women felt stigmatised by becoming mothers young. One described being heckled by a passer-by in the city's shopping centre when she was visibly pregnant and being told she was too young to be a mother. Those with partners preferred their boyfriend to accompany them in such public places in order to avoid such comments and counter the assumption that they had conceived outside an ongoing relationship.

Even their friends sometimes gave them a hard time. One young mother told us, 'None of my mates stood by me, they just slagged me off as soon as they found out I was pregnant', and another described slurs on her reputation which she felt were utterly unfair because, 'They were all sleeping with different people each week and I'd had the same boyfriend for three years' (actually since she was eleven). Another young woman suspected that some of her friends were jealous of her pregnancy.

Apparent ambivalence about teenage pregnancy among the mothers themselves came not from its clash with a government expectation of further educational opportunities but from the painful recognition of social condemnation, and sometimes direct hostility. Whilst common values emerged powerfully across the interviews, it is not necessary to find a value consensus among the group in order to show that the values assumed in the TPS and SEU (1999) cannot be assumed to be universal or uncontentious.

Motherhood and education: values and priorities

In contrast to their negative views of *school*, these young mothers were mostly positive about *education*. Most had ideas, although admittedly vague, of future courses at college, and four mentioned future training towards childcare or other care work. In fact, six were currently involved in some form of training (at college or through a voluntary organisation), one had had a home tutor in her final school year, and two had tried to return to school after having their babies, but without success. One was doing Business Studies at college, another was keen to work with children in sport, but would continue to think about exactly how while she tried for a second child. Unsuccessful attempts to return to education for two of them highlight the potential difficulties of combining motherhood with study: one was nudged back to school 'too early', felt completely alienated from her erstwhile friends and mortified at leaking breast-milk onto her school shirt, and another began a beauty course at college, but said she was 'thrown off' for missing a few weeks when her baby was in hospital. Another wasn't expected to return to school because it was recognised that she was a carer for her own mother. The degree of engagement with education or training testified to their good relationships with the SRO, but what these experiences highlight are education providers' assumptions that young people are necessarily free from care responsibilities and wholly free to attend courses. This freedom, celebrated in the neo-liberal subject, is a privilege that not all possess.

The three young women who already had prior children *did* talk about college courses and future training for work, but with one important caveat: they used the *future tense*. Those with younger babies—who had been subject to the SRO's influence during their pregnancies—thought they might continue with their education when the baby reached a year or so, and commonly spoke of 'being free to' go to college or get a job 'after having children' which meant when their children started school at four to five years-old:

> I can go to college later when I've had longer to work out what I want to do.

> By the time this [unborn] baby's in school, I'll only be twenty-two and with all three of my children in school, I'll be able to get a job then.

For them, being with their child throughout infancy was expected and preferred. Parenting was clearly much more important to their social identities than education (or employment) had been in their past, or than employment (or education) were to their imagined futures. Mothering came first in terms of both importance and timing:

'What's most important at the end of the day?' one young mother asked rhetorically of the interviewer and two other young mothers in the group, and everyone said 'Mmmm' in heartfelt agreement. It was possible to see mothering as conveying a valued social role, promoting their inclusion in their community and their elevation to responsible womanhood, in contrast to the policy construction linking teenage parenthood to social *exclusion* (Kidger, 2004). The policy link relies on a particular definition of social exclusion centring on paid work, but in common with other studies of young mothers (e.g. Kidger, ibid.) we saw how social and psychological inclusion was mediated through acquiring a mothering role.

The YWCA's study also identified a cultural norm of full-time mothering until children start school and that 'being a good mother meant staying with your baby': 'you'd be a bad mum if … you're not with your kid at all and you're working most of the time' said one young mum in their study, and another said: 'There are young girls in my estate and they leave their babies all the time with their mums, and … they get slagged off' (Harris et al., 2005: 11 and 10). Being responsible meant being there for your child, as we found, but also it was clear that 'time spent with [the] baby was precious and rewarding' (ibid.: 25). Harris et al. describe how this ideal of full-time mothering dominated their interviewees' thoughts over returning to employment or training and note how important being a good mother was to young women facing stigma about their parenting. As they point out, until recently, social policy reflected this same cultural norm of full-time or 'stay-at-home mothering'. There is a long history of punitive treatment of mothers deemed deviant, although the particular targets are historically contingent, and a current preoccupation is with age rather than 'legitimacy' (Alldred, 1999; David, 2003a and b), although 'illegitimacy' is sometimes assumed on the basis of age. It is the shifting policy climate that makes these young women's choices problematic. With benefit receipt frowned on (and practitioners deployed to reduce the number of claimants), young women such as those we interviewed, whose own parents are not high earners, are expected to shoulder the financial burden of raising a child individually whilst simultaneously showing that they are on a pathway into employment via education or training.

Parenting carried gendered expectations and young women's role as the primary carer was invested in by young men too. Some young mothers in the YWCA study and also in that by Lee et al. (2004) described their partners not wanting them to work: 'He doesn't want me to work, he tells me I shouldn't have to … he wants to look after me' (Harris et al., 2005: 10). We found similar gendered expectations including of male breadwinning, despite the local job market offering largely 'women's work' in the lighter side of local industry. This, alongside the fact that at least three of these young women lived with and helped care for babies born to their mother or sister, shows the importance of situating their decisions about participating in education, training or employment (EET) in the actual context of their lives, and seeing them embedded in family and other gendered relationships.

When these young women were publicly harassed by being told they were 'too young to have a baby', they understood this to mean 'too young' to parent a child adequately, not too young to leave education. The child's, not their own well-being, was the concern. This criticism draws on a discourse of mothering that can sacrifice a mother's needs for her child: distinct from the view that early parenthood was interrupting a mother's education, her earning or her pathway to a career. For such mothers/mothers-to-be, when day-to-day life with a baby is so absorbing even for non school-aged mothers (Gatrell, 2005), their consciousness of education seems notable, but perhaps not surprising given their prior contact with the Schools Reintegration Officer. The sense we gained was that the SRO was popular and influential— seemingly more so than any other professionals with whom they had had contact. This particular SRO was sympathetic to their wishes, and a warm, compassionate woman, but she clearly had an educational remit, albeit within a flexible framework that didn't assume schooling was the only form education could take. Their previous conversations with her had probably shaped their sense of their selves-to-be-educated, as well as their knowledge of what the local college offered. She had intentionally sought to shape their educational aspirations, and to 'encourage' them to engage with EET. She was often the only professional they could name, the only one they felt had shown concern for them and her support for them (often before and after the birth) was much appreciated. She maintained a fairly long-term relationship with the young women and was a positive presence even where she was technically failing because they were 'NEET'. In addition to this direct influence on the mothers, her educational orientation helped construct understandings of our research: it was on the strength of the trusting relationships she had built with young women that they agreed to talk to us, and our association with her probably shaped their perception of our interest in education.

Education and work: aspirations and expectations

The young mothers may have employed a discourse of education, but theirs was not an abstract education 'for-its-own-sake'. It was the instrumental recognition that education or training would improve their chances of future paid work and of better providing for their child/ren. Only the younger two mothers ever drew on the notion that teenage parenthood had interrupted their education—in line with the Government's concern with it as a route to social exclusion. But what was apparent was that their expectation of education was limited: one young mother said that ideally she would have waited until she was seventeen and had therefore 'finished her education' before having children, a second referred to her mother's hopes that she would have 'stayed on at school' and a third described the ideal time to have a child as 'Ideally eighteen to twenty. When you've got your education so you can fall back on it later, so you can get a job afterwards'.

None mentioned university, and college (for post-compulsory education) was the furthest 'staying on' envisaged. None were committed to particular careers nor had they already identified EET pathways, which must be seen in the context of the local labour market's unemployment given the 'downsizing' of the main regional industry. When they did talk about future employment, it was clear that they saw working as heavily contoured by their status as parents. It was not some idealised fantasy of future lives in hugely improved living situations, nor a glamorous career. It was motivated by pay and the desire to provide well for their children. These young parents could not assume they would find either particularly well-paid or fulfilling work since only two had completed compulsory schooling, one gaining some qualifications as a result of LEA provision of a Home Tutor. Rather than the individualised understandings of motivation that working-class girls are now taught to aspire to, their visions of the future preserved and supported their links to people and place, and thus reflected their particular class location and the absence of broader opportunities. Whilst being presumed single drew on a stereotype of teenage mothers that they objected to, in the sense of being unlikely to have a partner's income to draw on, the young mothers' financial situations was similar to that of lone mothers. Partners, where they had them, whilst usually older, were generally caught in the same structures: unemployed, on a training project or for other reasons peripheral to the household economy. These young people's instrumental view of education-for-work matched the Government's, but their view of work as coming *after* parenting deviated from the new expectation of paid work *alongside* parenting and subsequent need for formal childcare.

These young mothers rarely constructed their pregnancies as interrupting plans for study or training. Indeed, in their accounts paid work and mothering were constructed as fundamentally different pathways to adulthood. Similarly paid work was constructed as clashing rather than compatible with mothering by the white mothers in an earlier study of ours in London (Duncan et al., 2003b). This research found that African Caribbean mothers saw doing paid work as *part of* their mothering role, not conflicting with it, because they felt it important to model managing paid work alongside mothering. Mothers' decisions about combining paid work with mothering or about using childcare are not simply economic decisions, but are value-based and locally situated, reflecting their community values and gendered relationships and lived experiences (Duncan et al., 2003b). As we have described, several of the young mothers already had responsibilities for another family member, and/or helped care for another child. Two were in relationships with reformed 'bad boys' or ex-drug users, for which they had the respect and gratitude of their partners' families. Their identities as 'copers' and 'survivors' embodied gendered expectations of caring and responsibility for others in a working-class female archetype which was a source of positive self-esteem. By contrast, they did not have sources of self-esteem in their identities as learners or workers. Their identities and aspirations are formed in these contexts and they also applied *gendered* moral rationalities (Duncan and Edwards, 1999).

Thus values, rather than straightforward economics, determine choices about childcare and work and hence the model of 'rational economic man' is inappropriate for mothers' decisions about childcare (Duncan et al., 2003a). Government policies to create childcare 'markets', a central plank in neo-liberal reforms, therefore seem inappropriate.

Young women not in employment, education or training (NEET)

The structural factors limiting young mothers' success in the job market must be acknowledged. In an area of high unemployment, low social and geographical mobility, and male breadwinner expectations, young women without academic or vocational qualifications or experience will not easily find employment, and available employment may not meet any 'raised aspirations'. The YWCA study highlights the practical difficulties of combining motherhood with education or training:

> Only those with informal childcare, through family support, returned to EET relatively easily. Others felt childcare and a lack of support and flexibility in work or training made EET a struggle and forced them to sacrifice too much time with their children.   (Harris et al., 2005: 25)

For some, 'EET was out of the question because concerns about the baby's health, not knowing what to expect and learning to manage on a limited budget,

along with learning basic childcare skills, constituted a full-time job' (ibid.: 25).
Trying to combine EET with mothering placed considerable strains on their
lives, and the Government's 'pro-work' agenda puts too much pressure on young
mothers in particular (Harris et al., 2005; Kidger, 2004). Research shows that
even for mothers in their twenties and thirties who have the support of a partner,
the arrival of a child can be stressful (Gatrell, 2005). The young mothers in our
study also articulated particular values and standards for their mothering:

> I'd rather be poor and see my own kids, rather than like, be rich and
> never see them at all ... You need to be there ... if they've got problems
> they can talk to you.

The Government's target for sixty per cent of teenage mothers to be in EET
is unrealistic, given that it exceeds the employment rate among mothers in
general. The British Household Panel Survey (1991-7) showed that nearly
sixty per cent of all first-time mothers were not in employment when their
children were five years-old, so to expect the youngest group of mothers to
achieve a sixty per cent rate whilst their children are even younger is to expect
something highly exceptional. Even older mothers, of whom seventy per cent
have been in full-time employment *before* having a baby, do not nearly reach
the sixty per cent target for working afterwards. Second, the question remains
whether the objectives were ever appropriate given the different value women
attach to their mothering:

> social class shapes many young women's views of young motherhood as
> normal and respected, so strategies based on presumptions that teenage
> motherhood is 'a mistake', 'a problem' or 'abnormal' and that caring for
> children rather than paid working is a failure, are irrelevant to the lives and
> experiences of young mothers and are unlikely to succeed in encouraging
> young mothers into EET.   (Harris et al., 2005.: 31)

We share the conclusion of the YWCA report that the TPS presumes for
young mothers 'a life path not necessarily suited to their needs or reflected in
their families and communities' (ibid.: 25).

The conception rate among sixteen and seventeen year-olds remains more
resistant to intervention than that for older teenagers. Seen alongside our and
others' qualitative findings of (sub)cultural norms of 'early' childbearing, one

interpretation is that this 'older' group of teenage mothers—having children at seventeen or eighteen—are not seen as aberrant in their communities. If they reflect their own community norms, they are less amenable to pressure.

The Government's approach to teenage pregnancy as a social ill to be tackled, an individual failure to be redeemed, further reinforces the stigma. However there is some evidence that it is not being young, but being disapproved of that creates some of the problems of early childbearing. A study in Jerusalem compared young mothers from an orthodox Jewish community who marry young and receive considerable social and economic support from their community, with other young mothers across the city who were mostly poor and unmarried. Even controlling for exact age, marital status, ethnicity and smoking, the young mothers who received the support of their community had a significantly fewer low birth weight babies (Gale et al., 1989). Where adverse outcomes of teen pregnancies are observed, environmental disadvantage (poverty, limited pre-natal medical care, and lack of psychosocial support) may be key.

Conclusions

These young parents' views are notable to policy makers because they do not share the values the Government promotes regarding the role of paid work for parents or the undesirability of teenage pregnancy, and disregarding community/ peer group values may well limit the effectiveness of policy. Improved SRE may have been 'good for' these young women, but not necessarily through having the effect intended on teenage pregnancy rates. Instead their decisions about mothering and studying have to be seen in the context of gendered and class-based community norms and values about parenting, as more recent research has also confirmed (Heath et al., 2008). Even the interviews themselves illustrated how lives are embedded in relationships and for these young mothers that could mean being interviewed in the presence of their baby, their mother, their boyfriend or a professional.

Like other studies of the cultural norms in teenage pregnancy 'hotspots', we found a coherence among the young mothers' views of motherhood, education and employment, and an indication that community views were notably distinct from those assumed in Government thinking. Our critique of the pro-work agenda and ideas about social mobility through education shows how they allow young women to carry the burden of gender amid supposedly gender-neutral ideals. In addition, the particular position of these young women as *mothers* is not adequately recognised in the pro-education, pro-work climate and furthermore, the possibility of them not sharing Government (and hence professionals') values, and having alternative values, is systematically excluded.

The Government celebrates the 'good' old-fashioned values of the work ethic and self-reliance, but over-generalises it to undermine another old-fashioned value, that of full-time mothering. When the Government has blatantly sought to promote certain values to suit its economic priorities through education, their valorisation of 'old-fashioned community values' (Sennett, 2003) seems selective and disingenuous. The neo-liberal promise of social mobility through education (Walkerdine, 2003) sounds hollow in areas of multiple deprivation, social exclusion and male breadwinner expectations. One of the most insidious aspects is the individualisation of responsibility for failure to succeed in the job market and the expectation that teenage mothers themselves must avoid their own future 'social exclusion' by embarking on an education-to-employment pathway. Whilst we would challenge the 'epistemological fallacy' (Furlong and Cartmel, 1997) that individuals are to blame for the impact of socio-economic structures on their lives, the tacit question our interviewees perceived was about how they would take responsibility for their own education-to-earning pathway. In response, they narrated themselves as aspiring, future returners to EET. Research interviews, far from providing a window onto pre-formed selves, helped them perform a version of self-as-project and therefore produce themselves in line with expectations of the TPS and the neo-liberal ideal. However, this ideal is problematic, as we have seen, in terms of its masculine norms regarding participation in EET; its typically middle-class pattern of education then parenthood; its individualised responsibilities; and the assumption of the centrality of paid work to social inclusion.

References:

Alexiadou, N., (2002) Social inclusion and social exclusion in England: tensions in education policy, *Journal of Education Policy*, 17(1): 71-86.

Alldred, P., (1999) '*Fit to Parent?' Psychology, Knowledge and Popular Debate*, Unpublished PhD, London: University of East London.

Alldred, P. and David. M., (2007) *Get Real About Sex: The politics and practice of sex education*, Buckinghamshire: Open University Press.

Appola, S., Gonick, M. and Harris, A., (2005) *Young Femininities: Girlhood, Power and Social Change*, Basingstoke: Palgrave Macmillan.

Bullen, E., Kenway, J. and Hey, V., (2000) New Labour, Social Exclusion and Educational Risk Management: the case of 'gymslip mums', *British Educational Research Journal*, 26(4): 441-456.

Bunting, M., (2006) Behind the baby gap lies a culture of contempt for parenthood, *The Guardian*, 7th March, p31.

Coleman, L. and Cater S., (2006) 'Planned' teenage pregnancy: perspectives of young women from disadvantaged backgrounds in England, *Journal of Youth Studies*, 9(5): 595-616.

Corteen, K., (2006) Schools' fulfilment of sex and relationship education documentation: three school-based case studies, *Sex Education*, 6(1): 77-99.

David, M. E., (2003a) *Personal and Political: Feminisms, sociology and family lives*, Stoke-on-Trent: Trentham Books.

David, M. E. (2003b) 'Teenage Parenthood is bad for parents and children': A Feminist Critique of Family, Education and Social Welfare Policies and Practices, in Bloch, M., Holmund, K., Marquist, I and Popkewitz, T. (eds) *Governing Children, Family and Education: Restructuring the Welfare State*, New York St Martins Press and London: Palgrave Macmillan.

David, M., West, A. and Ribbens, J., (1994) *Mother's Intuition? Choosing Secondary Schools*, London: Falmer Press.

Department for Education and Employment, (2000) *Sex and Relationship Education Guidance*, Circular 0116/2000, DfEE.

Driver, S. and Martell, L., (1999) New Labour, Culture and Economy, in L. Ray and A. Sayer (eds) *Culture and Economy After the Cultural Turn*, London: Sage.

Driver, S. and Martell, L., (2002) *Blair's Britain*, Cambridge: Polity Press.

Duncan, S. and Edwards, R., (1999) *Lone Mothers, Paid Work and Gendered Moral Rationalities*, Basingstoke: Palgrave.

Duncan, S., Edwards, R., Reynolds, T. and Alldred, P., (2003a) Mothers and Childcare: policies, values and theories, *Children and Society*, Published online Nov 03/ paper Vol.18 (2004): 254-265.

Duncan, S., Edwards, R., Reynolds, T. and Alldred, P., (2003b) Motherhood, Paid Work and Partnering: Values and Theories, *Work, Employment and Society*, 17(2): 309-330.

Edwards, R.,(1993) *Mature Women Students: Separating and Connecting Family and Education*, London: Taylor and Francis.

Epstein, D. and Johnson, R., (1994) On the straight and narrow: the heterosexual presumption, homophobias and schools, in D. Epstein (ed.) *Challenging Lesbian and Gay Inequalities in Education*, Buckingham: Open University Press.

Epstein, D. and Johnson, R., (1998) *Schooling Sexualities*, Buckingham: Open University Press.

Franklin, J., (2000) What's Wrong with New Labour politics?, *Feminist Review*, 66: 138-141.

Furlong, A. and Cartmel, F., (1997) *Young People and Social Change: Individualisation and Risk in Late Modernity*, Buckingham: Open University Press.

Gale, R., Seidman, D., Dollberg, S., Armon, Y. and Stevenson, D.K., (1989) Is Teenage Pregnancy a Neonatal Risk Factor? *Journal of Adolescent Health Care*, 10: 404-408.

Gatrell, C., (2005) *Hard Labour: the Sociology of Parenthood*, Maidenhead: Open University Press.

Harden, A. and Osgood, J., (1999) Young women's experiences of arranging and having abortions, *Sociology of Health and Illness*, 21(4): 426-44.

Harris, J., Howard, M., Jones, C. and Russell, L., (2005) *Great Expectations: How realistic is the Government's target to get 60 per cent of young mothers into education, employment or training?* Oxford: YWCA Report.

Heath, S., Fuller, A and Paton, K., (2008) 'Networked based ambivalence and educational decision-making: a case study of non-participation in higher education', *Research Papers in Education* 23(2): 219-231

Kidger, J., (2004) Including young mothers: limitations to New Labour's strategy for supporting teenage parents, *Critical Social Policy* 24(3): 291-311.

Kiernan, K., Land, H. and Lewis, J. (1998) *Lone Motherhood in Twentieth Century Britain: From Footnote to Front Page*, Oxford: Clarendon Press.

Lee, E., Clements, S., Ingham, R. and Stone, N., (2004) *A matter of choice? Explaining national variations in teenage abortion and motherhood*, York: Joseph Rowntree Foundation.

Levitas, R.,(1998/2005) *The Inclusive Society? Social Exclusion and New Labour*, (1st/2nd edn), Basingstoke: Palgrave Macmillan

Mac An Ghaill, M., (1994) *The Making of Men: Masculinities, Sexualities and Schooling*, Buckingham: Open University Press.

McRobbie, A., (2000) Feminism and the Third Way, *Feminist Review*, 64: 97-112.

New, C. and David, M. E., (1985) *For the Children's Sake: Making Child Care More Than Women's Business*, Harmondsworth, Middlesex: Penguin.

Rees, T., (2007) Pushing the Gender Equality Agenda Forward in the European Union, in M.A. Danowitz Sagaria (ed.), *Women, Universities and Change. Gender Equality in the European Union and the United States*, Basingstoke: Palgrave Macmillan

Sennett, R., (2003) *Respect: The Formation of a Character in a World of Inequality*, London: Penguin.

Smith, L., (2006) Situations Vacant But Mums Need Not Apply, *The Times*, March 21.

Social Exclusion Unit, (1999) *Teenage Pregnancy*, Cm4342, London: The Stationary Office.

Tabberer, S., Hall, C., Prendergast, S. and Webster, A., (2000) *Teenage pregnancy and choice: Abortion or motherhood: Influences on the decision*, York: Joseph Rowntree Foundation.

Thomson, R., Henderson, S. and Holland, J., (2003) Making the most of what you've got? Resources, values and inequalities in young women's transitions to adulthood, *Educational Review*, 55(1): 33-46.

Van Every, J., (1995) *Heterosexual Women Changing the Family: Refusing To Be A 'Wife'!* London: Taylor and Francis.

Walkerdine, V., (2003) Reclassifying Upward Mobility: femininity and the neo-liberal subject, *Gender and Education*, 15(3): 237-248.

Chapter 3

Challenging the irrational, amoral and anti-social construction of the 'teenage mother'

Jan Macvarish and Jenny Billings

On election to power in 1997, the Blair administration moved teenage pregnancy to a central position as part of its agenda to tackle 'social exclusion'. Unlike the past, teenage pregnancy was problematised in apparently amoral terms: the mother's age, not her unmarried status was emphasised, and her sexual behaviour was framed as negatively affecting her and her baby's health and life chances rather than threatening the moral standards of the nation. Although the 'social exclusion' agenda posed the problem as one experienced by the 'socially excluded', it also put forward the existence of the 'excluded' as a problem for the rest of society, threatening the economic and social standard of living of the 'included'. Within this context, teenage pregnancy and motherhood was cast as being bad for teenagers, bad for children and bad for society.

This chapter explores the construction of the 'teenage mother' in policy discourse, and brings to bear upon it the findings from a qualitative research project that investigated the contemporary experience of teenage motherhood. It will be argued that qualitative studies such as this challenge the recent policy construction of the teenage mother in two significant ways. First, qualitative evidence calls into question the redefinition and the expansion of the category of the 'teenage mother' as a social problem. Second, it forces us to reconsider the way in which young motherhood has been constructed as both a cause and an effect of various 'deficits' at the level of individuals: in familial relationships, in particular, conceived of as a deficit of 'parenting skills'; in the rationality and moral agency of teenagers who become pregnant; and in the ability of those resistant to policy intervention to acknowledge and ameliorate their 'problems'. These misapprehensions, it is argued, result in policy seeking to engage with young mothers as inherently inadequate and in need of intensive state intervention, to reconstruct them as competent parents. Teenage pregnancy policy is setting important precedents in labelling as 'inadequate' a growing number of parents, pathologising them as a threat to their own children and as a cause of broader social problems. Such thinking is intolerant of varied family beliefs and practices, and dissolves the individual parent and child as subjects into mere embodiments of 'risk factors'.

Constructing the problem of teenage pregnancy

Expanding the category

A relatively unnoticed but significant feature of New Labour's teenage pregnancy strategy is the expansion of the category of 'problem young conceptions', from the under-sixteens to include the under-eighteens. Not only does this instantly inflate the perceived problem, it also redefines it. Older teenagers are far more likely to take a pregnancy to term, so the expanded category is very important in shifting the emphasis from the problem of girls experiencing unintended conceptions to the problem of young women pursuing their pregnancies to term and producing children. Although young, unmarried motherhood has a long history of moral condemnation, problematising pregnancy solely by virtue of the mother's young age is a more recent phenomenon. In current thinking, the mother's age is regarded as far more significant than her marital and relationship status.

So what does the age of the teenage mother signify? Within policy, claims are made that the category 'teenage' is strongly associated with measurable disadvantageous outcomes for young mothers and their offspring (Social Exclusion Unit 1999; TPSU 2005; NHS Health Development Agency 2003). The age of the teenage mother is argued to be significant because it is associated with inadequacy in her ability to care for the child owing to her lack of economic wherewithal, her emotional immaturity and her lack of education. While there has been a long-standing concern for the potentially negative impact of young motherhood on young women's lives, more recently thinking has shifted to a totalising narrative of harm to the child and an increasing problematisation of the young mother as a parent. 'The problem' therefore becomes expanded to include *all* teenage mothers and *all* of the children born to them. In recent years, critics have challenged these claims, arguing that the disadvantages associated with young motherhood are caused by the mother's socio-economic position, not her age (Ermisch 2003; Ermisch and Pevalin 2003, 2005).

The effect of a 'risk' framework

Another way in which the scale of the problem is expanded is noted by Dodds (forthcoming) in her article tracing the development of social exclusion policy.

Dodds illustrates how New Labour policy has shifted from concern with those who are 'excluded' from society's gains to a concern with those deemed to be 'at risk' of social exclusion. The influence of risk discourse within the context of teenage pregnancy policy has only recently begun to be explored (Dodds, forthcoming; Macvarish, forthcoming) but one of its effects is to expand concern from measurable, existing social problems to problems predicted in the future. In the case of teenage parenthood, this is embodied in the conceptualisation of babies born to young mothers as facing particular disadvantage through childhood and into adult life. This is evident in the 1999 Social Exclusion Unit report which launched the Teenage Pregnancy Strategy:

> Teenage parenthood is bad for parents and children. Becoming a parent too early involves a greater risk of being poor, unemployed and isolated. The children of teenage parents grow up with the odds stacked against them. (Social Exclusion Unit, 1999)

In the ensuing policy literature, a repeated claim has been that babies born to teenage parents will remain within their parents' social circumstances, held back by the stunted educational career of the mother and living within the limited economic opportunities of the community into which they are born. Additionally, the children of teenage mothers are cast as biologically 'vulnerable': a relationship is drawn between young maternal age and low-birth-weight babies, higher rates of infant mortality, a higher likelihood of being exposed to 'risky' antenatal behaviour such as unhealthy diets and smoking, and lower rates of breastfeeding. Thus the body and the brain of the baby are constructed as 'at risk'; it is claimed that low birth-weight (in fact only associated with the very youngest mothers) is associated with low-IQ (Bamfield 2007). Young mothers are also claimed to be more prone to post-natal depression, which is said to undermine maternal bonding and, in turn, claimed to affect the baby's neurological and emotional development. In this strongly deterministic framework, the baby is constructed as inherently disadvantaged at conception by virtue of its mother's age. The teenage mother is therefore posed as a risk to herself and to her baby. These apparently individual, privatised risks are 'socialised' through predictions of the mother's dependence on welfare and the multiple disadvantages which will render her child socially costly and potentially a threat to social order.

Zero-tolerance?

Such is the strength of the idea that young parenthood is inherently disastrous for mothers, babies and society, that at times policy has seemed to verge on a 'zero-tolerance' position on teenage pregnancy. In 2006, Minister for Children, Families and Young People, Beverley Hughes, took the unusual step of publicly responding to research claiming that some teenage pregnancies were planned and that teenage parenthood could have positive outcomes (Cater and Coleman 2006). A lengthy ministerial rebuttal was circulated and Hughes gave statements to the media:

> This is an unfortunate study which, on the basis of a very small and carefully selected sample, suggests that teenage pregnancy can be a positive option for some young people. We reject that view completely. There is overwhelming evidence that, overall, teenage parenthood leads to poorer outcomes both for teenage mothers and their children.
>
> (Beverley Hughes, BBC News Online, 17 July 2006)

In this way, on the basis of 'the evidence', policy asserts that all teenage mothers and their children are problematic.

The teenage mother as lacking in rationality or moral agency

Although the teenage mother is constructed as both parentally and socially 'risky', she is not held to be morally culpable for her behaviour. Because the teenager occupies the awkward position of being both adult and child, her autonomy or agency is often characterised as 'risky'. The teenage mother is a particularly potent symbol, therefore, of this 'risky subject', who is not capable of exercising moral or rational autonomy, but rather, in her actions, expresses the influences upon her from her environment or her past. Rather than making 'wrong choices', teenagers deemed 'at risk' of teenage pregnancy are constructed as being 'vulnerable' to the impacts of environmental and, increasingly, parental factors (NHS, 2003). As Castel points out, the new strategies of governance formed around the concept of 'risk', 'dissolve the notion of the *subject* or concrete individual and put in its place a combinatory of *factors*, the factors of risk' (Castel, 1991: 281).

Some aspects of risk discourse tend to emphasise 'raising awareness' and the dissemination of information so that individuals can make 'informed choices' based on an assessment of the risk. However, teenagers are not commonly constructed as working well with knowledge or as capable of acting rationally in their own best interests. High profile stories of very young teenagers having babies exacerbate prejudices that teenage parents are generally feckless, ignorant and immature. Knowledge of risk, which might be accepted as of advisory benefit to older populations, is less confidently held to produce the desired outcome among teenagers. Unplanned teenage pregnancies are blamed primarily on a lack of knowledge about sex and contraception or inadequate skills in negotiating sexual relationships. Planned teenage pregnancies are attributed, amongst other things, to naïvety about the demands of parenthood, or dysfunctional families and communities where traditional gender roles, a 'benefits culture' or low expectations thrive (see Arai 2003, 2005, for a critique of such claims).

The second half of the chapter draws on evidence from qualitative research to call into question the assumption that the teenage mother is inherently 'vulnerable'. The findings also challenge her construction as lacking in moral or rational agency, and challenge the tendency for policy discourse to reduce her to a mere embodiment of 'risk factors' and dysfunctions.

The problem of 'poor parenting'

The 'social exclusion' agenda increasingly explains 'exclusion' as the product of dysfunctional interpersonal relationships, in particular the relationship between parent and child. In the past three years, 'poor' parenting has become a key component of political explanations for the perpetuation of poverty and inequality. What Furedi (2001) has termed 'parental determinism' has come to dominate articulations of concern and shaped proposed solutions to an expanding range of problems. New Labour Health Secretary Alan Johnson stated to a conference of the relationship counselling charity Relate in 2007:

> Crucially, the quality of a child's upbringing plays a *colossal* role in determining what heights he or she will eventually be able to scale. At its *best*, a family's love and encouragement will provide a child with the confidence and self esteem to succeed. At its *worst*, and for a small minority, the experience can leave lasting scars ... Parenting outstrips every other factor: including social class, ethnicity or disability—in its impact on attainment.   (Johnson, 2007, emphasis in original)

In teenage pregnancy policy, the teenage mother's 'exclusion' is frequently explained by her own parents' attitudes and behaviour. For example, it is claimed that teenage motherhood is inter-generationally transmitted from mother to daughter or is a response to paternal absence. Parents are also said to lack the skills to communicate with their children about sex. In 2005, the Minister responsible for the strategy to reduce teenage pregnancy announced that the time had come to 'put parents at the heart of the teenage pregnancy strategy' (Hughes, quoted in *The Guardian*, 26 May 2005), admitting that its targets were unlikely to be met because there is no 'magic bullet from the government side and local authority side and all the partners on the ground' capable of making 'another substantial step forward'. She went on to say, 'we really need parents to now see themselves as making an absolutely unique and vital contribution to this issue … It is a contribution that I don't think anyone else can actually make' (op. cit.).

While this attempt to pass the responsibility for future policy success onto parents seems to flatter them as having a unique role, it can also be read as an attempt to blame parents for policy failure and as a statement of intent to target 'inadequate' parenting with policy interventions. Indeed, the Minister's words take a didactic turn when she suggests that, 'parents could start by asking their youngsters about sex education lessons at school, and perhaps discussing peer pressure about fashion, or talking about their friends' (op. cit.).

The implication of these ministerial statements is that the UK's 'shameful' (Blair in SEU, 1999) rate of teenage pregnancy can be explained by high numbers of parents neglecting to talk to their children about sex and relationships. This ministerial interview is also exemplary of policy defensiveness towards accusations of 'the nanny state' and 'old-fashioned' moralising. As the *Guardian* journalist writes, 'Ministers stress that they will not present parents with a 'birds and bees script' to run through with their teenagers, nor encourage parents to advocate abstinence' (op. cit.).

However, by moving away from rationales that are perceived to lack legitimacy, policy moves into the even more intimate terrain of how parents talk to their children about intensely private matters. The tendency for working-class teenagers to exhibit higher rates of parenthood than their middle-class counterparts is attributed to the inadequacies of their own parents' 'emotional literacy'. The solution is governmental intervention to improve the 'skills' and 'increase the confidence' of parents to enable them to talk to their own children. There is no evidence that teenage pregnancy is 'caused' by parental emotional 'illiteracy' and our findings will show that teenagers who become pregnant have often had very open and frank discussions with their mothers about sex and contraception. Reducing the explanation for teenage pregnancy to the level of intimate family relationships obscures the proven patterns that have much more convincing structural explanations and which demand political and economic solutions (Arai 2003, 2005; Lee et al. 2004). Blaming parents also 'opens up' people's personal lives to experimental state interventions in intimate relationships.

The teenage mother as evidence of 'family breakdown'?

A narrative that further underpins the shift in focus to parental inadequacy characterises the contemporary parent as being particularly isolated because of an alleged falling away of familial support. This decline is attributed to a number of factors including geographical mobility, women moving into the workforce, changing family forms, the burden of caring for elderly relatives and changes in the context of parenting, for example, due to technological developments (Every Parent Matters 2007). The construction of family life as being subject to unprecedented levels of strain is one that has become a 'commonsense' cultural truth. According to the government's Every Child Matters and Every Parent Matters reports, this has led to unprecedented need and demand for state and professional advice.:

> Government needs to consider carefully its role in enabling all parents to play a full and positive part in their children's learning and development. We want to create conditions where more parents can engage as partners in their children's learning and development, from birth, through the school years and as young people make the transition to adulthood. We are pushing at an open door here—75 per cent of parents say they want more help.
> (Alan Johnson, cover letter to the launch of *Every Parent Matters* report, 15 March 2007)

If parenting is more difficult in general then logically it must be even more difficult for teenage parents who must be particularly lacking in the resources and emotional maturity to cope.

Edwards and Gillies (2004) argue, however, that although some parents express the view that family support has lessened relative to the past, the policy perception that profound social changes have undermined family practices to such an extent that they need to be reconstituted via a 'pedagogical relationship' between parents and state agencies is out of step with the views of most parents.

Their study found that while most parents (with the notable exception of minority ethnic parents) viewed the state rather than family and friends as the most appropriate source of financial support and housing provision for those in need, the family was seen as most appropriate for providing child care, emotional support and advice about child health and behaviour. Interestingly, middle-class families were more likely to view the family as having become more fragmented (Edwards and Gillies, 2004: 643).

> Family, followed by friends, are (still) regarded as the people to turn to for most childrearing issues, with 'experts' only providing practical help and advice about long institutionalised areas of children's lives.
>
> (Edwards and Gillies, 2004: 627)

When we turn to the findings of our qualitative study, these viewpoints are echoed in the evocation of family support as overwhelmingly important in coping with young parenthood.

The qualitative challenge to the policy construction of the 'teenage mother'

So far we have discussed the way in which the teenage mother is conceived of in policy discourse. Qualitative research throws up a more complicated picture of the reality of life as a young parent. It brings to light alternative meanings attached to motherhood by young parents and their families that challenge those prevalent in policy discourse. The findings question the policy version of teenage motherhood in a number of significant ways, each explored in turn below. First, the very construct of a coherent category of the 'teenage parent' is disputed by the teenagers' diverse circumstances and their own self-definitions. Second, the picture of the peculiarly 'isolated' and 'vulnerable' teenage parent who requires intensive professional support is contradicted by descriptions of familial involvement both before and after the baby's birth. Finally, the portrayal of the teenage parent as the passive embodiment of 'risk factors' rather than being a moral and rational agent in her own right is also challenged by the young mothers' accounts of their decision-making regarding contraception, proceeding with the pregnancy and becoming parents.

Young parents were interviewed across the county of Kent in the South-East of England between December 2004 and March 2006. Pregnant teenagers aged between thirteen and eighteen were recruited, primarily via midwives, during the final trimester of pregnancy. Seventeen of the original thirty-five respondents were then followed up and re-interviewed around the time of the child's first birthday to gain information about their experiences of postnatal support and care. Male and female interviewees were sought, but most respondents were single females. All of the respondents were 'white-British' and most had lived in Kent since birth. The material discussed below is drawn from both the antenatal and postnatal wave of interviews with young mothers. The interviews with young fathers will not be discussed here because the chapter focuses on the particular policy construction of young mothers. However, many of the views expressed by young mothers were echoed by their partners. The age indicated in brackets following each quotation is that of the mother at the time of interview.

The 'teenage mother' as a homogeneous category determined by age

Young parenthood may be associated with particular socio-economic and educational circumstances over a broad population, but qualitative studies such as this one uncover the heterogeneity of individual lives. The pathways into teenage parenthood among our respondents were diverse and complex, and therefore very difficult to comprehensively capture and explain. The ways in which young parenthood was dealt with by individuals and their families were also varied, with few patterns formed along the lines of maternal age. Most displayed considerable fortitude in coping with a multitude of issues and seemed content with a minimal level of formal support, while some were more enthusiastic about state-provided services. All valued straightforward guidance with practical and financial matters such as benefits and housing, but even here, some prided themselves in finding their own way through bureaucracy while others felt let down by inefficient assessment procedures. While some of the mothers were keen to return to education or work either for reasons of sociability or for financial independence, others were protective of their time at home with a young child in the early years.

Some respondents found peer support groups targeted at young parents very useful in making them feel more normal and less judged, while providing practical, experiential advice. Others did not identify with other 'teenage' parents at all, challenging the value of emphasising a homogeneous identity and experience:

I didn't really go to that because I felt like, you know, I'm eighteen, I'm not that young if you know what I mean. I can do it myself because I'm quite independent … I don't know, I didn't really take much interest. I thought young and pregnant support would be like young people, like fourteen. You're eighteen years-old, you're older and you're more … not everybody's the same, but like you're more aware rather than when you're fourteen years-old. Some people know what they're doing and some people don't, I suppose but when you have a baby it all comes natural. No matter how much people tell you, you never do what they say. You end up doing it your own way anyway.   (18 years, antenatal)

Given the dominant political and cultural problematisation of teenage parenthood, there seemed to be a strong rationale for the mothers distancing themselves from rather than identifying with the category. For one girl, 'coping well' offered a refutation of belonging to the category of 'too young' for motherhood:

I think if you're able to cope with it then I wouldn't say I was young. I mean I've obviously … I think I cope well and I've been able to look after her and give her everything she needs so … you know?
                                        (16 years, postnatal)

Being 'lumped together' with thirteen and fourteen year-olds was also perceived as infantilising and conflicted with familial and community beliefs that cast young parenthood as something normal rather than deviant.

The 'teenage mother' as the product of inadequate familial relationships

As discussed earlier, in policy and broader public discussion, teenage pregnancy is represented as a symptom of family or social breakdown and inadequate parent-child communication, particularly concerning sex. Our findings challenge both of these conceptualisations.

Parental communication about sex

Our research found a surprisingly high level of maternal intervention in the sexual development of the young mothers. In many cases, mothers had proactively encouraged their daughters and their sons to use contraception and in some cases had taken them to sexual health clinics or GPs once they thought their child had reached an age when sexual experimentation was likely:

> Well my mum said about me going on to the pill ... (*Int*: Were you in a relationship at the time?) No, she just thought it was the best time, at the age of fifteen, in case I did decide to have sex or whatever and then she would feel happy about herself by helping me by getting on the pill instead of just letting me get on with it and going through all that stuff too early. (18 years, antenatal)

Some mothers seemed highly motivated to be open about sex from a young age:

> My mum is quite open about stuff like that because her mum never told her anything ... So she wanted to make sure we were all informed and that ... She was showing us a book and she was trying to get us to read it with her but we were laughing too much because we thought it was too funny ... I was about seven. (18 years, antenatal)

Some of the girls' mothers had been pregnant as teenagers themselves and were concerned to prevent their daughters from following a similar path:

> She said that she didn't want me to go the same way she did ... I think my mum was the one that explained it the best, because you can relate to your parents, can't you? (18 years, antenatal)

In the case of a girl who was estranged from her natural mother, her step-mother played an equally supportive role:

> I've spoke to like my step-mum quite a lot ... I wouldn't feel embarrassed to talk to her if I had a question or something ... I would ask her general stuff but when I started having sex I would tell her as well.
> (16 years, antenatal)

Perhaps surprisingly, grandparents could also be important sources of advice, whether instead of a parent or as well as a parent. This seemed to be so in families where grandparents had been very involved in the teenager's life:

> My mum was a young mum herself ... So she's more like my older sister
> and I don't go to her about anything because I'm too embarrassed. So I
> ask my nan. And my nan was the one that came to family planning with
> me ... she said, "right, we'd better get you on the pill" and she took me
> down the hospital and that was it.   (18 years, antenatal)

Family support during pregnancy

One of our key findings from the antenatal interviews was the centrality of family
support to the decision to proceed with a pregnancy and the ability to cope with
becoming a young parent. In most cases, this support had continued, although by
the time of the second interview many young parents were making the transition
to greater independence. Families tended to normalise the pregnancy experience,
creating a protective and supportive shield to buffer the negative stereotypical
image. Many of the young parents described relationships with their parents
as improving following their pregnancy:

> With my mum, it's made us closer because I mean before I even moved
> out, we hated each other ... not hated each other but we just really did
> not get along. Everything was an argument. We could never talk to each
> other. When I moved out it got easier. I fell pregnant and I think it got
> easier. But as soon as I had her we were like best friends—you can't
> separate us now!   (16 years, postnatal)

McDermott and Graham (2005) also found that the experience of pregnancy
and motherhood often helped to repair mother-daughter relationships which
had previously been fraught and conflictual.

During the pregnancy, mothers often played a vital role in calming the girls'
fears and reassuring them from their own experience that things were progressing
normally. Many of the girls anticipated their mothers playing a very active role in
helping them care for the new baby, whether or not they were living together:

> I normally phone my mum ... and say 'look, you know, the baby's not
> moving'. And mum will be like, 'you're alright' ... Because obviously, you
> know, you get told everything by loads and loads of people but you only
> really listen to your mum's advice.   (17 years, antenatal)

Having lost her mother at a young age, one girl's older sister was a vital source of support and affirmation even though she had initially tried to encourage her younger sibling to have a termination:

> She quite likes to come to the midwife and hear the baby's heartbeat. She loves hearing the baby's heartbeat, just to make sure she's all right ... My sister loves babies ... She can't wait to hold my baby. She keeps shouting at my belly saying, 'come out now, I want to give you a cuddle'. She felt her kick for the first time the other day. (16 years, antenatal)

In the antenatal interviews, family was overwhelmingly cited as the most helpful source of support during the pregnancy and was anticipated to be essential to coping after the birth. Parental support and that of the wider family, including witnessing other family members at close hand cope with young parenthood, seemed to normalise the experience and make it seem viable.

Family support in coping with parenthood

Financial dependence on their own parents was a strong feature of many of the young mothers' lives, whether in the provision of housing or material support to supplement welfare payments. Grandparents were more often a source of financial support than the father of the child. There were descriptions of families being very unhelpful, but these were the exception. For example, one girl's mother and sister were violent alcoholics and she moved out early on in the pregnancy. However, she was taken in by her boyfriend's family who were extremely supportive. Another girl, whose mother had died and who had been caring for her chronically ill and sometimes violent father was supported by her siblings in getting re-housed away from him once she became pregnant. Her relationship with her father subsequently improved and he was pleased about becoming a grandfather. Very few teenagers were left without any family support.

From providing a welcoming reaction to the news of the pregnancy to passing on second-hand baby equipment, the wider family can be very important to young parents' sense that they will be able to cope in the future. Like Speak (1995), we found that young mothers spent a large amount of time in their parental home even after getting independent accommodation. We found families providing childcare assistance, child-rearing advice, emotional support, financial assistance, housing and transportation. Most of the young parents described feeling indebted to their families, especially their mothers. Support was often forthcoming not just from the maternal grandparents but also from the paternal grandparents, who could also act as mediators between estranged or antagonistic young parents. Support was substantially material—especially providing housing and additional financial support, but also practical in providing childcare, freeing the girl to return to education or work, or offering respite from the pressures of being a parent:

> It's like my grandparents were so made up by him ... they bought the carpets for us.   (16 years, postnatal)

> I mean we've had a lot of support from my family and ... from members of his family and they have helped us out a lot. And my mum has been paying for me to have driving lessons ... And she's paid for my car ... So really it's just been family members that have helped us. We've had no real help from like the council or the state and it was really hard to get information about stuff we were entitled to.   (17 years, postnatal)

Another important role of family was in providing experience of babies and young children. Some of the respondents had siblings who were much younger than themselves and those who did, felt that parenthood was less frightening because of their direct experience of caring for small children:

> My mum's got five children but like I've got three sisters and a brother so I would ask her, my mum, things about it and she would just tell me her past experiences like through her pregnancies and what happened.
>   (18 years, postnatal)

Others saw family members cope with pregnancy and parenthood, often at a young age. One girl's observation of her cousin positively influenced her self-confidence as a future parent:

> Looking at how she copes has given me ideas on how I'm going to cope ... Because I was thinking, oh how am I going to do it? I've got my own responsibility now at the end of the day. What am I going to do? But actually seeing her cope has made me think yeah, think positive, you can actually do it. If you put yourself down obviously you're not going

to be able to do the things, but seeing her do it has made me a lot more confident. (18 years, antenatal)

The following respondent's brother became a father at a very young age, but speaking to him had confirmed the positive meanings to be found in parenthood:

I mean seeing my brother bring up a baby, it was difficult, you could see it was ... Well his girlfriend was actually fourteen and he was fifteen so ... And when I first told him I was pregnant he said it is hard but he said at the end of it it's worth it ... It is going to be hard but I think because we're both young we're going to be able to enjoy it more, seeing them grow up and doing the things that we want to do with the child ... I'm not gutted that I'm pregnant this young but it would have been nicer to do it in a few years time. (16 years, antenatal)

For most of our interviewees, professionals were looked to only to fill the gaps in expertise in the family network, usually identified as medical expertise, specific pregnancy and baby advice, and accessing welfare state benefits. In a review of the literature on teenage parents, McDermott and Graham (2005) found that young parents consistently make use of families and their own 'personal capacities'.

The 'teenage mother' as lacking moral and rational agency?

Pathways into pregnancy

Many of the young mothers spoke of being far more proactive in seeking contraceptive precautions than the policy picture presents:

I put myself on the pill when I was 15 ... I only put myself on the pill because I had read in these little books that it helped with your periods, like stops them being so heavy and stuff so ... I went to my doctor and asked to be put on to the pill. (18 years, antenatal)

When you're like fourteen or fifteen years-old you see boyfriends and whatever and I thought I was quite sensible getting on the pill ... I was

seeing a boyfriend at the time ... Although we wasn't intimate or anything
like that, still it's better to be safe than sorry.   (18 years, antenatal)

I was worried about getting pregnant most of all actually, because I really
didn't want it to happen. So I used to go ... and find out, and places that
I could go to find out and talk to someone about it and they told me like
all the things I needed to know.   (15 years, antenatal)

From these responses, a complex picture emerges of how pregnancy occurs
which suggests that in their levels of knowledge, sexually active teenagers who
get pregnant may not be so different to those who avoid pregnancy or who
have abortions. Surprisingly high levels of contraceptive use were reported, but
because this was not consistent over time, the risk of pregnancy was still high.
Other studies (for example, Luker 1996) have shown that it is not ignorance or an
unwillingness to use contraception that leads to pregnancy, but rather changing
patterns of use within relationships and through different relationships, bound
up with the complicated social and emotional vagaries of adolescent intimate
life. Luker writes that use of contraception tends to be 'relationship specific' and
sexual activity may be sporadic and unpredictable, making contraceptive use
more difficult (Luker, 1996).

The transition to parenthood

There were varied reactions to discovering the pregnancy and this variation
continued in the way the mothers came to terms with the situation. Some
embraced it as a positive experience very early on, while for others there were
continued feelings of regret about the timing of the pregnancy, mixed with
excitement about the future. Few of the girls regarded the timing of their
pregnancies as ideal. Although they did not regret having a baby, many did
regret becoming pregnant at a young age:

It's just stupid getting pregnant at a young age. I wish I'd never got
pregnant, I didn't want kids but when you know you've a person growing
inside you, you don't want to get rid of them.   (16 years, postnatal)

One of the couples admitted during the interview that they had planned to
have a baby but had not dared to tell anyone else this because they assumed

they would be thought of as foolish and irresponsible. Although most of the pregnancies were not described as planned, some respondents were still excited and pleased, seeing the pregnancy as an opportunity to change their lives:

> I didn't want to get rid of it. I don't know why. It's just a strange feeling but I just wanted to keep the baby so ... at the time I was only eighteen and I thought people would be like well you're only eighteen, you're not old enough to have a baby, you're not mature enough. But I was just ... I didn't really care at the time. I wanted to prove to myself, and prove to other people, that I could do it.   (18 years, postnatal)

The meaning of parenthood to young parents

A strong current running through the interviews was optimism that parenthood could provide a 'new beginning' and would allow the teenager to make the transition to adulthood in a way that might meet with approval from others. Even if getting pregnant was seen as an unfortunate accident, proceeding with the pregnancy was generally seen as a good thing by those surrounding the teenagers, and a number of them had clearly experienced affirmation that had not been available to them during their sometimes troubled adolescences. It was important for the girls to be able to see themselves as having made the right decision to proceed. Disavowing abortion and accepting responsibility for their 'mistake' allowed them to transform the pregnancy into something positive. These findings are in accord with those of McDermott and Graham (2005), who found that motherhood was an opportunity to enter into adult status and to take on the affirmed moral identity of the 'good mother'.

A number of the respondents described embracing the pregnancy and the prospect of parenthood as an opportunity to transform themselves and their lives. For some this was described as a transformation in their identity from 'bad girl' to 'good mum':

> I just think over the past like seven months I have grown up so much ... everybody has said to me you know you've grown up so much. You've got a beautiful place. You've got a lovely boyfriend who would do anything for you. You've got a baby on the way ... We're all really proud of you. And it's nice to be praised for that instead of going, 'you're out of order. You're all wrong. You do this and you do that'.   (17 years, antenatal)

I've got life in a different perspective altogether now, I've changed my attitude totally. I used to be a little bastard before I fell pregnant. Proper naughty, mouthy, always in trouble, just naughty. Just getting myself in trouble, going out fighting all the time ... and now I've got pregnant I've changed my mind totally, it's like turning your life around, when you've got a baby it's not like a part-time job is it, it's like a full-time thing you have to do really when you've got a baby. You have to have a straight head ... you have to look after the baby yourself if you decide to keep it.

(16 years, antenatal)

For others, having a baby promised to bring a more internal sense of meaning and purpose to their lives:

Because I wasn't really doing a lot with my life ... and I thought to myself to have a child would give me something to have and you know to ... not live for but you know what I mean? So that was one of the reasons ... well one of the main reasons. And yeah I just ... we just decided that's what we wanted.   (18 years, postnatal)

Although strongly rooted in systems of meaning about babies and parenthood and, in most cases, supported by family networks, for most of the interviewees, independence was highly valued and was most commonly understood as being demonstrated by autonomous problem-solving, 'coping well' or in producing a happy, 'well-behaved' baby:

I like to be independent. I always have. I would rather myself go without than have to ask someone ... I always have been ... I would rather do something on my own than have someone help me. I've always been like that.   (16 years, postnatal)

One young mother had been living at home in the early months after birth but had then moved into a flat of her own. She attributed her desire to breastfeed in part, to her need to draw a boundary around herself and her baby, marking the child as her own:

I loved living with my mum. I loved it ... But I like my independence so I like being on my own as well ... they seem to just take over and now

I'm on my own it's me and her so we get bonding sort of thing. I think that's why I breast fed as well, because everyone seemed to take over but I knew they couldn't take that over ... Me and my mum are very close so it was just like she thinks she's one of hers basically but I was just like she's mine!

(18 years, postnatal)

The lived experience of young mothers that emerges from qualitative research such as this, challenges many of the fundamental claims of policy. It calls into question the very category 'teenage mother' by revealing variations of experience and circumstance. Simplistic models of 'ignorance' or 'vulnerability' fail to capture the young mothers' complicated descriptions of their pathways into parenthood. The picture painted by young mothers of their familial relationships is very different to the policy one of family breakdown and 'inadequate parenting'. The meanings attached to the baby and to motherhood by young mothers and their families are not only absent from policy but actively denied by policy-makers.

Conclusion

In policy terms, the teenager who is 'at-risk' of pregnancy is the victim of 'low self-esteem', 'low aspirations' and 'inadequate parenting'. There is little space in policy for the idea that some individuals may simply wish to have children young or, if they find themselves accidentally pregnant, may value the child's life over their own adolescent fulfilment and gratification. Policy has a problem with finding meaning in teenage pregnancy and motherhood other than the acting out of dysfunctions and risk factors. As the findings of many qualitative studies show, however, whether planned or unplanned, and while difficult, parenthood offers hope of profound meaning to individuals, some of whom will be young.

The exercise of choice in the pursuit of a liveable moral identity, albeit in circumstances of limited real opportunity, suggests that for some young people, young parenthood is an effective way of achieving an adult social position, of fulfilling certain ambitions to create or enrich a loving family, and to move them on from a position of stasis in relation to formal education and the labour market. Many recent qualitative studies of teenage parenthood have found similar 'positive' experiences. In addition to the contributions to this book, Seamark and Lings (2004) found that becoming a mother during the teenage years was associated with an increased focus on career and life satisfaction. Coleman and Cater's (2006) study of planned parenthood found that having children was experienced as a source of satisfaction and fulfilment rather than as a cause of social exclusion. Wilson and Huntington (2005) question whether young parents themselves feel excluded, positing that it is more likely that they see themselves as being integrated into society by having children.

An alternative way of understanding young parenthood amongst working-class teenagers is offered by Bynner et al. (2002), contextualising it within a dual framework of 'fast' and 'slow' lanes to adulthood. Middle-class adolescents follow a slow, linear path with assumed progression from school, through higher education and into successively better-paid employment, while working-class adolescents are typically in a fast lane, without the mediations of progressive stages and without the surety of 'career' and improved circumstances as time passes. Geronimus (1997) suggests that for young people from poor backgrounds, having children young makes sense because they can still rely on intensive familial support; they have no guarantee that should they postpone parenthood they will be in a more secure financial position. This is not to suggest that amongst our sample, any more than a few of the pregnancies were planned. However, taking contraceptive risks that made pregnancy more likely, and deciding to continue into parenthood once the pregnancy was discovered, were choices shaped by a broader awareness of life's options, familial support and the young person's assessment of their own ability to cope.

The strengthened symbolic presence of the 'teenage mother' in policy and public discourse in recent years owes much to her dual status as both child and parent at a time when anxieties about both are peculiarly heightened (see chapter nine). The 'teenage mother' is both pitied and blamed, identified with and stigmatised because symbolically, she has come to embody a number of powerful contemporary concerns. The anxieties of our age which lend particular power to the problematisation of younger motherhood include: a concern with the role of the 'parent' and their ability, spontaneously, to rear the next generation; a concern with the particular vulnerability of twenty-first century childhood; a widespread concern with social disorder and moral decline but a recognition that past forms of social and moral ordering have an alienating rather than a cohering effect; and a need to legitimise state intervention at a time of low expectations of real socio-economic progress.

The existing literature on contemporary policy developments relating to 'teenage mothers' has engaged with some but not all of these trends. In particular, critiques have focused on the tendency within policy to devolve responsibility for social inequalities and associated social problems to individuals. Commentators of the category 'social exclusion' have argued that the 'neo-liberal' agenda is driven by sectional (capitalist) interests to deny the roots of social problems in socio-economic structures and to blame individuals in disadvantaged circumstances for the problems they face (albeit in sympathetic language). Consequent policy solutions tend to be non-economic and non-structural. These academic critiques have provided important insights into recent policy developments, in particular in challenging the decline in social understandings of the relationship between individual circumstances and larger social structures.

There is another dimension to contemporary policy that has been paid less attention in critical circles; the decline in social thinking has developed alongside a decline in the conceptualisation of the individual as a moral or rational agent, rooted in real social relationships. It has been argued here that policy concerned with the 'problem of teenage motherhood' clearly exemplifies this development. A less one-sided critique requires an exploration of how contemporary policy thinking largely constructs the individual as both abstracted from social relationships and alienated from their own capacity to be rational or moral agents.

References

Arai, L. (2003) Low expectations, sexual attitudes and knowledge: explaining teenage pregnancy and fertility in English communities. Insights from qualitative research, *The Sociological Review* 51(2): 199-217.

Arai, L. (2005) Peer and neighbourhood influences on teenage pregnancy and fertility: qualitative findings from research in English communities, *Health and Place* 13(1): 87-98.

Bamfield, L. (2007) *Born unequal: Why we need a progressive pre-birth agenda*. London: Fabian Society.

Billings, J.R., Macvarish, J. and Appleton, S. (2007) *Teenage parents' views and experiences of sex and relationships education, sexual health services and family support services in Kent. Service Users Report*, Antenatal. Centre for Health Services Studies, University of Kent, Canterbury.

Billings, J.R. and Macvarish, J. (2007) *Teenage parents' experiences of parenthood and views of family support services in Kent. Service Users Report, Postnatal.* Centre for Health Services Studies, University of Kent, Canterbury.

BBC News Online, Beverley Hughes, Minister for children, families and young people, 17 July 2006, accessed 18/11/08, news.bbc.co.uk/1/hi/health/5186614.stm

Bynner, J., Elias, P. et al. (2002). *Young people in transition: Changing pathways to employment and independence*. York: Joseph Rowntree Foundation.

Castel, R. (1991) From dangerousness to risk, in Burchell, G., Gordon, C. and Miller, P. (eds) *The Foucault effect: Studies in governmentality*, Chicago, IL: University of Chicago Press.

Cater, S. and Coleman, L. (2006). *'Planned' teenage pregnancy: Perspectives of parents from disadvantaged backgrounds*, Policy Press.

Department for Education and Skills (2007) *Every parent matters*, Department for Education and Skills.

Department for Education and Skills (2007) *Every child matters: Change for children*, Department for Education and Skills.

Dodds, A. (2009) Families 'at risk' and the Family Nurse Partnership: The intrusion of risk into social exclusion policy, *Journal of Social Policy*, 38: 399-514.

Edwards, R. and Gillies, V (2004) Support in parenting: Values and consensus concerning who to turn to, *Journal of Social Policy*, 33: 627-647.

Ermisch, J. (2003) *Does a 'teen-birth' have longer-term impact on the mother? Suggestive evidence from the British Household Panel Study*. Institute for Economic and Social Research, Working Papers, 2003-32, University of Essex.

Ermisch, J. and Pevalin, D.(2003) *Does a 'teen-birth' have a longer-term impact on the mother? Evidence from the 1970 British Cohort Study*, Institute of Economic and Social Research, Working Papers, 2003-32, University of Essex.

Ermisch, J, and Pevalin, D.J. (2005) Early motherhood and later partnerships, *Journal of Population Economics* 18(3): 469-489.

Furedi, F. (2001, 1st edn) *Paranoid parenting*. Continuum Press.

Geronimus, A.T. (1997) Teenage childbearing and personal responsibility: An alternative view, *Political Science Quarterly*, 112(3): 405-430.

Graham, H. and McDermott, E. (2005) Resilient young mothering: Social inequalities, late modernity and the 'problem' of 'teenage motherhood', *Journal of Youth Studies*, 8(1): 59-79.

The Guardian (2005) Beverley Hughes, *Guardian* interview Appeal to parents on teenage births, Lucy Ward (26 May 2005).

Johnson, A. (2007) Strong families, strong society, inaugural lecture to the Relate Institute, 27 February 2007, London, www.dcsf.gov.uk/speeches/media/documents/relatespeechweb.doc

Lee, E., Clements, S., Ingham, R., and Stone, N. (2004). *A matter of choice? Explaining national variations in abortion and motherhood*, York: Joseph Rowntree Foundation.

Luker, K. (1997) Dubious conceptions: The politics of teenage pregnancy. Cambridge, MA: Harvard University Press.

Macvarish, J. (forthcoming) The effect of 'risk-thinking' on the contemporary construction of teenage motherhood, *Health, Risk and Society*

NHS Health Development Agency (2003) *Evidence briefing summary, Teenage pregnancy and parenthood: A review of reviews*. C Swann, K Bowe, G McCormick and M Kosmin, www.nice.org.uk/niceMedia/documents/teenpreg_evidence_briefing_summary.pdf

Seamark, C. and Ling, P. (2004) Positive experiences of teenage motherhood: a qualitative study, *British Journal of General Practice*, November: 813-818.

S.E.U (1999) *Teenage pregnancy: Report by the Social Exclusion Unit*. London: Stationery Office.

Speak, S., Joseph Rowntree Foundation, et al. (1995) *Young single mothers: Barriers to independent living*, Family Policy Studies Centre.

Teenage Pregnancy Strategy Unit (2005) *Teenage pregnancy strategy evaluation. Final report synthesis*.

Wilson, H. and Huntingdon, A. (2005) Deviant (m)others: The construction of teenage motherhood in contemporary discourse, *Journal of Social Policy*, 35(1): 59-76.

Chapter 4

Just what difference does teenage motherhood make? Evidence from the Millennium Cohort Study

Denise Hawkes

1. Introduction

Teenage motherhood is often viewed as a bad outcome for the young mother herself and for her child. In attempting to correct for these bad outcomes government policy, as advanced by New Labour since 1997, has focused attention on three policy strands. The first is to try and prevent teenage motherhood through the initiatives launched by the Teenage Pregnancy Unit (Social Exclusion Unit, 1999) and the second is to alleviate the economic and social disadvantages experienced by the young mother and her child by promoting the employment and education through the New Deal for Lone Parents (Yeandle and Pearson, 2001). Finally, the third policy strand is to try to reduce the social, health and educational disadvantages experienced by the children of teenage mothers through the Sure Start programme (National Evaluation of Sure Start, 2008). Fundamentally, however, the starting point for all of these interventions is that the root of the problem is that the mother is young. But is this actually the case?

This chapter will present statistical evidence on the nature of early motherhood, for both the mothers themselves and their children, in Britain at the start of the twenty-first century. The statistical analysis presented will consider three snapshots of teenage motherhood:

1. The difference in life course experiences of teenage mothers, compared to non teenage mothers, prior to the birth of their first child,
2. The difference in the early life circumstances of children, by the age at which the mother had her first birth, and
3. The difference in cognitive, health and behavioural outcomes for children at ages 3 and 5, by the age at which the mother had her first birth

In the first set of statistical analysis I shall demonstrate that teenage motherhood is largely associated with the prior disadvantaged family background experienced by the teen before the birth of her child. Therefore teenage motherhood should be more correctly viewed as a signal of prior disadvantage. In other words it is not the existence of a teenage birth that is the problem, but rather the disadvantaged circumstances that lead to its occurrence. This view of teenage motherhood is found in other statistical studies, which also show the socio-economic determinants of the timing of motherhood (e.g. Kiernan and Diamond, 1983; Kiernan, 1992, 1997; Ermisch and Pevalin, 2003a; Rendall and Smallwood, 2003, Hawkes, 2008a, Jayaweera et al., 2005, SEU, 1999). In addition research using the British birth cohort study 1970 (Ermisch and Pevalin, 2003b, 2005) and data on British twins (Hawkes, 2008b) find that the socio-economic disadvantage of early motherhood is strongly associated with poor family background experienced by the teenage mother herself. This again suggests that teenage motherhood is really a symptom of a disadvantaged life course rather than the cause of it.

The second set of statistical analysis will document some of the circumstances the families find themselves in when the child is nine months old. Those children with teenage mothers are indeed born into families experiencing multiple disadvantages. These include being more likely to be living in poor areas, to experience poverty due to living in a family on benefits or having low income parents, to have a 'poor quality' father figure either due to unemployment or absence, and finally to living with a mother who is unhappy or depressed. Crucially, however, the analysis presented here shows that the mother's age at first birth is not the main driver of these disadvantages—rather it is the prior disadvantages experienced by the younger mothers during their own childhoods (see Hawkes, Joshi and Ward, 2004, for an extended analysis).

Similar results are found in the longitudinal studies carried out by Ermisch and Pevalin (2003b, 2005) which find that, once early life experiences of the teenage mother are controlled for; there are very few additional disadvantages to the family in terms of later household income and the education attainment of the young mother. However they do find a reduced chance of success for the teenage mother in the marriage market. Similarly Liao, (2003) using the same data source, finds some effect of early motherhood on a women's mental health. In summary many studies have found that given the poorer life course of most teenage mothers prior to the birth of their children, the often disadvantaged family situation experienced by the children themselves is likely to be a product of the mothers' poor life courses prior to becoming a mother, rather than a direct consequence of having a younger mother.

The final set of statistical analysis considers the impact on child cognitive, health and behavioural outcomes in the pre-school years. Many studies have used the British cohort studies of 1958 and 1970 to demonstrate that being born into a disadvantaged family may affect a child's experience of childhood and their subsequent success in adulthood (Gregg et al., 1999; Hobcraft and Kiernan, 2001; Feinstein, 2003; Blanden et al., 2005; Schoon, 2006). Given these findings we would expect the children of teenage mothers to attain poorer child outcomes given that teenage motherhood is a signal for intergenerational disadvantage. However, this is only the case for some aspects of child cognitive and behavioural outcomes, and again these largely disappear if prior disadvantage is accounted for.

2. The data—the Millennium Cohort Study and teenage mothers

The statistical analysis will be undertaken using the Millennium Cohort Study (MCS). The MCS is the fourth birth cohort study in the UK consisting of nearly 19,000 children born in the UK between September 2000 and January 2002 (Hansen, 2008). These children's families have been interviewed to date four times, when the children were nine months, three years, five years and seven years-old. The analysis presented in this chapter will use data from the first three sweeps. The MCS over samples those living in areas with high child poverty rates, large proportions of ethnic minority residents and those living in Wales, Scotland and Northern Ireland (Plewis, 2007). However, all the analysis presented in this chapter has been adjusted to correct for this survey design.

The main variable of interest for analysis in this chapter is the mother's age at first birth. This has been chosen rather than the mother's age at the birth of the cohort member (who may be a subsequent child). This is because those who had their first child in their teenage years, but where the cohort child is a subsequent non-teenage birth, have characteristics more like current teenage mothers than to other mothers their own age. Therefore, when the cohort member is the not the first born child of their mother, the age at which the mother had their first live birth is used.

Table 1 shows the distribution of the age at first birth of natural mothers in the MCS. When considering just those cohort members who are the first born of their mother, 14.9% are born to teenage mothers. The all births column includes those who had their first child as a teenager and for who the cohort member is a subsequent, non-teenage, birth. For all births 17.8% are born to mothers who were either teenagers at the time of the survey or who were teenage mothers when their first child was born.

Table 1: Age at first birth of the natural mothers in the Millennium Cohort Study

Age at first birth (years)	All births (%)	Cohort first births only (%)
under 20	17.8	14.9
20-24	25.7	20.3
25-29	29.3	28.4
30-34	20.9	26.0
35 and over	6.3	10.4

sample size of 18,726 natural mothers
percentages reported are adjusted to take account of the survey design

3. The life course experience of teenage mothers and non-teenage mothers prior to the birth of their first child

As noted in the introduction previous work using the MCS suggests that those who enter motherhood earlier have experienced more disadvantaged family backgrounds. The data presented here also demonstrates this—see Tables 2-4 and Figure 1.

Table 2 presents employment rates for the parents of the cohort member's mother (i.e. the child's grandparents) when she herself was fourteen. The first column shows that, of those who enter motherhood as teenagers, 61% had a mother who was employed when they were fourteen. This is insignificantly different to the proportion found for those who entered motherhood age 20-24—and indeed for those who became mothers over 35. Only those who entered motherhood between twenty-five and thirty-four are significantly more likely to have a working mother at the age of fourteen than those who entered motherhood as a teenager.

Table 2: Employment rates of the parents of the cohort members' mother when she was fourteen, by age at first birth.

Age at first birth (years)	Mother employed		Father employed	
	%	SE	%	SE
under 20	61	0.014	75	0.010
20-24	63	0.014	82	0.008
25-29	70	0.009	91	0.005
30-34	71	0.013	93	0.006
35 and over	65	0.019	93	0.010

sample size of 14,326 natural mothers
percentages and standard errors (SE) are adjusted to take account of the survey design

The second column in Table 2 looks at the proportion of teenage mothers whose father was employed when they were fourteen. (This excludes those whose father was not in contact). This shows that of those who were in contact with their parents, 75% of those who entered motherhood as a teenager had a working father when they were fourteen years-old. This is significantly lower than all other age groups (at the five percent probability level), although there is less difference to those who entered motherhood in their early twenties. Those entering motherhood as teenagers are more likely to have experienced the unemployment of a father figure than those who entered motherhood later. Clearly unemployment of a father figure would have implications for a family, at the least in terms of the mother probably having experienced life on benefits, and hence in poverty, in their mid teens.

Table 3 presents the country of origin of the cohort members' grandparents as well as the ethnicity of the cohort members' mothers. On average, within the UK, country of origin and ethnicity can be taken as a rough index of economic disadvantage (Plewis, 2007). The first column presents the data on the country of origin of the cohort members' grandmother. For children born to those who entered motherhood as a teenager, 88% had a grandmother born in Britain. This is insignificantly different to the proportion found for those who entered motherhood after their teens (and indeed is greater than the proportion for those entering motherhood between 20 and 24). The second column presents the data on the country of origin of the cohort members' grandfather. For those children born to a teenage mother, 88% also had a grandfather born in Britain. Again those who entered motherhood between twenty and twenty-four is the only group that is significantly different (at five percent probability level), for whom only 80% had a British father.

Table 3: Grandparent's country of origin and ethnicity of the cohort members' mother, by age at first birth

Age at first birth (years)	British grandmother		British grandfather		British mother		white mother	
	%	SE	%	SE	%	SE	%	SE
under 20	88	0.013	88	0.014	93	0.009	90	0.013
20-24	81	0.018	80	0.018	87	0.012	84	0.018
25-29	86	0.011	86	0.011	91	0.007	90	0.010
30-34	86	0.011	86	0.011	91	0.008	93	0.008
35 and over	83	0.019	83	0.018	89	0.016	92	0.011

sample size of 14,326 natural mother for country of origin data and 18,580 natural mothers for ethnicity data
percentages and standard errors (SE) are adjusted to take account of the survey design

Columns three and four in Table 3 look at the characteristics of the cohort members' mother. Of those who entered motherhood as a teenager, 93% were British and 90% were white. Again the only group in this column that is significantly different (at five percent probability levels) to the teenage mothers group are those who entered motherhood between twenty and twenty-four, who are even less likely to be British born (87%) and white (84%) than those who entered motherhood as a teenager.

In summary Table 3 shows that those who enter motherhood as a teenager are similar to all other groups in terms of their parents' (i.e. the child's maternal grandparents) country of origin and their ethnicity—with the exception of those who entered motherhood in their early twenties. For this age group, parents are significantly more likely to be born outside of the UK and to be from an ethnic minority group, compared to teenage mothers.

Figure 1 presents the proportion of natural mothers who left school at the minimum school leaving age (sixteen or for a few appropriate cases fifteen) by their age at their first birth. This figure shows that those who entered motherhood as a teenager are most likely to have left school by the compulsory school leaving age (79.5%), and this is significantly more likely compared to all other age groups. As the entrance to motherhood is delayed the chance of leaving school at the minimum school leaving age decreases substantially. However, there is less difference for those entering motherhood from twenty-five upwards in terms of the proportion of mothers leaving at the minimum school leaving age (24%—36%). In summary figure 1 shows that teenage mothers were more likely to leave school early.

Figure 1: Natural mothers who left school at minimum leaving age, by age at first birth

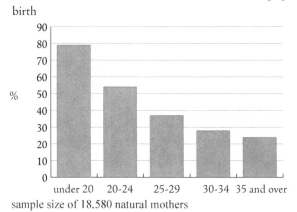

sample size of 18,580 natural mothers
percentages are adjusted to take account of the survey design

Table 4 presents some childhood experiences for the cohort members' mothers, and these give an indication of relative family stability and coherence. Column one shows the proportion of the mothers who experienced parental separation before they were eighteen years-old. Those who entered motherhood as a teenager were significantly more likely to have experienced parental separation than any other age group (48%), and this declines by age of first birth. The second column considers the proportion of mothers who lived away from home before they were eighteen, including experiencing time in care or living with other family members. As many as 32% of those who become mothers as teenagers had experienced time living away from home before they were eighteen. This is significantly more likely any other group. In summary those who entered motherhood as teenagers were significantly more likely to have experienced parental separation and have lived away from the family home, and hence—we can assume—more likely to have experienced instability, conflict and confusion in their childhoods.

Table 4: Family stability of the cohort members' mother, by age at first birth

Age at first birth (years)	Parents separated before cohort members' mother was eighteen		Cohort members' mother lived away from home before she was eighteen*	
	%	SE	%	SE
under 20	48	0.011	32	0.010
20-24	31	0.009	16	0.007
25-29	20	0.007	09	0.006
30-34	16	0.007	10	0.011
35 and over	14	0.012	12	0.012

sample size of 18, 580 natural mothers
percentages and standard errors (SE) are adjusted to take account of the survey design
* lived away from home includes time in care and living with other family members

Overall those who enter motherhood as a teenager were more likely to have experienced the unemployment of their father at the age of fourteen, to have left school at the minimum school leaving age, to have experienced parental separation and to have lived away from home than all other mothers. This amounts to a significantly more disadvantaged early life course experience for teenage mothers, compared to non-teenage mothers, prior to the birth of their first child. It is also worth noting that, for most of these measures, the 20-24 age group also appears relatively disadvantaged.

4. The early life circumstances of the children of teenage and non-teenage mothers

Table 5 presents four family circumstances, which we can take as indices of (dis)advantage, measured when the cohort member was nine months old. These measures will, of course, also indicate the living circumstances for the new mothers as well as their babies. The first column shows the proportion of families in each age group in which the mother had a partner living in the household, at least part time. Those who entered motherhood as a teenager are much less likely to have a partner in the household when the cohort child is nine months old. Column two repeats this exercise for owner occupied housing. Once again those who enter motherhood as teenagers are much less likely to be relatively advantaged, as measured this way, than any other age group. Column three shows that those entering motherhood as teenagers are least likely to have access to a car or van for personal use. Column four considers the chances of living in an advantaged area, and again teenage mothers are the most disadvantaged group on average. All of these results are statistically significant. However, as in the previous section, we find that whilst those who enter motherhood in their early twenties are significantly better off than those who enter motherhood as a teenager, they are still significantly less well off—for all four indices -than those who entered motherhood after twenty four.

Table 5: Family circumstances when the cohort member was nine months, by age at first birth

Age at first birth (years)	Partner present*		Owner occupier		Vehicle available+		Living in an advantaged area++	
	%	SE	%	SE	%	SE	%	SE
under 20	65	0.011	20	0.010	61	0.012	40	0.024
20-24	82	0.008	49	0.013	81	0.008	49	0.022
25-29	94	0.005	81	0.010	94	0.005	69	0.017
30-34	96	0.004	88	0.008	97	0.004	77	0.017
35 and over	95	0.008	88	0.012	95	0.008	74	0.028

sample size of 18,685 natural mothers

percentages and standard errors (SE) are adjusted to take account of the survey design

* partner present may or may not be the natural father of the cohort member

+ defined as access to a car/van for personal use (could own the vehicle or it could be a company vehicle)

++ defined as an electoral ward that did not have a high rate of child poverty in 2000

Overall those who enter motherhood as a teenager are less likely to have a partner present, to be owner occupiers, to have access to a vehicle for personal use and to be living in a relatively advantaged neighbourhood. This is a significantly more disadvantaged set of early life circumstances for the children of teenage mothers, and for these new mothers themselves, than for the children of non-teenage mothers.

5. Children's outcomes at three and five years-old

5.1 Cognitive outcomes

Given this double set of prior disadvantages for the teenage mother and her child it would be reasonable to expect lower cognitive scores for these children at both three and five years-old. The likelihood that teenage mothers will have experienced disadvantaged childhoods could make them less well equipped, on average, to help their child develop cognitive and behavioural skills. In addition the disadvantaged start to life experienced by these families probably means less resources available to them, which in turn would hinder cognitive development as measured in the tests undertaken on the MCS.

The first two columns of Table 6 consider two child cognitive tests administered when the cohort members were three years-old. The first column presents the results of the British Ability Scale (BAS) vocabulary subscale. In this test the children were shown a series of pictures and asked to name each item. Interestingly, although those with teenage mothers on average scored least, this difference is insignificant (at the ten percent probability level) to those with mothers in their early twenties. Rather, the significant difference comes at a later age, and those children whose mothers had their first child aged 25 and over score significantly better than those children whose mothers entered motherhood under this age. The second column in Table 6 considers the Bracken school readiness test. In this test the children are asked, among other things, to name letters and colours. Once again, while the children of teenage mothers score the lowest on average, this is insignificantly different (at ten percent probability level) to the children of those who entered motherhood in their early twenties. As with the BAS vocabulary test, the significant difference is between children born to mothers aged under and over 25 years. Furthermore, the analysis in Hawkes and Joshi (2009) suggests that—once the differences in prior family experiences are taken into account—these cognitive differences disappear all together. This

Denise Hawkes

suggests, yet again, that it is prior disadvantage rather than the age of the mother that is the main driver in child cognitive scores at age three.

Table 6: Child cognitive outcomes at three years and five years, by mother's age at first birth

Age at first birth (years)	Child cognitive outcomes at age three				Child cognitive outcomes at age five					
	BAS vocabulary subscale score		Bracken school readiness score		Naming vocabulary subscale score		Picture similarity subscale score		Pattern construction subscale score	
	mean	SE	mean	SE	mean	SE	mean	SE	mean	SE
under 20	46.7	0.31	97.6	0.46	51.5	0.25	54.1	0.39	49.1	0.31
20-24	48.4	0.31	101.7	0.43	53.5	0.30	54.5	0.26	50.5	0.27
25-29	52.1	0.23	108.2	0.41	57.3	0.25	56.7	0.24	52.4	0.23
30-34	53.9	0.31	111.8	0.52	59.5	0.28	57.8	0.29	53.4	0.28
35 and over	54.2	0.47	112.6	0.77	59.8	0.45	57.4	0.39	53.1	0.45

sample size of 11,509 cohort members
means and standard errors (SE) are adjusted to take account of the survey design

Columns three to five of table six present comparable results for the cognitive tests administered at age five. These three tests are all subscales of the British Ability Scale. Those children who have a teenage mother have a lower average score than the other groups for both the naming vocabulary and pattern construction subscales; however again this is insignificantly different to those with mothers who entered motherhood in their early twenties (at ten percent probability level). Similarly, for the picture similarities subscale those children who have a teenage mother also have a lower average score than the other groups, but again this is insignificantly different to those with mothers who entered motherhood in their early twenties (at five percent probability level). Analysis undertaken in Hawkes and Joshi (2009) finds that once prior family experiences are taken into account that these cognitive differences completely disappear.

Overall those children who have a mother who entered motherhood as a teenager do not do significantly worse than those who have a mother who entered motherhood in their early twenties on cognitive tests administered at age three and five. In addition the differences in the child outcomes in the pre-school years for the children of teenage and non-teenage mothers can be largely explained by the prior life disadvantage experienced and is not merely a consequence of having a teenager as a mother.

5.2   Child health outcomes at three years-old

Figure 2 considers the proportion of cohort members who are overweight at three years-old, where this can be taken as an index of overall health. Whilst there is some variation in the proportion of overweight children by the age at which their mother entered motherhood (and it is the children of mothers giving birth between 20 and 24 are most likely to be overweight) these patterns are not statistically significant. Therefore having a teenage mother does not significantly affect the chances of a pre-school child being overweight.

Figure 2: Proportion of cohort members who are overweight at three years-old, by age at first birth

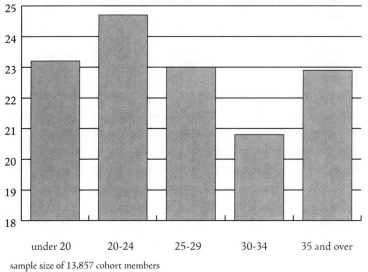

sample size of 13,857 cohort members
percentages are adjusted to take account of the survey design

Similar insignificant patterns were found for other reported health outcomes at age three, such as poor eyesight, acute illnesses like asthma, and health service for accidental injury. For all three of these health outcomes there was no statistical significant difference (at the five percent level) in the percentage of children experiencing these health concerns by age at motherhood. Therefore having a teenage mother does not significantly affect the chances of a pre-school child experiencing poor health.

5.3   Child behavioural outcomes at five years-old

Finally, I consider child behavioural outcomes as measured by the subscales of the 'Strengths and Difficulties' Questionnaire. This questionnaire is answered by the mother of the cohort member as part of the self-completion section of the third sweep of the MCS questionnaire.

Table 7: Child behavioural outcomes as age five years, by age at first birth

Age at first birth (years)	Prosocial subscale score		Hyperactivity subscale score		Emotional difficulties subscale score		Conduct problems subscale score		Peer problems subscale score	
	mean	SE	mean	SE	mean	SE	mean	SE	mean	SE
under 20	8.4	0.05	3.8	0.06	1.5	0.04	1.9	0.04	1.4	0.04
20-24	8.5	0.04	3.4	0.05	1.4	0.04	1.5	0.03	1.1	0.03
25-29	8.5	0.03	2.8	0.04	1.2	0.03	1.2	0.03	0.9	0.02
30-34	8.5	0.04	2.6	0.06	1.1	0.03	1.1	0.03	0.7	0.03
35 and over	8.4	0.07	2.7	0.10	1.0	0.06	1.0	0.05	0.9	0.05

sample size of 11,255 cohort members
means and standard errors (SE) are adjusted to take account of the survey design
each of these are subscales of the strengthens and difficulties questionnaire (SDQ) as reported by the cohort
    members mother

The first subscale, in the first column, considers pro-social behaviour—that is behaviour which is intended to benefit another person, such as helping, sharing and comforting. This is the only subscale where a higher score indicates better outcomes. We can see from the results in column one an average of 8.4 out of ten is scored by the children of those who entered motherhood as teenagers. This is little different from any other age group of mothers, and on this subscale the age of the mother at first birth is not a statistically significant determinant of the score obtained.

The second subscale records hyperactivity. In this case the children of teenage mothers have the highest score on average, and this is significantly larger than any other age group. However, again those with mothers in their early twenties also have significantly greater scores than those with mother aged twenty five and over. It is worth noting that it is the child's mother who reports these behavioural scores, and we might expect younger mothers to be more likely to report problem behaviours than older mothers.

The third column shows results for the emotional difficulties subscale. In this case the children of teenage mothers are not statistically significantly different to children of mothers in their early twenties. However both age groups are more likely to report such behaviours than those with mothers' age twenty five and over.

The fourth subscale measures conduct problems. The results here mirror those of hyperactivity, with the children of teenage mothers being significantly more likely to have conduct problems. The fifth subscale measures peer problems. Once again the children of teenage mothers are significantly more likely to have peer problems than the children of non-teenage mothers. However both the levels of conduct and peer problems reported for the children of teenage mothers are much lower than those for hyperactivity, and the differences with other age groups are not so great. This suggests that conduct and peer problems are not as much of a problem as hyperactivity for the children of teenage mothers.

Overall those children with a mother who entered motherhood as a teenager have significantly worse hyperactivity, conduct problems and peer problems than those who have a non-teenage mother. However they are not significantly worse, in these terms, than those children whose mothers entered motherhood in their early twenties. In addition there is no difference by age at first birth in terms of prosocial behaviour. Furthermore, Hawkes and Joshi (2009) find all but the hyperactive behaviour can be eliminated to insignificant difference once prior family disadvantage is controlled for. In other words most of the differences in child behavioural outcomes in the pre-school years for the children of teenage and non-teenage mothers can be explained by prior life disadvantages, and is not simply a consequence of having a teenager as a mother.

Conclusion

This chapter set out to consider three main aspects of teenage motherhood and the impact on their children at the start of the twenty first century:

1. *The difference in life course experience of teenage mothers and non-teenage mothers prior to the birth of their first child.*

The data shows that those who enter motherhood as a teenager were more likely to have experienced the unemployment of a father at the age of fourteen, to have left school at the minimum school leaving age, to have experienced parental separation and to have lived away from home than all other mothers. This is a significantly more disadvantaged early life course experience for teenage mothers than for non-teenage mothers prior to the birth of their first child.

2. *The difference in the early life circumstances of mothers and their children by the age at which the mother had her first birth.*

The data shows that those who enter motherhood as a teenager are less likely to have a partner present, to be owner occupiers, to have access to a vehicle for personal use, and to be living in a relatively advantaged neighbourhood. This is a significantly more disadvantaged set of early life circumstances for teenage mothers and her children than for non-teenage mothers and their children.

3. The difference in child outcomes in the pre-school years for the children of teenage and non teenage mothers

The data shows that those children whose mother who entered motherhood as a teenage do not score significantly worse at cognitive and some behavioural indices than those who have a mother who entered motherhood in their early twenties. In addition what differences there are in these scores can be largely explained by the prior life disadvantage experienced and is not merely a consequence of having a teenager as a mother. The one exception, where the children of teenage mothers still score less well, even when disadvantage has been controlled for, is hyperactivity. Finally no significant difference is found in health outcomes.

All of this statistical evidence points to the conclusion that the incidence of teenage motherhood is a signal of the prior disadvantage of the mother. Similarly, most of the subsequent disadvantage of their children is associated with their mothers' prior disadvantages and those subsequently experienced, because of this, by the children themselves. Even so, for some indices of cognitive development, behaviour and health there is little difference between the children of teenage mothers and other children, while on many outcome indices mothers who first gave birth between 20 and 24 also do relatively poorly. Being a young mother does not in itself lead to poorer outcomes for the children of teenage mothers, or for the mothers themselves. Rather teenage motherhood often signals a life of exposure, both for mothers and children, to a range of social and economic disadvantages.

What do these results imply for government policy surrounding teenage motherhood? Put simply, they suggest a shift in government policy towards the social and economic causes of teenage motherhood, rather than the incidence of teenage motherhood itself. This is not only because it is prior disadvantage, not the age of mother, that predisposes teenage mothers and their children to less favourable outcomes. In addition this policy shift would be sensible because the factors associated with becoming a teenage mother appear to be the same factors as those influencing the life chances of their children. Therefore government policy aimed at targeting disadvantages such as father's unemployment and area poverty would help to directly reduce the incidence of teenage pregnancy as well as to improve the life chances of those who are the children of teenage mothers.

Acknowledgements

I would like to thank the Economic and Social Research Council for funding this research (grant number RES-163-25-0002). A special thanks to Heather Joshi for all her helpful comments and suggestions on various stages of this work. I would also like to thank the participants of the Centre for Longitudinal Studies internal seminar series 2008 and the Understanding Population Trends and Processes annual conference in Leeds 2008 for their comments and suggestions. All remaining errors are of course my own.

Bibliography

Blanden, J., Goodman, A., Gregg, P. and Machin, S. (2005) Changes in intergenerational mobility in Britain, in Corak, M. (ed.) *Generational Income Mobility in North America and Europe*, Cambridge University Press, Cambridge, pp. 112-147.

Ermisch, J., and D. Pevalin. (2003a) Who has a child as a teenager? *ISER Working Paper 2003-30*, Institute of Social and Economic Research, University of Essex, Colchester.

Ermisch, J., and Pevalin, D. (2003b) Does a teen birth have longer-term impact on the mother? Evidence for the 1970 British Cohort Study, *ISER Working Paper 2003-28*, Institute of Social and Economic Research, University of Essex, Colchester.

Ermisch, J. F. and Pevalin D. J. (2005) Early motherhood and later partnerships, *Journal of Population Economics*, 18: 469-489.

Feinstein, L. (2003) Inequality in the early cognitive development of British children in the 1970 Cohort, *Economica*, 70(277): 73-97.

Gregg, P., Harkness, S. and Machin, S. (1999) *Child Development and Family Income*, Joseph Rowntree Foundation, York.

Hansen, K. (2008) *Millennium Cohort Study. A Guide to the Datasets*, Centre for Longitudinal Studies, Institute of Education, University of London, London.

Hawkes, D. (2008a) The UK Millennium Cohort Study: the circumstances of early motherhood, in Edwards, R. (ed.) *Researching Families and Communities: Social and Generational Change*, Routledge, Abingdon, pp. 147-163.

Hawkes, D. (2008b) The socio-economic consequences of early child bearing: evidence from a sample of UK female twins, submitted to *Journal of Population Economics*.

Hawkes, D. and Joshi, H. (2009) Unequal entry to motherhood and unequal child outcomes: evidence from the UK Millennium Cohort, work in progress

Hawkes, D., Joshi, H. and Ward, K. (2004) Unequal entry to motherhood and unequal starts in life: evidence from the first survey of the UK Millennium Cohort, *Working Paper 6*, CLS Cohort Studies, London, www. cls. ioe. ac. uk/core/documents/download. asp?id=299andlog stat=1

Hobcraft, J., and Kiernan, K. E. (2001) Childhood poverty, early motherhood and adult social exclusion, *The British Journal of Sociology*, 52(3): 495-517.

Jayaweera, H., Joshi, H., McFarlane, A., Hawkes, D. and Butler, N. (2005) Pregnancy and child birth, in Dex, S. and Joshi, H. (eds.) *Children of the 21st Century from Birth to Nine Months. The UK Millennium Cohort Study Series*, The Policy Press, Bristol, pp. 109-132.

Kiernan, K. E. (1992) The impact of family disruption in childhood on transitions made in young adult life, *Population Studies*, 46: 213-234.

Kiernan, K. E. (1997) Becoming a young parent: a longitudinal study of associated factors, *British Journal of Sociology*, 48: 406-428.

Kiernan. K. E. and Diamond, I. (1983) The age at which childbearing starts -a longitudinal study, *Population Studies*, 37(3): 363-380.

Liao, T. F. (2003) Mental health, teenage motherhood, and age at first birth among British women in the 1990s, *ISER Working Paper 2003-33*, Institute of Social and Economic Research, University of Essex, Colchester.

National Evaluation of Sure Start (2008) The impact of Sure Start local programmes on three year-olds and their families, *Research Report NESS/2008/FR/027*, Institute for the Study of Children, Families and Social Issues, Birkbeck, University of London, London.

Plewis, I. (2007) *Millennium Cohort Study: Technical report on sampling*, Centre for Longitudinal Studies, Institute of Education, University of London. www. cls. ioe. ac. uk/studies. asp?section=00010002000100050004

Rendall, M. and Smallwood, S. (2003) Higher qualifications, first-birth timing, and further childbearing in England and Wales, *Population Trends*, 111: 18-26.

Schoon, I. (2006) *Risk and Resilience: Adaptations to Changing Times*, Cambridge University Press, Cambridge.

Social Exclusion Unit (SEU) (1999) *Teenage Pregnancy*, TSO, London.

Yeandle, S., and Pearson, S, (2001) New Deal for Lone Parents, *Working age and employment report esr89rep*, Department for Work and Pensions, TSO, London.

Chapter 5

Pathways to adulthood: Reflections from three generations of young mothers and fathers

"You just do your best and you be the best parent you can".

Eleanor Formby, Julia Hirst and Jenny Owen

Introduction

This chapter reflects on findings from a qualitative study of women and men from three generations, who all became parents during their teenage years. Our aim is to offer some insight into lived experiences, and to illustrate the importance of life course, upbringing, and social context in understanding experiences of pregnancy and of becoming—and sometimes being labelled as—a 'young parent'. This approach facilitates understanding of the diverse ways in which the identity of 'young parent' can have both immediate and longer-term implications for individuals, with commonalities and differences across and within generations, genders, and social classes. What appears to characterise the accounts of all our study participants is that having a baby as a teenager is not necessarily predictive of adversity. This is not to suggest that young parenthood is problem-free; rather, our findings suggest that if problems are experienced, they arise from the particular social and economic circumstances that form the context for pregnancy and parenthood, rather than from the age at which pregnancy occurs.

Below, we outline our starting-points and study design, and then present our findings in a sequence that mirrors the ways in which participants told their stories. We begin with reflections on the discovery of pregnancy, including the ways in which opportunities to learn about sex and relationships (or the lack of such opportunities) were seen as influencing this transitional period. We then move on to accounts of the experience of parenthood, including access to formal and informal support networks, and finally to themes concerning stigmatisation and identity. In conclusion, we highlight the ways in which this three generation study contributes to broader debates and perspectives on teenage parenthood in the UK.

Background to the study

In the UK, recent research and policy discourses concerning teenage pregnancy and parenthood have commonly revolved around issues of class, disadvantage, and poverty, either implicitly or explicitly. Analyses of conception and termination rates, for example, demonstrate that continuation of a teenage pregnancy is more common among young women from relatively poor socio-economic backgrounds than among more affluent young women; currently, those from professional and managerial households are more likely to terminate a pregnancy than to continue it (Berthoud et al., 2004). There have been contrasting arguments about the extent to which teenage parenthood is an outcome of poverty and disadvantage, and the extent to which it is a cause. Some studies have focused on early parenthood as contributing, in itself, to problems in later life, including poverty (via dependence on benefits or low-paid work), limited educational achievements, and poor health status (Hobcraft and Kiernan, 2001). Commonly, these patterns are seen as being reproduced inter-generationally (see for example SEU, 1999). This is the reasoning that underlies the current UK Teenage Pregnancy Strategy, with its focus on reducing teenage conceptions and births, and also reducing 'social exclusion' among young parents.

However, other empirical studies and theoretical critiques have raised a number of questions about this emphasis. A 'review of reviews' related to teenage pregnancy concluded that 'socio-economic disadvantage can be both a cause and consequence of teenage parenthood' (Swann et al., 2003: 1). Berthoud et al. (2004) found that the negative consequences of having a child while a teenager are considerably less marked than current Government policy suggests. There is evidence, however, of a likelihood of poorer mental health for teenage mothers than older mothers; there is also evidence that the children of teenage mothers are at greater risk of low educational attainment, unemployment, and eventual early parenthood themselves (Berthoud et al., 2004). This, of course, begs important questions: how far is 'teenage parenthood' itself really the problem? Or, do problems arise from the ways in which young parents are positioned in society, whether they are characterised as the passive victims of 'social exclusion', or stigmatised as deviating from culturally- and historically-specific constructions of 'normal' parenthood (Bonell, 2004)?

The inter-related themes of disadvantage, identity, and stigmatisation are explored in depth in the systematic review of qualitative research about teenage motherhood completed by McDermott, Graham and Hamilton (2004). This illustrated the ways in which many young mothers asserted views of themselves as coping responsibly with pregnancy and parenthood, in marked contrast to the public reactions they encountered:

> The studies in the synthesis suggest that as the young mother's pregnancy became visible, their bodies became physical markers of immorality, irresponsibility, and inappropriate sexual activity … the 'good' mother is defined through a discourse of her children's needs, and this discourse was heavily drawn on by the young mothers.
>
> (McDermott, Graham and Hamilton, 2004: 28-30)

As Pam Alldred and Miriam David (this volume) demonstrate, there are clear pressures on young mothers to enter into discourses of self-improvement that may result in reproducing very negative constructions of young parenthood (see also Kidger, 2004). Since we had no policy or evaluation agenda to pursue in our research, we hoped to avoid some of these pressures, and to create an opportunity for our participants to reflect on the ways in which early parenthood has been experienced in very different time periods and sets of social and family circumstances. We now move on to outline briefly how we went about this.

Study design

Our study was based in South Yorkshire, UK; participants came from the Sheffield and Doncaster localities. With a population of around 500,000, Sheffield is a large and socially diverse city, encompassing some of the most affluent and some of the most deprived wards in England. As in other large Northern cities, there has been a transition from large-scale employment in steel, mining and other forms of manufacturing to employment in various forms of service industry. Doncaster is smaller, with a population of nearly 300,000, but has experienced a similar transition.

In order to reach participants from different generations, we adopted a range of purposive and snowball sampling strategies. Interviews and features in local media (radio and press) were most successful in recruiting parents from the oldest generation. We also designed and distributed leaflets, in consultation with current young parents, and advertised the project via local health, education, and other support services in the region. This mix of approaches has shaped the sample in particular ways: for example, the oldest generation of participants includes a majority of people who described themselves as being from middle-class backgrounds, while our youngest participants all saw themselves as being of working-class origin. In this connection, it is important to point out that the study was not designed as a wide-ranging or generalisable survey, but as an exploratory piece of work. We wanted to find out how taking a biographical and multi-generational approach might inform research with, and about, teenage parents, perhaps identifying new themes and insights for further research on a larger-scale.

Before discussing the main themes in our findings, we briefly introduce below the participants from each generation, to offer a sense of the characters behind the disclosures, and the contexts that shaped their lives. Pseudonyms are used, in order to preserve anonymity. Table 1 provides an overview.

Table 1

Generation	Male	Female	Total
Oldest (aged 54-68, had their 1st child in the period 1958-1972)	6	6	12
Middle (aged 30-49, had their 1st child in the period 1976-1995)	6	3	9
Youngest (aged 15-25, had their 1st child in the period 1998-2006)	2	5	7
Total	14	14	28

Oldest generation mothers

Eileen, Kate, Hilary, Linda, Kay, and Barbara were all in their fifties and sixties at the time of the study and had their first child in the 1950s, 1960s or early 1970s. Most came from middle-class backgrounds, with parents who were employed in white-collar professions, and adopted 'strict' approaches to raising their daughters. These family circumstances proved salient in their accounts of reactions to their pregnancy, and of their own feelings, in that the need for respectability was paramount. Each mother married the father of their baby.

Oldest generation fathers

Robert, Paul, Colin, James, Dave, and Charlie were also in their fifties and sixties and had become fathers in the 1950s, 1960s or early 1970s. They described growing up in working-class or lower middle-class families. Two out of the six went on to become senior professionals. Despite different career trajectories, there are significant commonalities in their experiences of being fathers. All had two or more children, with the first being conceived when they were between sixteen and nineteen. All but one married the mother of the child soon after discovering she was pregnant, the exception being a couple who were already married before the pregnancy.

Middle generation mothers

Helen, Rachael, and Ruth were in their thirties or forties during the research and had their first child in the 1970s, 1980s or 1990s. These women came from middle-class professional or lower middle-class backgrounds. Each of these mothers described a somewhat disrupted childhood; experiences included domestic violence (resulting in spending time in refuges or with other relatives), parental separation and/or divorce, and severe bullying at school.

Middle generation fathers

Pete, Nick, Patrick, Craig, Tim, and Matt were in their thirties or forties and had their first child in the late 1970s to early 1990s. These fathers grew up in loving families and had fond memories of their mother, father, and siblings. All described coming from working-class backgrounds and neighbourhoods; they saw themselves as having avoided some of the contexts and temptations that led some of their peers into crime or other difficulties. For some, community activities and hobbies were seen as being very significant in helping to avoid this. Examples cited included church youth club, brass band membership, and football.

Youngest generation mothers

Joanne, Katrina, Beth, Chantelle, and Debs were aged fifteen to twenty-five during the study and had their first child in the period 1998-2006. Some were pregnant with a first or subsequent child at the point of taking part. All were engaged with a voluntary sector support service at the point of participation in the research. Each described themselves as being from a working-class background, and a majority had had a disrupted childhood; they had experienced bullying or abuse, domestic violence and/or had been in the care system. The majority had already left school when they became pregnant, aged sixteen or seventeen. Most were still with the father of their child(ren), though relationships were relatively new at the point of conception (three to five months). Most of the fathers were a few years-older than the mothers, and most of the pregnancies were unplanned, though not unwanted insofar as all the women chose to continue with their pregnancy.

Youngest generation fathers

Dave and Damian were both under twenty-one when they took part, and had become fathers in the period 2005-2006. They chose a very brief form of involvement in the project—through short, filmed interviews—and so our data on their backgrounds is much more limited than the data for other participants.

Participants were invited to choose their level of involvement, in one or more of the following forms of data collection:

- biographical-narrative interviews;
- photographic diaries and photo-elicitation interviews/discussion groups;
- participation in radio phone-in;
- group discussions, and
- short, filmed interviews.

Table 2 summarises the pattern of participation: some participants were involved in more than one method, hence the figures below are more than the total number of participants (see Table 1).

Table 2

Method	Number who participated in each method
1: Biographical-narrative interviews (2-3 interviews per participant)	9 (= 23 separate interviews[1])
2: Group discussions (+ potential individual interviews)	8
3: Photographic diaries	6
4: Group discussions facilitated by sharing of photographs (from method 3)	10
5: Video-recorded 'talking heads' documented on DVD	6
6: Radio phone-in	5 callers

Biographical-narrative interviews (Bertaux and Thompson, 1997; Seidman, 1998) involved either two or three interviews, spread over a number of weeks. These moved from an initial, open-ended 'life-story' approach to a more focused reflection on key aspects of the 'story' (Plummer, 1995). This three-stage process facilitated the development of a strong relationship between the interviewer and interviewee. Many commented that the process had enabled them to think about aspects of their experience in new ways:

---

1   Six participants had three interviews; two participants had two interviews, and one participant had one interview and chose not to continue.

I've told some people some stuff and I've told other people other stuff …
but … never ever told anybody everything … I'm quite amazed … hearing
it meself … I'd not put that piece of the jigsaw in place before now … it
was a fairly difficult home situation really, when I think about, when I
kind of put it all in context.   (Kate, oldest generation mother)

Those involved in photographic methods were provided with a disposable
camera and invited to take photographs to reflect their current or former lives
as young parents, using short, written guidance. Most took photographs over
a two to four week period and the resultant 'diary' provided a visual record to
illustrate 'portfolios' of experience. Some participants chose to use pre-existing
photographs and albums, either instead of, or in addition to, those taken
specifically for the research. Group discussions were then held to discuss the
diaries, drawing on images, memories, and stories evoked by the photos. Images
included children and partners, other family members and friends, homes, cars,
pets, social gatherings and significant family events, family holidays, and various
representations of hobbies and interests.

Discussion groups were also held with participants who had not participated
in photographic diaries. These focused on issues relating to experiences of
pregnancy or parenting (for example experiences of family life and/or support
services), and sometimes involved discussing photographs they would have
taken had they had the opportunity. In general, both the use of actual photos,
and reference to ideas for potential photos, proved particularly successful in
eliciting experiences that otherwise might not have come to light.

All discussions and interviews were recorded, transcribed, and then
analysed using thematic analysis. As researchers, we read and coded transcripts
independently, and then compared emerging themes and interpretations.

Study findings: from discovering pregnancy to reflecting on life as a 'young' parent

1.   *Sex, pregnancy and childbirth*

For most parents, pregnancy was reported as unplanned. Both mothers and
fathers recalled how shocked they were; however, two of the middle generation
mothers wondered, with hindsight, if they had 'subconsciously planned' their
pregnancy as they took no action to prevent it. Another mother from the oldest
generation actively planned the pregnancy following the termination of her first

pregnancy under pressure from her mother. Fathers did not recall having much input into decision-making about the pregnancy, whereas for all mothers, the initial sense of 'shock' at being pregnant was followed by a clear and immediate decision to reject abortion and 'take responsibility' by progressing with the pregnancy. The sense of 'it's my fault, I can't blame the baby', and hence rejecting termination, echoes findings from other studies (e.g. Hoggart, 2006; McDermott and Graham, 2005). Many took this action despite strong family pressures to have an abortion.

Within the sample, class differences emerged in relation to family reactions. Older mothers, from middle-class backgrounds, described being subject to harsh reactions and condemnation, because of a perception that this did not and should not happen:

> It was unknown in my sort of social background.
>
> (Kate, oldest generation mother)

As indicated earlier, for mothers and fathers in the oldest generation, irrespective of social background, marriage was perceived as the 'only option', with pregnancy outside marriage regarded as more unacceptable than pregnancy as a teenager:

> The sooner you got married the sooner you could convince people it were a honeymoon baby.
>
> (Eileen, oldest generation mother)

However, regardless of experiences during pregnancy, all parents relished telling detailed stories about the birth of their baby, remembered with feelings of joy and delight. Fathers were particularly effusive about their sense of pride:

> I was very proud to be a dad ... I loved pushing him in the pram and changing him and feeding him.   (Robert, oldest generation father)

It was at this early stage in their parenting stories that mothers and fathers made explicit references to the positive 'turning-point' offered by pregnancy: the opportunity to make new plans, including the beginnings of a strong family unit or renewed efforts to gain qualifications and secure more certain futures. This concurs with young parents' views in other studies (e.g. Cater and Coleman,

2006; McDermott and Graham, 2005). Some mothers in our study explicitly pointed out their need to maintain or aspire to autonomous lives without surveillance from external services and, if possible, to reject dependency on the State and/or support services. This was described with reference to a strong sense of pride in independence and firm views on the 'right' way to parent. For most, across all generations, this 'right way' included a desire to ensure 'quality time' with family, such as eating 'healthy' meals together 'around a table', and to prioritise or aspire to family holidays. For many, this was underpinned by explicit strategies for managing a career plan that could minimise dependence on childcare provided outside the family, as well as offering a positive role model:

> I personally feel that the way that my life's panned out and the job that
> I do, having my children earlier [has] been beneficial, rather than doing
> it the other way round. For me, it was the right way to do it because my
> life's now worked out that way.   (Ruth, middle generation mother)

> Originally I wanted to get my career first before having kids ... I've done
> it the other way round. But I don't regret not having a career first. I've
> got qualifications behind me ... because I've done part-time work and
> stuff in-between ... But I prefer to be at home with my kids.
>   (Joanne, youngest generation mother)

We turn now to some observations about sex education; our findings include parallels between the views of parents in different generations. A lack of formal learning and knowledge about sex and relationships might be seen as a predictable aspect of the context for parenthood for our oldest participants, whose formative years were the 1940s and 1950s. However, younger parents who grew up at the turn of the twenty-first century commented just as strongly about the lack of appropriate opportunities to discuss and learn about sex, either because it was easy to miss the one day in the school year on which sex and relationships education was offered at school, or through finding it inadequate for their needs. No participants had experienced any input on relationships and many reported finding it difficult to discuss contraception or safer sex, even with their partners. This meant that for many in our study, the period leading up to pregnancy was associated with the lack of a clear sense of confidence or control over fertility. Many considered or took steps to use contraception where they could, but often this was not straightforward. Kate and Eileen provide some insights from the oldest generation:

> You couldn't even say the word 'sex'. You had to say S-E-X. You're talking about the late nineteen-fifties, early sixties here. It was taboo.
> (Kate, oldest generation mother)

> When I started my period ... I was only ten and a half and I woke up with this blood and I'd not a clue what it was and I was absolutely panic struck. I stopped in bed and refused to get up because I didn't want to tell my mother about this blood ... so I stopped drinking. I tried not to drink. I mean it's stupid. I tried not to drink because I didn't want to make too much blood you see ... The first time I had sex I thought, 'God, this is disgusting' ... I just found it absolutely violent, I suppose and animal-like really ... I mean you're the first person I've ever talked to about it really, yeah. No, my generation didn't talk about sex and I still find it difficult.
> (Eileen, oldest generation mother)

Irrespective of age group, all lamented that sex education was too biologically-based and/or too late to be of use:

> We had sex education at school. Obviously it didn't work very well ... It was rubbish ... biology teachers who really don't want to cover the subject.
> (Rachael, middle generation mother)

> My mum didn't talk to me about it. School ... didn't go into much depth about it, so basically ... I found out myself because my mum never talked about sex.
> (Joanne, youngest generation mother)

Most sought information about sex and contraception from other sources. For middle-class mothers and fathers from the older generation this included literature such as Lady Chatterley's Lover by D. H. Lawrence, as well as reference books:

> I was very conscientious and I went to the reference library ... I looked up ... contraception and pregnancy and so on. Of course I got it wrong

... looked in an encyclopaedia ... Well, I can't remember all the details, but it said something about it is reasonably safe without contraception at these particular times and I think that's what I picked and then ... It's just that we decided not to use contraception at a certain time because I thought I understood it ... And of course because [my girlfriend] then trusted me, she was right to some extent to blame me [for the pregnancy] because I'd got it wrong, but ... it was incompetence rather than being a bastard, if you see what I mean.   (Robert, oldest generation father)

Working-class parents (of all generations) relied on informal sources such as brothers and sisters, colleagues, partners or friends, and occasionally parents. Most participants were aware of the potential unreliability of such information and learnt most from practice:

They [my sources of information] weren't parents and they weren't sex education. That much is absolutely crystal clear to me ... I think I can remember ... you know, the smutty talk with small boys and ... basically it was just peer group stuff actually and supplemented as we got older by a certain amount of clumsy self-help and experimentation.
                    (James, oldest generation father)

For some from the oldest generation, cost was also an issue:

I hadn't got a clue about contraception. I mean you just went and bought Durex and in the coming years before the availability of the pill we couldn't afford Durex sometimes ... They were quite expensive given the other pulls on your budget.   (Barbara, oldest generation mother)

Other issues pointed to a lack of confidence or competence to use contraception:

You just didn't think about using condoms at all ... you'd just be too embarrassed to use them if you're having sex when you're young. It's bad enough having sex ... you'd just rather just have unprotected sex than use a condom.   (Rachael, middle generation mother)

When I did find out about the pill ... I'm not one for taking tablets so I either forgot or, and like men had their ways ... they expected you to put them [the condom] on ... and I didn't like touching them.

(Joanne, youngest generation mother)

Moving on to accounts of childbirth, poignant stories reflect how difficult it was for some mothers, particularly among the oldest generation:

I can remember that they put me in a delivery room ... I don't know what they're like now but then it was like an operating theatre ... with lots of lights around and all shiny steel whatever they were ... instruments ... And they left me in there for hours on my own and I was so frightened ... nobody came in to see how I was doing, nobody really explained why I was in this ... delivery suite ... I can see the lights above me 'cos I was flat on me back on this really narrow, narrow high bed that I was scared of falling off ... And I was so frightened that I ended up screaming and they all came rushing in and they didn't half tell me off. I got really, really told off. For, well, for being naughty really.

(Kate, oldest generation mother)

I was taken into the labour ward, the labour room and there were all these trolleys with things covered over which I've got a vivid imagination so I'd gradually worked myself up into such a state that they knocked me out because I got the shaking and I was shaking from head to foot, I couldn't stop so they knocked me out ... I can remember shaking myself so badly that I was going to fall off the bed and there was a woman in the other labour room screaming and I can remember this nurse saying, 'She's frightening her to death'. (Eileen, oldest generation mother)

Some of the younger generation mothers also felt poorly informed about childbirth but were more likely to have received information or advice from a dedicated support service.

We turn now to experiences of being a parent and highlight, in particular, observations on some commonalities and differences in mothers' and fathers' accounts. Following this, we consider the salience of context in relation to formal and informal support networks.

2.   *Being a young mother or young father*

Gendered experiences of parenting

Differences in women's and men's experiences of being a parent might to some extent be predictable, particularly in relation to domestic and caring responsibilities, but the gender distinctions we discuss here are broader than this; they are also evident in all generations.

While mothers across all generations and social classes spoke of their parenting in positive terms and never regretted the decision to continue with the pregnancy, they felt their initiation into the role while still young, had also been accompanied by a degree of 'loss'. Where fathers reported no sadness over 'lost youth', a sense of 'what might have been' was common and endured for all women, whether in their thirties or sixties. Many mothers had lost friends and missed activities they associated with being young, such as dancing, clubbing, or holidays with friends.

For some older and middle generation mothers this is explained to a degree by their particular circumstances in living with partners who were rarely involved in the care of their baby:

> My husband wasn't very interested in being a parent so he ... literally wasn't around very much, didn't come home very often.
>
> (Hilary, oldest generation mother)

> He resented the commitment and responsibilities that came with being a parent and that was reinforced twice fold when [my second child] was born because he didn't really have much to do with her.
>
> (Ruth, middle generation mother)

Though fathers did not signal any change to their life's trajectory on becoming a parent, it is notable that their stories highlight three issues which helped maintain pre-parenthood lifestyles and continuation of their education and/or employment. First is the considerable practical and emotional support some fathers received from family members, especially older sisters:

> It was absolutely crucial ... I couldn't say that too strongly. Without that I don't think anybody would have managed.
>
> (Robert, oldest generation father)

I, for example, have never felt that I've been prevented from doing anything I've wanted to do by virtue of the fact that I was a dad very early, but in terms of what enabled me to cope with that, then I think there's a whole set of informal and formal things helped me cope with it.

(James, oldest generation father)

Second, some ome single parent fathers felt their status conferred some kudos, as James explains:

As a bloke on his own with kids I got all kinds of allowances made for me ... I got all kind of brownie points just by virtue of being a bloke and coping ... I occasionally, shamelessly, played up to it because it was useful, but more often than not I got pissed off with it, partly because I felt it wasn't actually very flattering as if, you know, blokes shouldn't be able to deal with this.   (James, oldest generation father)

Both single fathers from the older generation, and middle generation single mothers, felt that their 'single parent' identity was more significant than that of being a 'young parent', in relation to professional and lay reactions, as well as the everyday practicalities of caring. However, social class and the localities where they lived were also salient in this respect and we return to this issue shortly.

A third reason for differences in parenting experience perhaps more predictably relates to the gendered use of time, domestic roles, and uses of money. This was particularly marked in photo elicitation discussions when participants were asked to select the images most significant to them. Mothers selected photographs of family members or particular family events and none took photographs of anything other than those of their family, home and/or locality. When explored through further questioning no mothers appeared to prioritise or assert a right to a social life, or identified money and time to pursue leisure, hobbies, sport, or adult relationships. In the same exercise with (middle generation) fathers they too selected photographs of children and partners but also some which depicted their hobbies e.g. football ground, music collection, book collection, mountain bike, computer. In explanations fathers said hobbies were an important aspect of their parenting in allowing them to 'de-stress'.

(Un)supportive contexts for parenting

Now we broaden discussion to consideration of some contextual issues that had direct influence on everyday aspects of being a mother or father, including experiences of maternity care and other forms of professional support.

Irrespective of generation and gender, all participants described poor experiences of maternity care. Problems included insensitivity and judgemental attitudes from professionals, actions that excluded fathers, and a lack of information and consultation on choices available for birth and pain relief.

Mothers of all ages described unsettling memories of their experiences of health care. They found it difficult to be assertive about their wishes or needs, and sometimes experienced professionals' disregard for their wishes. Some women retained a fear or distrust of professionals in health or social care:

> It's more the barriers with professionals that I found ... one of the hardest aspects ... more difficult and more challenging, communicating with them ... Their attitude as well ... I found some of them ... very condescending and, 'We know best', and they don't necessarily always.
> (Ruth, middle generation mother)

> Because I had two midwives ... the first one ... she weren't actually explaining things to me and ... I asked questions and ... she answered them and ... I didn't really understand so I'd ask again and, I don't know, I just felt that she got sick of me a bit because I were asking questions and she weren't giving me it in enough detail. Where[as] my new midwife ... I didn't really ask her questions because I go in and she tells me ... straight away.
> (Katrina, youngest generation mother)

Fathers, particularly from the older and middle generations, animatedly described experiences of female-dominated care which enhanced their sense of exclusion as a young father, in both formal (e.g. with medics and midwives) and informal domains (e.g. with mother-in-laws). Most, however, acknowledged that this was probably a product of the time (1970s-1980s). Those who had more children later in life, however, were less forgiving of similar experiences occurring in the 1990s-2000s. Some fathers suggested that, despite social and political commentary that ostensibly aims to include fathers, maternity services still view them as of secondary importance compared with mothers (and children). One father felt he was viewed as the 'cause' of pregnancy and that once the baby was born, policy and provision focused on the mother. Examples of feeling excluded included radiologists obscuring fathers' views of prenatal scans, and obstetricians excluding fathers from decisions around pain control or the care of the mother and/or child. Fathers felt they could be 'best prepared' for dealing with health care professionals by "reading up" as much as possible from "books and the internet" on options for birth, pain control and postnatal care:

> As you're going through the antenatal things … as a young man you get a sense of women who are in authority; midwives, mothers-in-law, female doctors and you get … definitely a sense of you being blamed and them visiting on you as a man all of their disdain for maleness, as it were … there was definitely a sense of people visiting some sort of vengeance … [my girlfriend] who was pregnant being sympathised with because, 'That's what men are like', as it were. So there was a kind of joining together and an exclusion, a very strong sense of that.
>
> (Robert, oldest generation father)

Earlier we flagged up the significance of supportive family and community contexts and now we explore this in more detail. Where one lives/lived was cited as hugely influential by both mothers and fathers who highlighted the social and practical benefits of living in a community where young parents were not unusual. This contrasted with the isolation experienced by some (older and middle generation) mothers who lived in middle-class communities where young parenthood was less visible:

> If you live on a middle-class street somewhere, nobody speaks to you. You take your kid to a middle-class school, nobody speaks to you. They've all got Range Rovers, they've all got cars … so you don't walk home with other sets of kids. They're all working … I never felt judged by a lot of working-class mothers and I always felt judged by a lot of middle-class mothers … none of the kids were allowed to play out on the street. They were all booked up going to ballet lessons and cello and horse riding and being driven around from here to there and I never really did much of that. Well, I did as much as I could.
>
> (Rachael, middle generation mother)

Though we have no directly comparable data from fathers, references (made above) to the immense help and support they had received from their families might well have buffered the impact of wider local contexts. For younger generation mothers, external support services offered a similarly buffering effect in helping them foster new friendships and support networks in recognition of the loss of friendships that new parenthood can bring:

> I don't talk to any of my friends any more because now I've got a baby they don't want to know me … because they're all going out clubbing and things like that. They just … they all say "Oh, I'll come down and see you" and stuff like that, but you never see anything of them, so … I've made new friends who've got babies themselves.
>
> (Charlene, youngest generation mother)

> They say "Oh, I'll come and visit you," but … most of my friends from school … they never do … we've met new friends which have got babies or are pregnant, through going to like different things, attending different courses and stuff.
>
> (Kim, youngest generation mother)

The youngest generation of mothers viewed dedicated support as very important, emotionally, socially, and practically. By comparison, mothers from previous generations were disadvantaged if they did not have family support, as other forms of support had not been widely available. It is worth reiterating that some women in our study explicitly linked negative responses to their pregnancy with subsequent diagnoses of depression, and improving health was associated with access to appropriate support services. This suggests that understanding and sympathetic support services may be significant to decreasing the potential for long-term negative impacts of stigmatisation, particularly where mainstream provision may be experienced as judgemental and/or inappropriate.

Dedicated support was particularly important for younger generation mothers who had experienced isolation from friends and, for some, lack of support from family or lack of family for those who had been in the care system. Support came in various forms, including assistance with housing and benefit applications, emotional support from project workers, the facilitation of peer support, access to childcare, and education and/or training opportunities. Taking part in educational activities could be a source of pride and self-esteem, with some mothers attending one course after another. The encouragement they received from support workers boosted their confidence and helped to counteract the stigma they often felt elsewhere:

> I like to hear that I am a good parent and that ... I've achieved something or I've done something in an appropriate way and in a good manner ... The more places ... that you get, the more you feel better within yourself and the more you think, 'I can do it. I've got this far. I've done this', and it gives you more confidence to go out and do more successful things, i.e. go and get a job and not worry about it.
>
> (Joanne, youngest generation mother)

Another influential factor was housing. Unlike mothers across all three generations, no fathers brought up the practical difficulties of inappropriate housing and/or financial circumstances. All mothers spoke of the importance of appropriate and timely access to housing, as a 'nest' that facilitated planning and a sense of control, security, safety, pride, and legitimacy in the parenting role. However, not all women were able to access such housing and ridiculed the enduring myth that young parenthood can be used as a tool to secure housing, with many citing evidence of the difficulties experienced. Younger generation mothers who had their own home felt extremely grateful and fortunate:

> It's my house, it's not anybody else's. It's mine and I pay for it and it's where I feel safe and where all the love in my life is ... that's why it's so important to me.   (Ruth, middle generation mother)

> [The council] didn't give me a house until after the baby's born. I'm trying to sort the baby out and the house out and everything else. How can I sort it out when I've got no carpets down, no curtains up and everything and you've just shoved me in this house with a new-born baby and you've not given me the chance to get it done?
>
> (Charlene, youngest generation mother)

Practical problems included a lack of appropriate or available council housing (such as an eight-year waiting list). Experiences of stress and uncertainty when staying with friends or family, and experiences of living in cramped housing, were familiar to all, with unsuitable housing compounded by financial hardship and/

or social isolation. For older generation mothers, the similarity to the influential 1960s realist television play *Cathy Come Home* were often noted:

> The place we lived in … was one very small room … like a sort of bed-sitting room with a tiny little kitchen and a little bathroom, which didn't have a toilet. So there was nowhere to put a cot and for the first six months my baby slept in the pram and we used to get him off to sleep in the kitchen and then wheel the pram into the bathroom because … we only had one room, but then he got too big to leave in the pram, so we had to move to a place that had two rooms because we couldn't put a cot up in this bathroom.   (Hilary, oldest generation mother)

For mothers living with family, there were difficulties in balancing the advantage of support on-hand with the disadvantages of potential interference, overcrowding, lack of privacy and/or loss of independence. This had led to mothers feeling disempowered by the situation or specific family members. In contrast, some of the fathers in our sample felt they had clearly benefited from support within the extended family.

To summarise, we have illustrated that gender and supportive (or unsupportive) family, community and professional contexts are key influences in the experiences of parenthood. For mothers, a number of practical problems loomed large in personal accounts, for example difficulties in accessing appropriate housing. Fathers did not emphasise these points, but rather commented on their sense of exclusion or marginalisation from the processes of antenatal care, childbirth, and postnatal care. We now turn to a final theme that was prominent in parents' accounts as they looked back over life course transitions: a sense of stigmatisation and the impact of others' views on their own identities.

3.   *Looking back on experiences of parenting*

Stigma

Despite the pleasure and pride that all participants described, stigma was also a feature of parenting that each generation, but mostly mothers, highlighted. This again points up the importance of context and the significance of others' views in how parenting is lived on an everyday level. The effects are not transitory but rather they endure; for some, the stigma felt as a teenage mother is still an issue some fifty years later.

Stigma was, and continues to be, experienced in many forms, including being insulted in public:

> Getting filthy looks off some people ... anybody and everybody ... and snide comments from school kids, 'Slag, slut, tart'. Even when ... [son] was going to school, I still got them ... I got used to it and I just shrugged it off. Sometimes I'd not say owt or just walk away or I'd just ignore it and then go home and then probably cry.
>
> (Joanne, youngest generation mother)

Mothers also recounted vivid memories of negative responses from various health practitioners, children's teachers, landlords, and other parents. Though present, the fear or experience of stigma appeared less significant for fathers[2] than it was for mothers across all generations:

> Being pregnant and ... having a child is quite a public thing. Visually people can see ... you're not old enough to have a child when it looks as if you're their older brother, you know, taking them for a walk ... I think that still is there ... It's ... sort of moral religious ... a sort of status. It's a social status thing because you're not old enough to have had that ... you shouldn't have done that at that age and you're out of the ordinary ... there's a stigma still.   (Robert, oldest generation father)

> You did get quite negative reactions from people ... school friends were a bit shocked ... Actually the main problem was schools ... so it wasn't really 'til you got a bit older that you were starting to feel disapproval ... It was more to do with ... interactions with teachers ... it was the teachers, which remained a problem all the time ... I just always felt they weren't taking me seriously. Always. I mean even when I was in my thirties ... there was a feeling that they were looking down on you ... I thought I was treated quite badly actually by the schools ... I was shocked.
>
> (Hilary, oldest generation mother)

> I just wish there was more ... help and support for young mums and to actually listen and not judge us, not judge us too much because the judging can pull somebody down, it can hurt ... we just want

2   By contrast, Hirst's (2003) study highlighted young fathers' experiences of feeling stigmatised, particularly in relation to their mixed heritage or black identity.

acknowledgement. We want positive feedback from people. We don't need the sniggers. We don't need the remarks. We'd get on fine, we wouldn't be no problem to people if they'd just give us the chance instead of pushing us aside and branding us straight away.

(Joanne, youngest generation mother)

By way of explanations for stigma, participants felt that the media were culpable in sustaining inaccurate portrayals of teenage pregnancy or young parenting, and that no effort was made to highlight the contradictions or other problems:

> [The media] never mention that … until you're eighteen you can't get a bill in your own name and you can't get benefits, they have to be paid to your parents or to some responsible adult, which implies … you're not responsible enough … you've had a baby but you're still not responsible. You're responsible for their life, but you can't be responsible to pay a bill.   (Ruth, middle generation mother)

Some (middle generation) fathers held strong feelings about explicitly rejecting the stereotype which they felt existed about young (irresponsible) fathers in the media and public opinion, both for themselves, and for other young men.

Perceptions of judgement and possessing a stigmatised identity were difficult to live with and for many mothers manifested in feelings of constant surveillance, of potential for condemnation and punishment. Some individuals confided fears that their child could be 'taken away', though they were not able to explain why they thought that this might happen. These participants felt they had to prove themselves as good parents over and above the expectations of older parents, and had to do 'more' or 'better' to be accepted. More surprising was the degree to which this sense of stigma endured long after their children were grown, with some participants avoiding disclosing the age of their children or grandchildren in work situations to avoid being exposed as a former young parent. For one woman in the oldest generation, the extreme reaction to her pregnancy from her (middle-class) parents and teachers at the grammar school she attended created a series of exclusions which she appeared to have internalised and retained some forty years on, in her strong sense of "letting her family down" and "bringing shame" to her family and neighbourhood:

Everything in my life ... came together to make me feel humiliated and embarrassed and immoral and not worthy of consideration, because that was the message I was getting from everywhere, it was what I was getting from my parents, it was what I'd got from school, it was what I was getting ... from antenatal services, so I hadn't got anybody to tell me anything different, so ... that's what I believed. I was just this ... person that was completely unworthy of attention and respect.

(Kate, oldest generation mother)

Young mothers in the current generation made comments that echoed some of the same feelings:

I used to be ashamed ... [and] feel angry and frustrated ... and scared because I thought, 'Does everyone actually think the same?'... And that's when I started pulling myself down as well and saying, 'I'm not a good mum and I don't deserve to be a mum'.

(Joanne, youngest generation mother)

I always felt like I had to justify what I was doing with my life because I'd had a baby so young, so whenever people asked me what I did I said 'well I've got a baby but I'm at college' ... I always felt like I had to justify it.

(Debs, youngest generation mother)

An advantage of a three generation study has been the ability to identify shifts in attitudes over time. Some parents, for example, were subject to dominant (negative) perceptions of young parenting at the time they were bringing up their child(ren) but with reflections over time they have come to hold different views, as illustrated by a former teenage mother now in her sixties:

The next door neighbour came into my house and the first thing she said was, 'Oh isn't it clean?' and my husband said, 'Well why shouldn't it be?' People had expectations of you that if ... you were young and you'd got all these children, A, you couldn't manage your money, B, you were thick and C, you were dirty ... So these were the sort of expectations people had of you. You were young and therefore you were bound to be dirty. You were bound to be feckless really ... That's how everybody saw me as being, feckless ... I was aware of being proud that people thought

I was coping, not angry at being patronised. That's come with years. I'm very angry now at being patronised, but then I was proud that people thought I was keeping my end up. (Eileen, oldest generation mother)

Not surprisingly, experiences of stigmatisation were influential on parents' (changing) identities, as we explore below.

Identities of parenthood

Our findings suggest that the identity of being a 'young' mother or father is not unitary: over-writing the various complex codes for parenting identity are other inscriptions or expectations that these participants explicitly linked to their age. Most parents had experienced contrasting constructions of self-identity at different times in their lives. One version was a fragile self, linked to stigma, and negative public and professional discourses about young parents; these were experienced as undermining parenting skills, decision-making, and self-worth. In some extreme cases this led to severe depression. A second version was more positive, associated with a sense of responsibility and achievement experienced through becoming a parent, and sometimes contrasted directly with a previous self-identity of being a 'bad kid'.

A fragile sense of self was often referred to in connection with notions of being seen as the stigmatised 'other'. Some parents resisted this sense of being 'other' by belonging to a specific support group or service aimed at young parents. Having friends and acquaintances who were also young parents appeared to contribute to a more positive sense of self-worth. However, this option was much less available for older and middle generation parents, some of whom had experienced significant levels of social isolation, for example through being the only young parent in a middle-class neighbourhood. A positive parenting identity was often built on notions of being responsible, mature, and in control. For some, and not only among older participants, getting married added further legitimacy or acceptance to their new status as a parent:

Actually settling down as well, that's a big achievement for me because I've had dreams and ... hopes and they've never turned out. This is the only dream I've actually managed to keep or managed to succeed in and that's getting married ... and being settled.

(Joanne, youngest generation mother)

Conclusion

Our three generation study has shown that experiences of parenting and self-identity were inextricably linked to particular types of formal and informal support, and a sense of being labelled or 'othered'. Thus, the wider social context is immensely important to an understanding of these experiences. Here, we highlight the factors that we consider particularly important within that context.

First, we have illustrated above some continuities in the ways in which learning about and discussing sex, relationships and contraception often remain difficult, particularly in adolescence. Women and men from every generation in the study could give examples of a sense of unease, embarrassment, and inhibition. Despite successive layers of policy about sex education in schools, this sense of unease endures. We are not suggesting here that the usually unplanned pregnancies described by our participants resulted simply from ignorance. Rather, there was a broader sense of a lack of confidence and control in relation to sex and relationships.

Second, and in contrast, a sense of resilience and active determination to 'cope' dominated accounts of living as a young parent—whether alone or with a partner. This underlines McDermott and Graham's findings (2005) about young parents' assertions of positive identities in the face of both stigmatisation, and practical difficulties. Looking across the generations, we can see strong parallels in the accounts of feeling 'branded' and humiliated, perhaps by a midwife or health visitor, or by a comment or critical glance on the street. Strikingly, this sense of being stigmatised can continue into grandparenthood. These accounts come from mothers in particular; for fathers, the enduring theme is one of feeling marginalised, even among the youngest generation. Changing policies and public attitudes, which have become more affirming of fathers' participation in antenatal care, childbirth and postnatal care, were not seen as offering a welcome, or a genuine sense of inclusivity, by the young fathers in this study.

Third, our study was designed partly to address the complexities of representing oneself and being represented as a 'young parent' through research processes. We set out to avoid the superficial 'snapshot' limitations of one-off, interview-based studies, and to create various avenues for women and men to reflect on and describe their experiences in depth. For some participants, this was the first opportunity to air feelings and experiences that still evoked painful or difficult memories. The particular contribution of the range of methods that we used was to offer insights into the diversity and the complexity of social, economic and interpersonal contexts in shaping experiences of teenage parenthood. For some, the immediate family context was the major source of practical support and emotional recognition, counteracting both practical difficulties (such as access to affordable housing or childcare), and public messages of disapproval. For others, the presence or absence of peers, in neighbourhoods or schools, was crucial: in this respect, some older participants had found that relative affluence did not protect them from an enduring sense of shame and exposure, associated with being the only visible young parent in a particular social setting. Overall, the study adds weight to the increasing range of research that seeks to reject an homogenising view of 'teenage parenthood', both in terms of parental identities, and in terms of experiences over the life course.

The study suggests a number of implications for policy and service development. First, the youngest participants gave clear examples of the positive impact of the kinds of dedicated support services for young parents that have been established in voluntary sector and health and education services over recent years. These provide examples of non-judgmental, facilitative services that need wider recognition and dissemination. This study, like some earlier ones (e.g. see Jones, 2002), illustrates the ways in which becoming a parent can form part of a successful transition to adulthood, given appropriate family, community and/or professional support. Second, however, the study findings underline the importance of acknowledging and responding to the enduring emotional and material impact of marginalisation and stigmatisation among young parents. Our findings reflect the ways in which being a single or unmarried parent no longer attracts the level of disapproval that was prevalent for our oldest participants. Being a 'young' parent in the early twenty-first century, however, remains symbolic of failing to pursue the 'right' path to 'responsible' citizenship. The YWCA's recent public campaign—'Respect Young Mums'[3]—stands out, because it is such a rare example of a challenge to the dominant discourse of risk and deficiency that still dominates policy concerning teenage pregnancy and parenthood. Building on our findings (and a strong body of other research in this area) we would advocate a more supportive and inclusive policy environment that recognises the diversity of experience (and need) among young parents.

Acknowledgements

The authors gratefully acknowledge the participants' involvement in this project, and the financial support provided by Sheffield Health and Social Research

3   See www.ywca.org.uk/youngmums [last accessed on 15/3/09].

Consortium between 2004 and 2006. We would also like to thank various projects and individuals in South Yorkshire for their assistance with, and support for, this research, including: Father Figures, Manor and Castle Development Trust, Rotherham YMCA Developing Dads, Sheffield Hospital and Home Education Service, Sheffield Sure Start Plus, The Standhouse Centre, Ben Yeger, and YWCA Doncaster Women's Centre.

References

Bertaux, D. and Thompson, P. (1997) *Pathways to social class: a qualitative approach to social mobility*, Oxford: Clarendon Press.

Berthoud, R. et al. (2004) Long-term consequences of teenage births for parents and their children. Teenage Pregnancy Research Programme research briefing March 2004. [online]. Available at: www.dfes.gov.uk/teenagepregnancy/dsp_showDoc.cfm?File Name=ACFA6CE%2Epdf.

Bonell, C. (2004) Why is teenage pregnancy conceptualized as a social problem? A review of quantitative research from the USA and UK, *Culture, Health and Sexuality* 6(3): 255-272

Cater, S. and Coleman, L. (2006) *'Planned' teenage pregnancy: Perspectives of young parents from disadvantaged backgrounds*, Bristol: The Policy Press.

Hirst, J. (2003) *Voices of experience: Muslim and African Caribbean teenagers' insights on pregnancy and parenting (MACTIPP)*, Sheffield: Sheffield Hallam University and Sheffield City Council.

Hobcraft, J. and Kiernan, K. (2001) Childhood poverty, early motherhood and adult social exclusion, *British Journal of Sociology* 52(3): 495-517.

Hoggart, L. (2006) Risk, young women and sexual decision-making, *Forum: Qualitative Social Research* 7(1): Art. 28.

Jones, G. (2002) *The youth divide: Diverging paths to adulthood*. York: York Publishing Services Ltd.

Kidger, J. (2004) Including young mothers: limitations to New Labour's strategy for supporting teenage parents, *Critical Social Policy* 24(3): 291-311.

McDermott, E., Graham, H. and Hamilton, V. (2004) *Experiences of being a teenage mother in the UK: A report of a systematic review of qualitative studies*. [online]. Available at: www.sphsu.mrc.ac.uk/Evidence/Research/Review%2010/ SR%20Executive%20Summary.pdf.

McDermott, E. and Graham, H. (2005) Resilient young mothering: social inequalities, late modernity and the 'problem' of 'teenage' motherhood, *Journal of Youth Studies* 8(1): 59-79.

Plummer, K. (1995) Life story research, in Smith, J.A., Harre, R. and Van Langenhove, L. (eds) *Rethinking methods in psychology*, London: Sage.

Seidman, I. (1998) *Interviewing as qualitative research: A guide for researchers in education and the social sciences*, New York: Teachers College Press.

Social Exclusion Unit (SEU) (1999) *Teenage pregnancy*, London: Teenage Pregnancy Unit.

Swann, C., Bowe, K., McCormick, G. and Kosmin, M. (2003) *Teenage pregnancy and parenthood: a review of reviews—Evidence briefing summary*, Wetherby: Health Development Agency.

Chapter 6

Great Expectations: teenage pregnancy and intergenerational transmission

Ann McNulty

1. Introduction

'You'll never stop young people round here getting pregnant.'[1] This assumption about an inevitable cycle of teenage pregnancy is apparently widely held by health professionals in areas of disadvantage, such as the locality in North East England where this chapter is set. This assumption is also reflected in New Labour policy-making. For example the national Teenage Pregnancy Strategy (Social Exclusion Unit 1999) has been influenced by ideas about a problematic 'long-standing culture of early pregnancy' (Department for Education and Skills 2006:37) in some geographical areas where young women who become pregnant are assumed to lack aspiration. Both Tony Blair (1999), then Prime Minister and personally involved in the Teenage Pregnancy Strategy, and Hazel Blears (2002), then Minister of State responsible for the Strategy, gave this assumption some emphasis in their public pronouncements. This in turn links with theories of the transmission of worklessness, poverty and disorder in particular 'underclass' cultural settings (Murray 1990, Dennis and Erdos 1992). In response to all this, the local Teenage Pregnancy Coordinator decided to sponsor research on young women's pregnancies from an intergenerational perspective. Using the study[2] that resulted, the chapter examines notions of culture and intergenerational transmission of teenage pregnancy and disadvantage.

Despite a substantial body of 'teenage pregnancy' literature, relatively little attention has been given to women's representations of their pregnancies in relation to their other life experiences such as growing up, going to school and

---

1. This comment, recorded at a Teenage Pregnancy Action Plan Day in the research area in 2003, was one of many that set the Coordinator thinking about the possibility of researching young women's pregnancies from an intergenerational angle.

2 The research was funded through a CASE PhD studentship, a partnership between the Economic and Social Research Council (Award PTA-033-2002-00047) and a North East England NHS Trust. Professor Diane Richardson (Newcastle University) was principal academic supervisor, supported by Dr Robin Humphrey.

moving into paid employment. The research addressed this gap in the context of a particular locality. Thirteen women, each of whom had had a child under the age of twenty, and who were connected as mothers and daughters across three generations within six family groups, composed versions of their life stories in biographical narrative interviews (Chamberlayne et al. 2000, Wengraf 2005). The chapter begins in section two with a brief methodological note and an introduction to the women and the place in which, for the most part, they grew up and imagined their futures. There follows an examination of the construction of some young women's pregnancies as problems to be tackled (as discussed for example by Bonell 2004), the most recent permutation of which is the late twentieth and early twenty-first century teenage pregnancy discourse (see chapters one and nine).

2. Research context and methods

The criterion for recruitment to the study was that within each family there should be women connected both as mothers and daughters across three consecutive generations, each of whom had given birth under the age of twenty. The women also had to be prepared to take part in at least two biographical narrative interviews. This produced a small and tightly defined group of participants. However, although not a representative sample, the women's accounts of life events did provide an opportunity to explore the variety of experiences often collapsed into the stereotypical term 'teenage pregnancy' (Robinson 2002, Rustin 2006). The biographical narrative interview method proved effective in encouraging the women to be narrators (Lawler 2002, Skultans 2004), and to produce individual life story versions covering the period from the 1930s to the 2000s and illustrating changing social contexts and norms (Greenhalgh 1999, Duncan 2004).

The research participants

The women who took part in the research spanned generations within six discrete family groups, and at the point of interview they were between seventeen and sixty-nine years of age. They were white, from working-class backgrounds, and had lived all or most of their lives in the research area. Four of the thirteen women had always lived there, and five more had never lived outside of North East England. Four women had moved away temporarily, three as girls following fathers' employment opportunities within the UK and abroad, and one moving as a young woman because of her male partner's job. In the box below the women are grouped in their generational positions at the time of fieldwork, some having moved into them well ahead of the majority of women of similar age. The decades refer to the broad historical points at which they gave birth between the ages of sixteen and nineteen (four were sixteen, three were seventeen, one was eighteen and five were nineteen). The names[3] of the women who took part in interviews are italicised. The women whose names are in regular font did not participate in interviews for various reasons, for example one woman decided that she did not want to "go over the past", and one was seriously ill at time of interview. These women appeared however in their daughters' and granddaughters' interview accounts.

Great-great grandmothers (1930s):	Hannah and Isabella
Great-grandmothers (1950/60s):	*Iris, Brenda, Norma, Dorothy, Barbara, Mary*
Grandmothers (1970/80s):	*Susan, Joan, Carole, Emma, Dawn and Linda*
Mothers (2000s):	*Natalie, Sara, Laura, Joanne, Hayley*

A strength and limitation of the study was the focus on women's accounts. The women's experiences were not researched in isolation however, as they positioned themselves intergenerationally in relation to men (fathers, grandfathers, sons, brothers and uncles) as well as to women, as significant others in their lives. I made no assumption about the sexual identities of the women who took part in interviews, and all of them described relationships with men as sexual partners, which may reflect the teenage pregnancy focus of the study. At the time of their interviews six of the thirteen women (five grandmothers and one mother) were no longer in a relationship with the man who was the father of their first child. Four had no ongoing contact with, or support from, their former partners and in three cases this was because of domestic violence. Between them the women had relationships of one to fifty years to review, and their life story versions illustrated social changes that are inextricably linked with shifts in the organisation and meanings of heterosexual sex and relationships (Stanley 1995, Hockey et al. 2003).

The women's life stories showed diversity *within* their small generational groups, as highlighted in previous research (for example Heron 1985, Phoenix

---

3   To protect the women's confidentiality, the names used are pseudonyms and some biographical details have been changed. Name, age group and generational position are in brackets following quotes from the research interviews.

1991), and also diversity *between* generations, reflecting changing social and economic circumstances in one geographical area, as well as areas of commonality and overlap. The range of similarities and differences contrasts with the current one-dimensional story of teenage pregnancy, and supports the suggestion made by Chamberlayne and Rustin (1999:14) that social problems are frequently 'not what they seem'.

The first research finding, during the recruitment phase, was that it was more difficult than local professionals had anticipated to identify the supposedly typical families that met the three generation criterion. Several said they were surprised that 'there aren't more'. The following quotes are from telephone conversations with health practitioners.

> I think there probably will be loads. That's the culture round here. But that's an assumption, because I haven't asked them about their grandmothers.

> I had a feeling that there might be a lot, and then I could hardly think of any. I initially thought 'Oh, she'll have had her baby young', and then you found that she was twenty-two or twenty-three, still a young woman but not a teenager. It was interesting for us (reference to the practitioner's team) to see there were fewer three generation families than we thought there would be.

> A lot who we thought were three generations weren't. There was one who had her daughters young, whose daughters had children young, and we really thought that she was born when her mam was young, and she was the child of an older mam, so we learnt something from it. It just shows you how you assume things.

One health practitioner identified herself, her mother and her grandmother as having had a baby under the age of twenty and having lived for most of their lives in the research area. The involvement of this family group in the research was significant in challenging both the idea of a link between teenage pregnancy and cultural 'otherness', including lack of aspiration, ambition and achievement, and the assumption of a boundary between personal and professional experience of pregnancy under the age of twenty. This was a theme that recurred in the research.

The ethics of intergenerational biographical research

The study also highlighted ethical issues in researching intergenerational relationships. For example, recruitment to research interviews was via the youngest woman in all but one family group, which meant that almost all of the young women had to ask their grandmothers, and some had to ask their mothers, how old they were when they had their first baby. These knowledge gaps punctured the idea of intergenerational transmission of a message that having a baby as a teenager is not a problem because women within the family 'have always done it', and they also highlighted the potential for harm to participants. For example one woman talked about how she found out that her maternal grandmother had had her first child as a young unmarried woman, while researching her family history for a homework task at school.

> I was doing English at school and we did a family tree thing, and I found out a lot about my granma's life, because I was doing something on her. She gave me a lot of stories and showed me photos of before she was married, with her baby, so we sort of discussed it then, and she said she considered it lucky that, you know, somebody had taken her on with the child. At that time, most people who got pregnant then, their babies were taken off them and put up for adoption, so to actually keep the baby was quite an achievement.   Emma (in her thirties, grandmother)

Emma's grandmother transmitted a story of contemporary success in managing to keep her baby and subsequently marry. Although this situation had a positive outcome, with the grandmother prepared to share a version of a sensitive life event, it was a reminder of the risk of exposure of family secrets in intergenerational work.

A practical consideration was how to represent the women's local accents. I decided to transcribe phonetically, although this was inevitably a partial form of translation that could not reproduce the cadences and qualities of the women's speaking voices (Karpf 2006). However I did not want to translate them out of the ways in which they spoke, which represented a particular form of intergenerational transmission.

The research locality: "They need to know where we come from …"[4]

The accounts of the women who took part in the research placed their teenage pregnancies in particular historical contexts in one geographical area that has changed significantly over the time period (1930s to early 2000s) covered by interview data, challenging the uniform view of teenage pregnancy (Buxton et al. 2005). Contrary to the idea of intergenerational transmission of worklessness and acute social disadvantage, heavy industries used to be a source of relatively well-paid jobs for men in the research area, and several older women referred to fathers working in the mining and other local industries.

> Me dad was somebody that the house revolved around, in that it woke up when me dad had to get ready to go to work. Me dad came home for his dinner at dinnertime, and the dinner was being put on the table as me father walked in. He would go and get a wash (laughed) cos he was always black greasy, and he would have his dinner, have his cup o' tea and then he would walk back to work again (laughed) and the whole household went by what me father had to do. Friday night he used to get paid, and as he came home he always bought a big bar of Wall's ice cream (laughed), a packet o' wafers and six teacakes, and that was Friday night.   Barbara (in her sixties, great-grandmother)

One of the women's fathers relocated from the research area to another part of North East England in the 1970s, following what Hudson (1989:357) describes as 'alternative male-employing manufacturing activities away from the coalfields'. These mining and manufacturing jobs disappeared with the restructuring of the British economy from the 1960s onwards. More recently, 'light' manufacturing companies provided employment for women, although these too are now moving elsewhere and twenty-first century employment opportunities for women without higher qualifications, who want to work locally, are generally restricted to low paid and insecure jobs in the service sector. This means increasing social inequalities linked to levels of income and class position (Doran et al. 2004, Meyer 2005, Schoon et al. 2005, Wheeler et al. 2005). The women's stories reflected challenging socio-economic problems for communities such as those in

---

4   Kathleen Buxton is quoted in a commentary *Teenage Pregnancy: More than meets the eye* (Buxton et al. 2005), suggesting that people "need to know where we come from, and not just point the finger". She and other women with experience of pregnancy under twenty designed and regularly facilitate a workshop for Newcastle University medical students. They use 'teenage pregnancy' as a way in to discussion of health inequalities.

the research locality, that originally formed around heavy industries (Whitehead 1992 [1988], Stonebridge 2002, North East Strategic Health Authority 2007) and the impact of globalisation on local employment opportunities, with a shift to an economy based on consumption rather than production. A striking visual reminder of these processes was located near the Teenage Pregnancy Team office in the research area, namely a shuttered factory that was mentioned by several women as a previously reliable source of paid manual work. The factory closed when a large UK high-street retailer moved production of goods abroad, following cheaper labour costs.

3. Changing conceptions of deviance, from 'illegitimacy' to 'single parenthood' to 'teenage pregnancy'

Ideas about what constitutes an expected sequence of life events are historically specific (Paechter 2001). For example, Hockey and James (1993) discuss processes of categorisation and normalisation by people's age, based on ideas about who should do what, and when. Women deviating from contemporary norms have risked, and still risk, being categorised, disparaged and stigmatised.

> When me mother had her baby (in the 1930s), she was lucky me grandparents accepted it, because a lot of her generation were put away (in mental institutions) for the same thing … their lives had been wasted because they had been locked away for it. And you never actually thought of yourself as being in the same position, but really it's the same, isn't it. When I had (first baby in the 1960s), it happened in a few families and it was covered up and not spoken about. It was something that was sort of whispered about, you know "Oh, so and so's pregnant (whispered), no better than she should be" (laughed). It definitely wasn't something that was accepted.   Barbara (in her sixties, great-grandmother)

Framed by a contemporary teenage pregnancy discourse that constructs young women's pregnancies as problems to be tackled (see chapters one, two and three) the pregnancies of all of the women who took part in the research are *retrospectively* defined as having happened when they were too young, and as being part of an intergenerational cycle of deviance. This definition is however not relevant to the older women who became pregnant at a time when marital status rather than age was a marker of convention (see chapter one). Reference to a 'cycle' suggests repetition of 'the same thing', but in fact women's pregnancies under the age of twenty have had various meanings over time in relation to in/out of marriage and in/out of an expected chronological order of life events, as shaped by social change, geographical place and symbolic space.

Women who became pregnant as married teenagers in the 1950s and 1960s were not out of the ordinary. Mary had been married for more than a year when she became pregnant at nineteen, and the announcement of her pregnancy was hoped for and immediately celebrated.

> We were just ower (over) the moon because I was married for a year. Me mam and dad just cuddled us, ower the moon.
>
> Mary (in her sixties, great-grandmother)

During these decades heterosexual encounters outside of marriage were constructed as socially disruptive (with same gender encounters viewed as deviant, and illegal for men until the late 1960s). Monogamous heterosexual relationships within marriage were seen as ideal forms of sexual and social organisation (Peplar 2002, Duncan and Phillips 2008). Some Family Planning Association clinics even asked women for proof of intention to marry, for example a receipt for a wedding dress, before providing them with contraception (Dear 2005). Similarly official discourse in the UK at the time promoted the institution of 'the family' (a concept appearing to require no explanation) as the foundation of post-war socio-economic reconstruction. Against this social background, women tended to marry earlier and have children younger than in the previous generation (Thomson 1969) and in 1962 as many as a fifth of all live births were to young women aged fifteen to nineteen (Haste 1992). During the 1960s and 1970s, however, reliable contraception became more available,[5] and there was a general downwards trend in fertility (Fox Harding 1996). The marriage rate peaked in 1970 and then dipped, and the proportion of children born to unmarried women rose from approximately five per cent in the 1950s to eleven per cent by the end of the 1970s (see chapter 1).

By the 1980s most women under the age of twenty who gave birth were unmarried, and these 'teenage' mothers were increasingly demonised by the

---

5   Proof of marital status was not needed to access contraception via the Brook Advisory Centres established in 1964 (Ferris 1993). While the oral contraceptive pill was available from the mid-1960s, it was 1966 before the Royal College of Obstetrics and Gynaecology made a statement in support of contraception (Ferris 1993), and it was not until the 1970s that the National Health Service incorporated contraception services into core provision.

Conservative governments and the tabloid press (Selman 1998). A stereotypical single mother was constructed, who dared to have babies on benefit, babies who in turn grew into delinquent youth (Millar 1997). During the 1990s, having a baby as a teenager became increasingly extraordinary from a demographic perspective, as the mean age of women at the birth of a first child in England and Wales increased from 24.3 years in 1976 to 26.8 years in 1997 (Population Trends 1998). In response 1990s 'pro-family' pressure groups warned of social breakdown (e.g. Dennis and Erdos 1992). Supposedly, women with children who lived with men were deserving, able, reputable, honest, while mothers who did not were undeserving, feckless, disreputable and manipulative of the welfare system (Murray 1990). Murray's underclass theory went so far as to directly connect 'single motherhood' with the collapse of social cohesion in 'lower working-class communities everywhere' (Murray 1994:11).

Emma (in her thirties, grandmother) refused to marry when she became pregnant at seventeen in the 1980s, cohabiting instead with her partner, the father of the baby. He was in a well-paid job and they bought a house together. At the point of interview Emma had been separated from her partner for ten years, having never expected to be a 'single mother', and having subsequently managed to care for three children (with her parents' support), train for a career and work full-time. Emma's life story confounds ideas about the 'threat' of single mothers. Generally, most women who live in circumstances that put particular pressure on their mothering do not have children who behave anti-socially (Graham 1987, Richardson 1993, Phoenix 1996, Roseneil and Mann 1996). The notion of 'underclass' appears crude in relation to the complexity of individual biographies and the changing economic and social circumstances in different geographical areas (Macdonald and Marsh 2001).

At the point of being interviewed, Mary and Barbara (great-grandmothers) had been married for almost fifty years. Mary, in her biographical account, compared her own joyful experience of finding out that she was pregnant for the first time, with the respective 'problematic' first pregnancies of a daughter and granddaughter. One of her daughters became pregnant when she was seventeen and single in the 1980s because of condom failure (Mary's other daughters did not have teenage pregnancies). One of her granddaughters became pregnant at sixteen while still at school in the early 2000s through not being clear about how to use the contraceptive pill effectively.

They haven't really had a, whay, to me they haven't had a life. They're straight into motherhood aren't they, and I mean I'm ard (old)-fashioned you see, I think people should be married. But she (granddaughter) *has* got her partner.   Mary (in her sixties, great-grandmother)

Following the Second World War women received a clear message about the importance of their unpaid work as wives, domestic managers and child carers (Haste 1992). Mary stopped working when she married and did not move back into paid employment until her children were at school, at which point she worked part-time to fit in with school-day hours. In contrast, her daughter who brought up a child during the 1980s was determined to be financially self-supporting and never stopped working. She was able to remain in paid employment because of childcare support from her extended family. Mary's granddaughter was working when she became pregnant at the beginning of the 2000s (she met her partner at work), lost her job at that point, and, at the point of interview, was planning to return to paid employment when her child started school.

Hadley (1996) refers to the historical and cultural specificity of what is taken for granted or considered socially unacceptable. In the 1930s, at the beginning of the period covered by the women's life stories, anxiety about population replacement after the first World War (Peplar 2002) was paralleled by eugenic concerns about socio-economic differentials in family size, as people in heterosexual relationships in working-class communities tended to have children from an earlier age and therefore often had more children (Selman 1998). The threat of the fertility of working-class heterosexual women to social order is a thread running through the discourses of unmarried and lone motherhood (Carabine 2001). Most recently, this 'hazard' discourse has focused on teenage pregnancy (chapter nine). The first pregnancies of eleven of the thirteen women who participated in the research were unexpected and marked out as 'illegitimate', 'single parent' or 'teenage', with the changing vocabulary reflecting shifting moral panics about deviance from the contemporary 'carefully calibrated norms of motherhood' (Smart 1996:47). Barbara talked about the difference between being pregnant as an unmarried teenager in the 1960s, and being pregnant as a married woman several years later, with the same man.

When I had (first baby in 1960), for all you were sort of excited and over the moon about it (laughed), you couldn't show that because it wasn't the done thing to be pregnant an' not married, cos I always remember that was the difference between having the first and the second child, that you could be really excited about being pregnant and show it with the second one, where with the first one you had to sort of keep your feelings in check cos you knew you'd, as they said in those days, 'done wrong' (laughed).   Barbara (in her sixties, great-grandmother)

Emma's parents expected that she would marry before her baby was born, as she was engaged to be married when she became pregnant in the 1980s. In her interview she criticised contemporary veiling of pre-marital sex and pregnancy.

It must have only been within a week of me finding out I was pregnant that it was said to me about getting married. "Makes it look nice". I don't see how (laughed) because at the end of the day I was still pregnant (laughed). I would still have been pregnant when I got married, so I don't see how it actually fits in, but I suppose in society's eyes.

Emma (in her thirties, grandmother)

4. Changing culture and intergenerational transmission

As already discussed, the suggestion of an inevitable relationship between young women's pregnancies and serious social problems is problematic, as it supports the idea of transmission of cultural deficits that predispose towards deviant behaviour and disorder. The conceptions of culture that underpin professionals' anecdotes about a generational cycle of teenage pregnancy, appear to be largely assumed rather than evidenced. Research suggesting that economic marginalisation is a significant factor in social instability (e.g. MacDonald and Marsh 2005), challenges the underclass theory of the transmission of disorder in particular 'cultural landscapes'. It is therefore important to critically consider cultural aspects of explanations of teenage pregnancy. The intergenerational feature of this study provided an opportunity to think differently about the relationship between changing social and material conditions on the one hand, and on the other the flexible concept of culture that covers values, opportunities, aspirations and expectations in different social settings (Williams 1983). Phoenix (1988:154), for example, proposes a dynamic definition of culture that includes 'analyses of material factors', and she argues elsewhere (Phoenix 2001) that economic practices are implicated in processes of gendered inequality, that in turn produce sets of circumstances in which unintended teenage pregnancies happen.

Growing up

Although three women referred to the disruption and 'disorder' of violence perpetrated by fathers and male partners of their mothers when they were girls, the other ten defined their experiences of growing up as 'normal', in places that they described as 'safe' and 'quiet'. One woman for example talked about a 'textbook perfect upbringing'.

> Nobody in my family was ever in trouble. I was surrounded by me family, which is a very secure environment for any child to grow up in. It was a very secure happy environment.   Susan (in her thirties, grandmother)

Others told similar stories:

> I had a good childhood, ermm me and me brother, me mam, me dad. Me mam used to take wor (us) everywhere. During the summer holidays there used to be her and a few other women, they used to get together and they used to take wor all swimmin'. We used to gan on the bus. She would take wor over to what we used to call the burn, which was just like a stream where the old pits used to be.   Linda (in her forties, grandmother)

> I grew up in quite a quiet place, I lived with me mam an' dad an' me brother and sister in a quiet place, and I was just like normal really. I wasn't a little rebel or nothin' like that. I was just normal. I was just in the normal school, an' normal house wi' me brother and sister, just grew up wi' them.   Sara (teenager, mother)

Educational aspiration

The absence of all of the youngest research participants from further education settings might be interpreted, in current policy terms, as cultural deficit, intergenerationally transmitted in the form of 'poor' expectations (Social Exclusion Unit 1999) and 'low' aspiration (One North East 2007). But in fact twelve of the thirteen women in the study mentioned that a career had been part of their hopes for the future when they were girls, and that their parents had transmitted this aspiration for a 'good' job. Similarly the women who were grandmothers (in the late thirties and forties age group) talked about their parents' hopes for them, their own aspirations, and their ambition for their children.

> They (parents) didn't want me to grow up and have a, you know, just a factory job. They wanted me to make something of myself. None of me friends had children when I was pregnant. I mean, sounds snobby, but people who were in the same classes as me at school, the sort o' high achievers, didn't get pregnant.   Emma (in her thirties, grandmother)

However, participants' life stories illustrated the difficulty of achieving social mobility through a career route. Educational plans were variously reported as having been interrupted by misinformation or lack of information about career routes, disruption at home, and school absence because of caring responsibilities. Teenage pregnancy disrupted the education or training of only four of the thirteen women (a great-grandmother, a grandmother and two mothers). Hayley for example talked about an unexpected pregnancy interrupting her plan to move into further education when she left school.

> I wanted to go to college and do a business studies course. The whole family had high hopes for me about going to college, and I just felt like I'd let me mam down   Hayley (teenager, mother)

Susan had already left school when she became pregnant unintentionally. She described being an A grade student in the 1980s, and the first in her family to study to A level.

> I was going to go to college and be a physiotherapist. I went on me work experience with the physiotherapy team, who said "Actually you need a science subject to do this". So I'd been wrongly advised on what to take. And then you can't, it's like hard to correct that. Then it's like 'Oh I'll just get a job for a while'. And then you get caught up in it. And then I met her Dad and then I fell pregnant and then I wasn't doin' anything. I still don't know that I wouldn't go to university, I have thought about it every year for the last few years.   Susan (in her thirties, grandmother)

Unsure as to what to do with the 'wrong' A' levels, Susan shifted to unskilled employment. Her account illustrated the complexity of negotiating entry to an employment area that was unknown within her family group. This issue is discussed by Thomson et al. (2002) who describe the enormity, for the young people whose experiences they researched, of entering unfamiliar territory in order to pursue social mobility through careers. Kenway and McLeod (2004) who studied the trajectories of individual young women and pairs of mothers and daughters living on low incomes also found gaps in knowledge about how to negotiate entry to higher education institutions in order to turn career aspiration into reality. Whereas politicians and policy documents often assume that young women who become pregnant have a 'low' level of motivation to pursue higher education in order to gain a 'good' job (Blair 1999, Connexions Service et al. 2001, Blears 2002, Department for Education and Skills 2006), the women in this study did not appear to lack aspiration. Their references to achievements at school challenged the idea of deficit.

> I was a quiet kid (laughed). I always had me nose in a book, What was that they used to say at school ?"If you want to find Linda, she's in the corner with her nose in a book". I still enjoy readin', I love readin'. I got grade ones and twos in the exams, came in the first two for maths as well.   Linda (in her forties, grandmother)

Carole missed the opportunity to gain qualifications to become a nurse, which was her dream when she was a girl, when her mother left her father (because of domestic violence) and had to become an income earner.

> I was kept off school to keep an eye on the house while me mam was away at work, to make sure the other ones were alright. An' it was like arl I seemed to dee was babysit. I had to watch the little ones, mek tea for them arl. "You'll have to stay off school to keep an eye on the house" an' what not. I would say I lost a good two an' a half year at school for arl the time I took off. Me last year at High School I was never there. I left school. I had nay qualifications or anythin' so it was just like try for a job, any sort of job, so I went to work in a factory, which I couldn't stand. I hated it.   Carole (in her thirties, grandmother)

Joan recalled her husband's expression of anger and frustration at the news of their daughter's pregnancy at sixteen at the beginning of the 2000s. His outburst reflected the current construction of teenage pregnancy as a disruptor of educational achievement, (see Dawson et al. 2005, Hosie and Selman 2006), interrupting a supposedly straightforward route to employment and personal success.

> He just says "Oh, she's wrecked her life", cos she was still at school, "wrecked her life". He used to keep goin' on "You've wrecked your life" an' "You could ha' like getten (got) on at school, an' stuff like gettin' a job".
>
> Joan (in her thirties, 'grandmother')

Carole's daughter talked about her interrupted route to academic (and assumed economic) success, and her family's response. Mimicking her mother's voice, she said that Carole had always wanted her to "get a good career an' make something of meself before I tied meself down and had children". Carole corroborated that she had actively transmitted a message about the importance of doing things differently to herself and not having a teenage pregnancy, and described her feelings of shock and disappointment when her daughter became pregnant under the age of twenty.

> I was devastated actually when she said she was expectin'. Whay, because you dee, you spend that many years fetchin' them up, you want what's better. You wanted somethin' better for them than what we had, d'you know what I mean. An' to see her come in an' tell you she's expectin, it's like "Oh, what!"
>
> Carole (in her thirties, grandmother)

Carole described her adjustment to grandparenthood, "But I mean now we've got him we wouldn't be without him, cos I mean, he is gorgeous, and he's such a well-behaved babby for her". This highlights the disjunction expressed by other women in the grandmother group, between initial negative assessment of a daughter's pregnancy in the context of an expected future of paid employment and opportunity, and reappraisal of the situation from the pleasurable position of grandmother.

Dawn's plan to be a health visitor changed with her desire for financial independence, linked to easy availability of local employment when she left school without qualifications at the end of the 1970s. She acknowledged that unskilled work was not what had been expected for her, illustrating her parents' aspiration for social mobility at a time when it was easier to achieve than in subsequent decades.

> *Dawn*: Never got there. I ended up working in factories and that, what a let down.
>
> *Ann*: Did you ever talk about that at school, about what you wanted to be?
>
> *Dawn*: Aye, but I didn't want to go to (college), three or four years in college. It's alright to gan to college but it's the money, you've got to have money in your pocket, and I think you only got £25 a week, when we were younger, to go to college, and arl the rest o' your friends was workin', bringin' in money and oot every weekend, where you couldn't on £25 a week, so I opted to gan into the factories, more money
>
> *Ann*: How old were you then, sixteen ?
>
> *Dawn*: Aye, sixteen I left school and I've worked ever since. I never stopped on for me exams. I regret that now like, but I had left because everyone else was leavin'. You could stop on at school, but there was nee money in it so we just left and went to factories. Them that stayed on at school eventually hoyed the towel in, because they needed money, the same as what we did, which was stupid really, cos education gets you a long way nowadays, rather than leaving school and deein' stupid factory work, but you need money to live. The factory work was very well paid. But after a couple of years, you got fed up with it. I dee wish I'd stopped at school.
>
> Dawn (in her thirties, grandmother)

Mary had wanted to be a nurse. When I asked if she had made any moves towards nurse training, she laughed as she replied.

> No, no, I ended up workin' in the breweries, believe it or not (laughed) aye, at Newcastle, I worked at a factory first mind, when I first left school, then I went to the breweries and I was there till I got married, so that was the nurse's career away (laughed), it was just a thought
>
> Mary (in her sixties, great-grandmother)

The careers mentioned most frequently were those stereotypically linked with women such as nursing, midwifery and teaching, involving emotional as well as intellectual and practical skills. Mary recognised the gendered nature of her aspiration to become a nurse, when she said: "I think it was just a lassy's thing really, you kna". Young women and young men continue to opt for gender-typical subjects in secondary school and to aspire to gendered types of paid work with different rates of pay, generally lower for women (Buswell 1992, Equal Opportunities Commission 1999, Furlong and Biggart 1999, Harrison 2001). One of the findings of Tinklin et al.'s (2005) research was that girls from working-class backgrounds are more likely than middle-class girls to pursue gender-typical jobs, which may reflect difficulty in accessing information about other options. Seaman et al. (2005:4) found that many of the young women (and also the young men) in their study of resilience in disadvantaged communities 'had high educational aspirations but opted for traditional non-professional jobs, often gender-related'.

The under-achievement of young people who grow up in disadvantaged areas is highlighted in many recent studies (Gillborn and Mirza 2000, Yeandle et al. 2003, Wiggins et al. 2005, Osler 2006). In the research area in the North East of England educational attainment is below local and national averages at all stages, and the women's stories highlighted a connection between unfulfilled hopes for careers on the one hand and ease of access to the full range of learning and training resources on the other, rather than 'low' aspirations. A recent report (Equality and Human Rights Commission 2008:13-14) points out that working-class young women, together with women from an ethnic minority background, 'suffer the most detriment in an education system that fails to widen choices and challenge stereotypes; their relatively fewer resources to break free of the low paid, low status work exacerbates the problem of gender stereotyping'. When young women do achieve in educational settings, their efforts are still 'not translating into well-paid jobs' (Equality and Human Rights Commission 2008:13)

Employment opportunities

Low *economic* aspirations can also suggest a realistic assessment of local employment opportunities, with the career trajectories of women who have had a baby as a teenager being influenced more by external structural factors, such as available employment opportunities, than by some inherent 'cultural deficit' (Diamond et al. 1998, Hobcraft and Kiernan 1999, Berthoud et al. 2004). The participants' life stories illustrated the influence of such economic and material constraints, paradoxically often co-existing with a strong sense of the importance of paid employment:

Everybody in me family worked, cos we all did, that's what we did. That's
what I came from, that ethos. *Everybody* worked in my family, nobody
signed on, I didn't know what the dole was, *everybody* worked.

(Susan, in her thirties, grandmother)

The transmission of a work ethic was referred to by all of the grandmothers
(women in their thirties and forties), and makes sense in the context of the
industrial history of the research area. However, it does not fit the current
environment of insecure and often low paid employment, to which the majority
of the women and their partners are restricted because of a lack of qualifications
in secondary or higher education.

All of the women, apart from the two youngest who became pregnant while
at school and who had not been in any paid employment at time of interview,
referred to experiences in various jobs. The great-grandmothers, Mary and
Barbara, had had periods of full-time employment in the National Health
Service and the hospitality sector respectively. Their jobs were relatively low-paid,
reflecting their lack of qualifications, and each had worked part-time, doing early
morning and night-time shifts to accommodate childcare responsibilities. Three
of the grandmothers had been employed in the service sector, mainly part-time,
from the point at which their children were, as one said, "well settled at school".
One grandmother had always worked full-time in the retail sector, one had been
promoted into a management position within a public sector organisation (from
which she had had to take prolonged sick leave because of the effects of domestic
violence), and one had reconnected with higher education, with childcare support
from her mother, and gained a degree and subsequent position as a youth worker.
The youngest women with experience of paid employment referred to short-term
contracts, for example in a local recycling plant.

The interview accounts also illustrated shifting local employment prospects
for men in the different generational groups (Nayak 2006). The husbands of
the two great-grandmothers were retired, from a managerial position and from
a job in the construction industry respectively. The husbands and partners
of the grandmothers had all had experience of full-time employment, two in
unskilled jobs, one self-employed, one in a skilled manual occupation, one as
a health professional and one in the armed forces. Of the youngest women's
partners, three were in work, one in a small business, one in a skilled manual
job and one in a temporary job with a minimum wage. The remaining two were
unemployed at time of interview.

The life stories produced by the women included examples of resources that are generally unacknowledged in contemporary teenage pregnancy discourse, including skilful management of low income.

> Me and me partner didn't have a job then. We didn't have any money when we first got our house. That was dead hard. I can remember his (Natalie's partner) sister used to make our teas, cos she used to live just round the corner, and she used to bring our teas round for us, because I couldn't afford to go shopping. We used to give her ten pounds a week and she used to make our teas every day. Givin' her ten pounds a week was easier than goin' and spendin' ten pounds on shopping, because that wouldn't have fed us for a week.   Natalie (in her twenties, mother)

A common thread in the accounts of the youngest women who had recently become mothers, was their motivation to reconnect to the sorts of jobs they had hoped for before they became pregnant. They appeared however to be generally excluded from access to information about routes to 'good' jobs. Raffo and Reeves (2000), who researched the schooling, training and further education experiences of thirty-one young people aged fifteen to twenty-four in socio-economically disadvantaged areas of Manchester, found that young people were living in situations in which it was difficult to find ways of accessing new information about jobs and how to equip themselves for them. Family connections were the main source of information about jobs for those young people who took part in UK research that explored the concept of social capital in relation to children and young people (Swann et al. 2003). Similarly, several of the youngest women in this North East England study talked about finding temporary and insecure paid employment through their extended family networks.

> Ermm, one of my Dad's relatives worked there in the factory an' he was leavin', so I asked him for the number an' I rang them up an' I got the job. They asked us to go for an interview an' told us there and then I had it, cos you didn't really need any qualifications or (laughed) anything like that. I did quite good there, an' I stayed there. I was seventeen when I started there. They fired us, cos that's when I found out I was pregnant.
>   Laura (in her twenties, mother)

Conclusion

Thirteen women composed versions of their life stories, highlighting the complexity of the circumstances and relationships that produced their teenage pregnancies. Their compositions showed diversity within and between the generational groups, rather than sameness, and suggested no intergenerational transmission of a message encouraging teenage pregnancy. The absence of all except one of the women from contemporary further education settings and their lack of professional qualifications and careers is interpreted in current UK policy terms as an intergenerationally transmitted cultural deficit, manifesting itself in 'poor' expectations, 'low' aspirations and exclusion from paid work. This 'story' is not borne out by the women's stories, as all except one of them had hoped for a career when they were growing up, and all, apart from the two youngest who became pregnant while at school, had been in paid employment. All of their male partners had also been employed, although the younger men were struggling to find or stay in work at the beginning of the millennium. In their accounts of growing up women referred to career aspirations interrupted by a variety of structural factors, including lack of access to information about career routes, school absence because of caring responsibility, desire for financial independence, and the effects of domestic violence.

Now, as the women move through the future they were imagining in their interviews, there is the question of 'what happened next?' in relation to their great expectations for themselves, their daughters and their granddaughters.

References

Berthoud, R., Ermisch, J., Fransesconi, M., Liao, T., Pevalin, D., Robson, K., (2004) *Long-term Consequences of Teenage Births for Parents and their Children*, Teenage Pregnancy Research Programme Research Briefing Number 1, March 2004, London: Teenage Pregnancy Unit.

Blair, T., (1999) Foreword by the Prime Minister, in Social Exclusion Unit, *Teenage Pregnancy*, pp. 4-5, London: The Stationery Office.

Blears, H., (2002) Foreword, in Department of Health, *Government Response to the First Annual Report of the Independent Advisory Group on Teenage Pregnancy*, p.1, London: Department of Health.

Bonell, C., (2004) Why is teenage pregnancy conceptualized as a social problem?: A Review of Quantitative Research from the USA and UK, *Culture, Health and Sexuality*, preview article, http://www.tandf.co.uk/journals, accessed 11 March 2004.

Buswell, C., (1992) Training girls to be low-paid women, in Glendinning, C. and Millar, J.,(eds) *Women and Poverty in Britain: the 1990s*, pp. 79-94, Hemel Hempstead: Harvester Wheatsheaf.

Buxton, K., Buxton, D., McGlen, S., Baker, M., McNulty, A., Drinkwater, C. (2005) Teenage Pregnancy: More than meets the eye, *British Journal of General Practice*, 55(513):315.

Carabine, J., (2001) Constituting Sexuality through Social Policy: The Case of Lone Motherhood 1834 and Today, *Social and Legal Studies*, pp. 291-314.

Chamberlayne, P. and Rustin, M.,(1999) *From Biography to Social Policy: Final Report of the SOSTRIS Project* (SOE2 — CT96 — 3010), Centre for Biography in Social Policy, University of East London.

Chamberlayne, P., Bornat, J., Wengraf, T., (2000) Introduction: The biographical turn, in Chamberlayne, P., Bornat, J., Wengraf, T., (eds) *The Turn to Biographical Methods in Social Science: Comparative issues and examples*, pp. 1-30, London: Routledge.

Connexions Service, Teenage Pregnancy Unit and Sure Start (2001) *Working together: Connexions and teenage pregnancy*, DfES Publications: Nottingham.

Dawson, N., Hosie, A., Meadows S., Selman, P. and Speak, S., (2005) *The Education of Pregnant Young Women and Young Mothers in England*, Universities of Bristol and Newcastle upon Tyne.

Dear, M., (2005) *A Social and Sexual Health Revolution, 75: A lifetime of fighting for sexual health*, pp. 5-7, London: Family Planning Association (fpa).

Dennis, N. and Erdos, G., (1992) *Families without Fatherhood*, Choice in Welfare, No 12, London: The Institute of Economic Affairs (IEA) Health and Welfare Unit.

Department for Education and Skills (2006) *Teenage Pregnancy Next Steps: Guidance for Local Authorities and Primary Care Trusts on Effective Delivery of Local Strategies*, London: DfES.

Diamond, I., Clements, S., Stone, N., Ingham, R., (1998) *Spatial Variation in Teenage Conceptions in South and West England*, Paper, Applications of Random Effects/ Multilevel Models to Categorical Data in Social Sciences and Medicine Conference, 20 October 1998, London: Royal Statistical Society.

Doran, T., Drever, F., Whitehead Margaret (2004) Is there a north-south divide in social class inequalities in health in Great Britain? Cross sectional study using data from the 2001 census, *British Medical Journal*, 328: 1043-1045.

Duncan, S., (2004) *Combining intensive and extensive research: Discovering issues and interpreting evidence*, ESRC Seminar Series, Knowing Families, Seminar 5, Combining Qualitative and Quantitative Approaches in Family Research, 19 March 2004, Leeds University: Centre for Research on Family, Kinship and Childhood.

Duncan, S. and Phillips, M., (2008) New families? Tradition and change in partnering and relationships, in *British Social Attitudes 2007/8*, London, NatCen, Sage.

Equal Opportunities Commission (1999) *Facts about Women and Men in Britain: 1999*, Manchester: EOC.

Equality and Human Rights Commission (2008) *Submission from the Equality and Human Rights Commission (EHRC) on the Sixth Periodic Report of the United Kingdom to the United Nations Committee on the Elimination of all forms of Discrimination Against Women (CEDAW)*, London: Equality and Human Rights Commission.

Ferris, P., (1993) *Sex and the British: A Twentieth-Century History*, London: Michael Joseph.

Fox Harding, L., (1996) *Family, State and Social Policy*, Basingstoke: Macmillan Press.

Furlong, A. and Biggart, A., (1999) Framing Choices: A Longitudinal Study of Occupational Aspirations among 13- to 16-year-olds, *Journal of Education and Work*, 12: 21-35.

Gillborn, D. and Mirza, H., (2000) *Educational Inequality: Mapping Race, Class and Gender, A synthesis of research evidence*, London: Office for Standards in Education.

Graham, H., (1987) Being Poor: Perceptions and Coping Strategies of Lone Mothers, in Brannen, J. and Wilson, G. (eds) *Give and Take in Families: Studies in Resource Distribution*, Hemel Hempstead: Allen and Unwin.

Greenhalgh, T., (1999) Narrative based medicine in an evidence based world, *British Medical Journal*, 318: 323-325.

Hadley, J., (1996) *Abortion: Between Freedom and Necessity*, London: Virago.

Harrison, W. C. (2001) Truth is slippery stuff, in Francis, B. and Skelton, C (eds) *Investigating Gender: Contemporary Perspectives in Education*, pp. 52-64, Buckingham: Open University Press.

Haste, C. (1992) *Rules of Desire: Sex in Britain: World War 1 to the Present*, London: Chatto and Windus.

Heron, Liz (ed) (1985) *Truth, Dare or Promise: Girls Growing Up in the 50s*, London: Virago.

Hobcraft, J. and Kiernan, K. (1999) *Childhood Poverty, Early Motherhood and Adult Social Exclusion*, CASE Paper 28, Centre for Analysis of Social Exclusion, London School of Economics.

Hockey, J. and James, A. (1993) *Growing Up and Growing Old: Ageing and Dependency in the Life Course*, London: Sage.

Hockey, J., Robinson, V., Meah, A., (2003) *A Cross Generational Investigation of the Making of Heterosexual Relationships*, Workshop, 8 December, University of Sheffield.

Hosie, A. and Selman, P., (2006) An exploration of disengagement and re-engagement from the education system, in Holgate, H., Evans, R. and Yuen, F. K O (eds) *Teenage Pregnancy and Parenthood: Global Perspectives, Issues and Interventions*, pp. 77-94, Abingdon:Routledge.

Hudson, R. (1989) *Wrecking a Region: State Polices (sic), Party Politics and Regional Change in North East England*, London: Pion.

Karpf, A., (2006) The power of speech, *The Guardian: Review*, 6 June 2006, pp. 14-17.

Kenway, J. and McLeod, J. (2004) Bourdieu's reflexive sociology and spaces of points of view: Whose reflexivity, which perspective?, *British Journal of Sociology of Education*, 25(4): 525-544, http://www.tandf.co.uk/journals, accessed 30 September 2004.

Lawler, S. (2002) Narrative in Social Research, in May, T. (ed) *Qualitative Research in Action*, pp. 242-258, London: Sage.

MacDonald, R. and Marsh, J. (2005) *Disconnected Youth?: Growing up in Britain's poor neighbourhoods*, Basingstoke: Palgrave Macmillan.

Meyer P. C. (2005) *Age 05 — Internationaler Soziologiekongress "Gesundheit und Alter(n)"*, 25-27 August, Neuchâtel, Switzerland.

Millar, J.,(1997) Gender, in Walker, A. and Walker, C., (eds) *Britain Divided: The Growth of Social Exclusion in the 1980s and 1990s*, pp. 99-110, London: Child Poverty Action Group.

Murray, C.,(1990) *The Emerging British Underclass*, London: Institute of Economic Affairs.

Murray, C.,(1994) *Underclass: The Crisis Deepens*, London: Institute of Economic Affairs.

Nayak, A., (2006) Displaced masculinities: Chavs, Youth and Class in the Post-Industrial City, *Sociology*, 40(5): 813-831.

North East Strategic Health Authority (2007) *Annual Report 2006-07*, Newcastle upon Tyne: North East Strategic Health Authority.

One North East (2007) *Raising Aspirations and Attainment*, http://www.onenortheast. co.uk/page/raisingaspirations, accessed 1 July 2007.

Osler, A., (2006) Excluded girls: Interpersonal, institutional and structural violence in schooling, *Gender and Education*, 18(6): 571-589, http://www.tandf.co.uk/journals, accessed 16 May 2007.

Paechter, C., (2001) Using poststructuralist ideas in gender theory and research, in Francis, B. and Skelton, C., (eds) *Investigating Gender: Contemporary Perspectives in Education*, pp. 41-51, Buckingham: Open University Press.

Peplar, M.,(2002) *Family Matters: A history of ideas about family since 1945*, Harlow: Pearson Education.

Phoenix, A., (1988) Narrow definitions of culture: The case of early motherhood, in Westwood, S. and Bhachu, P., (eds) *Enterprising Women: Ethnicity, Economy, and Gender Relations*, pp. 153-176, London: Routledge.

Phoenix, A., (1991) *Young Mothers?* Cambridge: Polity Press.

Phoenix, A., (1996) Social constructions of lone motherhood: A case of competing discourses, in Silva Elizabeth Bortolaia (ed) *Good Enough Mothering?: Feminist Perspectives on Lone Motherhood*, pp. 175-190, London: Routledge.

Phoenix, A., (2001) Racialization and gendering in the (re)production of educational inequalities, in Francis, B. and Skelton, C., (eds) *Investigating Gender: Contemporary Perspectives in Education*, pp. 126-138, Buckingham: Open University Press.

Population Trends (1998) Birth Statistics: Recent trends in England and Wales, *Population Trends*, 94(Winter 1998): 12-18, http://www.statistics.gov.uk/downloads, accessed 16 February 2005.

Raffo, C. and Reeves, M., (2000) Youth Transitions and Social Exclusion: Developments in Social Capital Theory, *Journal of Youth Studies*, 3(2): 147-166.

Richardson, D.,(1993) *Women, Motherhood and Childrearing*, Basingstoke: Macmillan Press.

Robinson, E., (2002) *Why do Primary Care Trust's (sic) need to buy in to the Teenage Pregnancy Strategy*, Presentation, Third Anniversary of the Teenage Pregnancy Strategy Launch, 27 June, London: Mermaid Conference Centre.

Roseneil, S. and Mann, K., (1996) Unpalatable choices and inadequate families: Lone mothers and the underclass debate, in Silva, E. B. (ed) *Good Enough Mothering?: Feminist Perspectives on Lone Motherhood*, pp. 191-210, London: Routledge.

Rustin, M.,(2006) *Biographic-Narrative Interpretive Method Review Day*, 11 July 2006, University of Central Lancashire.

Schoon, I., Martin, P. and Ross, A., (2005) *Teenage Pregnancy and Social Class*, Paper, Seminar on the Teenage Pregnancy Strategy, Gender Statistics Users' Group, 10 November 2005, London: Royal Statistical Society.

Seaman, P., Turner, K., Hill, M., Stafford A. and Walker M. (2005) *Parenting and children's resilience in disadvantaged communities*, Findings, February 2006, http://www.jrf.org. uk/knowledge/findings/socialpolicy, accessed 25 February 2006.

Selman, P., (1998) Teenage Pregnancy, Poverty and the Welfare Debate in Europe and the United States, Paper, Poverty, Fertility and Family Planning Seminar, pp. 139-166, http://www.cicred.ined.fr/pauvrete/actes.selman, accessed 16 February 2005.

Skultans, V. (2004) Narratives of displacement and identity, in Hurwitz, B., Greenhalgh, T., Skultans, V. (eds) *Narrative Research in Health and Illness*, pp. 292-308, Oxford: Blackwell with British Medical Association (BMA).

Smart, C, (1996) Deconstructing Motherhood, in Silva, E. B. (ed) *Good enough mothering?: Feminist perspectives on lone motherhood*, pp. 37-57, London: Routledge.

Social Exclusion Unit (1999) *Teenage Pregnancy*, London: The Stationery Office.

Stanley, L. (1995) *Sex Surveyed 1949-1994, From Mass-Observation's 'Little Kinsey' to the National Survey and Hite Reports*, London: Taylor and Francis.

Stonebridge, J., (2002) *Teenage Pregnancy in the North East*, Directorate of Health and Social Care North, Public Health Group North East, London: Department of Health.

Swann, C., Bowe, K., McCormick G., Kosmin, M.,(2003) *Teenage Pregnancy and Parenthood: a Review of Reviews*, Wetherby: Health Development Agency.

Thomson, D., (1969) *England in the Twentieth Century*, Harmondsworth: Penguin Books.

Thomson, R. Bell, R., Holland, J., Henderson, S., McGrellis, S. and Sharpe, S. (2002) Critical moments: Choice, chance and opportunity in young people's narratives of transition, *Sociology*, 36(2): 335-354.

Tinklin, T., Croxford, L., Ducklin, A., Frame Barbara (2005) Gender and attitudes to work and family roles: The views of young people at the millennium, *Gender and Education*, 17(2):129-142.

Wengraf, T., (2005) *Interviewing for life-histories, lived situations and experience: The Biographic-Narrative Interpretive Method (BNIM), A Short Guide to BNIM Interviewing and Interpretation*, London East Research Institute, University of East London.

Wheeler, B., Shaw, M., Mitchell, R., Dorling, D. (2005) *Life in Britain: Using Millennial Census data to understand poverty, inequality and place*, Bristol: The Policy Press in association with the Joseph Rowntree Foundation.

Whitehead, M. (1992 [1988]) The Health Divide', *Inequalities in Health*, pp. 215-400, Harmondsworth: Penguin Books.

Wiggins, M., Oakley, A., Sawtell, M., Austerberry, H., Clemens, F., Elbourne, D. (2005) *Teenage Parenthood and Social Exclusion: A multi-method study*, Summary report of findings, London: Social Science Research Unit, Institute of Education.

Williams, R. (1983) *Key Words: A vocabulary of culture and society*, London: Fontana.

Yeandle, S., Escott K., Grant L., Batty, E. (2003) *Women and men talking about poverty*, Working Paper Series, No 7, Manchester: Equal Opportunities Commission.

Chapter 7

'Just a mum or dad': experiencing teenage parenting and work-life balances

Claire Alexander, Simon Duncan and Rosalind Edwards

> Ain't he cute?
> No he ain't
> He's just another burden
> On the Welfare State
>   (*Too Much Too Young*, The Specials)

Introduction:

As we have argued in the introduction to this collection, the dominant view of teenage parenting presented by the media, politicians and policymakers has been concerned with the construction of young mothers and fathers as constituting a 'problem'—for children and families themselves, for policymakers and practitioners, and for society as a whole. Further, this has been taken to -signal a breakdown in moral values as well as proliferating social and economic 'costs'—creating 'another burden on the welfare state' by teenage mothers and their children. However, what has been missing from this externally imposed, state-driven and overly economistic model of 'welfare' are the voices and experiences of young parents themselves, who are more usually positioned as the passive *objects* of policy intervention than as active *subjects* in their own lives.

The current chapter is concerned with two distinct, but related aspects of teenage parenting from 'the inside': firstly, the chapter describes the experience of teenage parents themselves, exploring their views on parenthood and their social networks for support. Secondly, it focuses on the aspirations of young mothers and fathers in relation to education and employment. The chapter is based on a small scale qualitative study of teenage mothers and fathers in Bradford, which was carried out for the local authority teenage pregnancy service (Upfront) in 2006 and 2007 (Alexander, Duncan and Edwards 2007). The aim of the project was twofold. First, it hoped to contribute to the growing body of qualitative literature in this area, which challenges the dominant pathologised and problem oriented accounts of teenage parenting. Second, and consequently, the project would aid local policy formation and practice in providing insights into the lived experiences and everyday support needs of young parents.

What the study found, in essence, was that teenage parents saw themselves primarily as 'just a mother or a father', contesting their categorisation as a problem group. Additionally they were embedded in strong support networks and were highly motivated towards education and employment as a means of providing a stable future for their children. The chapter argues that such lived experiences contest dominant policy discourses in two ways: first, by promoting an alternative model of social participation which centralises family and parenting; and second, by challenging the portrait of teenage parents as lacking aspirations around education and employment. Indeed, the ambitions for future success in study and work are often rooted in the desire to fulfil the responsibilities of good parenting.

Constructing teenage parenting: an economic or moral agenda?

As discussed in earlier chapters, New Labour's Teenage Pregnancy Strategy, launched in 1999, had an expressed dual goal: to halve the number of teenage pregnancies, and to increase the number of teenage parents (usually mothers) entering into education, training or employment. Policy across the following decade has remained highly consistent around these two core related themes— the 'problem' of teenage parenting and the pivotal role of the labour market—and are of particular interest to the present chapter in two related ways. The first is what might be seen as the 'culturing' of the teenage parenting problem—teenage mothers are seen as emblematic of an 'underclass' which is outside of mainstream British society, and which is defined through pathologised moral and cultural values, 'lifestyles and behaviour', seemingly transmitted across generations (Wilson and Huntington 2005, McNulty, chapter six). The second is around the positioning of education and employment as the normative pathway to social inclusion and full citizenship, and the assumption that these aspirations are incompatible with the status of teenage parents by default (see chapter one). It is significant, for example, that Charles Murray's exploration of 'the underclass' in the UK took the presence of single mothers and high levels of illegitimacy[1] as highly indicative, along with long term unemployment (and violent crime) as identifying markers of 'the British underclass'. Murray asserted:

---

1. Murray attributed to the increase in rates of illegitimacy to the reduced stigma of single motherhood and, tellingly, to the provision of welfare services that enabled single mothers to keep children.

Britain has a growing population of working-aged, healthy people who live in a different world from other Britons, who are raising their children to live in it and whose values are contaminating the life of entire neighbourhoods.   (1990: 4)

This attribution of deviant moral and cultural values to teenage mothers is echoed in the following comment by then Prime Minister Tony Blair in an article on teenage pregnancy in *The Times* in 1999 entitled 'Teenage mums are all our business':

I believe now that it is the *decent majority, who play by the rules*, who want us to take a lead in defining *a new moral purpose*.
                                 (Blair cited in Rolfe 2005: 236, our emphasis).

Teenage mothers here are placed beyond the pale of 'decent' society, and are seen—by no less a figure than the Prime Minister—as immoral rulebreakers. This position is reinforced by their supposedly effectively 'opting out' of the education and employment system, and the attributed combination of low expectations, poor aspirations and ignorance (SEU 1999; see also Duncan 2007, Wilson and Huntington 2005, Arai 2003 for critique). Indeed, some have argued that young people from poorer backgrounds, and particularly teenage mothers, are in 'the fast lane' to adulthood (Brynner and Pan 2002, cited in Graham and McDermott 2005), which is itself a fast lane to social exclusion. Brynner and Pan thus argue that 'teenage motherhood, perhaps more than any other status, epitomises the problem [of social exclusion]: early school leaving, no qualifications, poor job or youth training, pregnancy and childbirth, poor prospects of ever getting a decent job, family poverty' (cited in Graham and McDermott 2005: 25-6).

The danger of such culturing of teenage parenting is three-fold: first, it runs the risk of blaming teenage mothers themselves for their social exclusion rather than broader social processes and constraints (Duncan 2007, Graham and McDermott 2005; Kidger 2004); second, it ignores or overrides the presence of alternative (class or ethnic) value systems in favour of a dominant middle-class set of 'norms and values' which renders young parents' choices, 'lifestyles and behaviour' illegitimate, irrational and pathological (Arai 2003; Duncan and Edwards 1999; Duncan et al. 2003b; Graham and McDermott 2005; Duncan 2007); third, it predicates social inclusion and acceptance on the entering into the labour market in a way which delegitimatises motherhood and family (especially for the poor and the young) in favour of an individualistic, masculinised and professional economic model of waged employment (Duncan 2005, 2007, Duncan et al. 2003a). Rather ironically, at a time where the government is promoting notions of 'active citizenship' amongst young people as a way of generating social and community cohesion (Goldsmith 2008; H. M. Government 2005; Alexander 2007), the idea of motherhood as a valued social role is being undermined—for the young, poor and unmarried, at least. This suggests an ambivalence at the heart of New Labour policy on teenage parenting, and parenting more generally—a tension between the valorisation of 'the family' as the bedrock of a stable and cohesive society (Edwards 2004) and the insistence on economic participation in the labour market which sees mothers and fathers as, first and foremost, workers (Duncan et al. 2003a). Such ambivalence poses particular problems for parents who are unable, or unwilling, to balance the requirements of family and work as laid out in this framework, most notably those in non-traditional, non-normative family arrangements, whether this is defined through ethnicity, class, single or teenage parenthood[2].

While the policy discourse maps neatly onto the media and political construction of the 'problem' of teenage parenting, what is less clear cut is its relationship to the empirical evidence (see chapter nine). Indeed, many researchers have argued that the evidence presented by the government on teenage parenting represents a highly selective quantitative evidence base which overlooks the more complex qualitative picture emerging from teenage parents themselves (See chapter one for review, and other chapters for recent empirical evidence, also Graham and McDermott 2005; Arai 2003, Wilson and Huntington 2005; Kidger 2004; Duncan 2007). Graham and McDermott have argued (2005) that while a quantitative approach underscores the view of teenage parenting as a route to social exclusion, a qualitative approach reveals that it is experienced by teenage parents themselves as an act of social inclusion (see also Kidger 2004). However, quantitative research has also clearly demonstrated that poor health, social and economic outcomes are predicated on social status irrespective of teenage pregnancy (see chapter four), so the implication seems to be less a methodological than an ideological one (see chapter nine). Other qualitative studies challenge strongly the foundational assumptions of policy around low expectations and aspirations, ignorance and benefit culture that

---

2. Wilson and Huntington thus assert that 'middle-class aspirations for well-paid professional jobs have come to set the parameters for social inclusion' (2005: 69).

define teenage parents (Duncan 2007, Arai 2003, Wilson and Huntington 2005) and draw attention to the broader social context and barriers to social inclusion against which educational success, labour market participation and the choice to become parents need to be understood (Wilson and Huntington 2005, Arai 2003, Duncan 2007). Such studies draw attention too to the ways in which young parents experience parenthood as a positive and enriching experience, which defines their sense of entry into adult roles and responsibilities and which speaks to an alternative set of values based on family, kinship and community (Duncan 2007, Arai 2003, Kidger 2004, Graham and McDermott 2005, Rolfe 2005, Bell et al. 2004, SmithBattle 2000) within particular 'local economies of value' (Thompson 2000). Thus Arai comments

> Policymakers find it hard to believe that young women, often in the least auspicious circumstances, might actually *want* to be become mothers.
> (2003: 212)

Similarly, Wilson and Huntington note,

> interview studies found that most young women were proud to be parents … keen to be good parents … and found motherhood enjoyable and/or satisfying … [T]here is evidence that by having a baby mothers have claimed independence and/or adult responsibilities.   (2005: 65)

It is ironic, then, that the insistence on Education, Employment and Training (EET) as the route to 'official' sanctioned social inclusion often carries with it the necessary reduction or abandonment of the parental role, which in effect sets young parents up to fail both as workers and as parents (Kidger 2004). However, research on the attitudes, experiences and aspirations of teenage parents themselves points to a dual response which demonstrates both their awareness of the external moral discourses which position them as deviant and failing in the eyes of wider society, and their own set of alternative individual, family and community based measures for success—which particularly posit being a 'good parent' as a primary source of identity and esteem. While these alternatives can be characterised primarily through class, other factors like ethnicity and location, along with age and family background, are also important, suggesting a greater heterogeneity within the category of 'teenage parent' than is usually recognised in policy. As Duncan (2007) and Duncan and Edwards (1999) have argued, this qualitative evidence suggests that policymakers are guilty of a 'rationality mistake' in assuming that teenage parents subscribe to economically driven cost-benefit type plans around education and employment in a drive to maximise personal benefits. As Duncan comments:

> becoming a young mother or father can be rational and moral in terms of their everyday worlds of family, community and locality, and parenting can be seen as more valuable than employment.   (2007: 325).

Research by Duncan et al. (2004) on mothers' assessments of childcare provision similarly points to complex moral and emotional decisions that make up part of the 'choice' to return to work and how best to combine this with parental responsibilities—what Duncan and Edwards (1999) term 'gendered moral rationality'. This research demonstrates clearly the place of class, ethnicity and social location in shaping these decisions. And, where teenage parents are 'just a mum or a dad' like any other, our findings here are not dissimilar from research on parenting more generally.

The focus on the 'everyday worlds' of young mothers and fathers provides compelling insights into these alternative moral rationalities, which contest the moralising certainties of policymakers and the media, and the cold abstractions of quantitative analyses. An up-close-and-personal approach allows too for the recognition of the diversity of experience and subjectivity of young parents (for example, around class, ethnicity and location) and looks at what young parents actually want and need, and how they are dealing, in practice, with the demands of combining parenthood with education and employment. What follows is an account of the lives of some young mothers and fathers in Bradford in these terms.

Listening to young mothers and fathers: the study

The study is drawn from the narratives of young mothers and fathers who were part of a small qualitative study of teenage parents undertaken by the authors for the Upfront Pregnancy Team, funded by Bradford City Council Youth Service in 2006 (Alexander et al. 2007). The interviews were conducted by three 'peer researchers'—Yasmin Akhtar, Kayleigh Anderson and Amy McKay—who carried out a total of eight interviews with young parents (six mothers and two fathers). A table outlining the key characteristics of the interviewees is included below[3].

3. Names of participants have been changed to ensure anonymity

Table 1   The mothers and fathers in this study

	Age at interview	Children		Partner status	Household type	Ethnicity	Education Qualifications	Income source
		No.	Age					
Mothers								
Maryam	20	1	11 mths	married	extended	British Pakistani	none	husband's job
Nicole	18	1	9 mths		nuclear	white British	GCSEs + vocational	partner's job
Siobhan	18	1	9 mths		nuclear	white British	GCSEs	benefits
Shamina	20	1	9 mths	married	extended	British Pakistani	GCSEs	husband's job
Steffi	21	1	3 yrs		extended	white British	GCSEs	partner's job
Susie	18	1	2 yrs	single	lone	white British	GCSEs	benefits
Fathers								
Darren	21	1	3 yrs		nuclear	white British	GCSEs + vocational	job
Liam	18	1	2 yrs		nuclear	white British	none	job

Source: Interviews, May 2006

The location of the study in Bradford, though largely a result of the funding source, is serendipitous in terms of shedding light on the broader issue of teenage parenting. Bradford is a northern city which features highly in social indices of social deprivation[4], a result of decades of deindustrialisation and economic neglect. It also has a unique demographic make up, with a concentration of long-settled British Asian (mainly Pakistani) families in the inner wards[5] (Alam and Husband 2006), and white British families in concentrations in the outer wards. This enabled the researchers to explore the neglected issue of ethnicity in relation to teenage parenting, particularly around the community expectations of marriage and parenthood in Asian/Pakistani/Muslim households[6].

All interviewees were aged between eighteen and twenty-one years-old at the time of interview, and had one child born while they were aged between sixteen and nineteen years-old. The semi-structured interviews explored a

4. In 2001, Bradford was ranked 30th most deprived out of 354 local authority areas in England, while in 2004, 14 of Bradford's 307 Super Output Areas were ranked in the most deprived 1% in England, mainly in inner-city locations (Alam and Husband 2006)

5. 2001 Census records 19% of the population as 'Asian or British Asian' with high concentrations in inner-city wards such as Manningham (79%), Toller (75%), Bradford Moor (70%), City (63%).

6. Although the DCSF Strategy document (2007) notes that 'All Asian ethnic groups have a lower than average incidence of teenage motherhood' (p9), the younger age of marriage and childbirth in Pakistani and Bangladeshi communities, combined with high rates of economic inactivity for women and high

continued overleaf

range of themes covering the experience of motherhood/fatherhood, support networks, neighbourhood and community, education and employment. Of the peer researchers employed, two—Amy and Kayleigh—were teenage mothers themselves, while the third interviewer -Yasmin, was slightly older—but had been a young mother when her first child was born. The former two peer researchers were both white young mothers living in outer areas of Bradford, while the latter was of Pakistani descent living in inner city Bradford. Due to the small size and limited resourcing of the project, the peer researchers were paid on an hourly rate (as well as travel and childcare expenses), and were responsible for finding interviewees (two mothers and one father each) and conducting the interviews. The peer researchers were given a day of training by the research team and ongoing mentoring by Simon Duncan, as well as taking part in final exit interviews, and Simon was able to arrange for their work on the project to be accredited. Interviews were transcribed within the University of Bradford and analysed by the research team (see Edwards and Alexander, forthcoming, Kidger 2004 for a further discussion of using peer researchers/educators).

While such a small study cannot claim to be representative of the experiences and attitudes of young parents in Bradford, or more broadly, the interviews did reveal some compelling insights into how young mothers and fathers experience parenting, and their concerns and aspirations for the future. These insights challenge the dominant construction of the issue by the media and policy makers. Indeed, one finding was that the young parents we interviewed were acutely aware of the dominant negative images around teenage pregnancy and consciously struggled to distance themselves from this picture and the attitudes of the public and service practitioners with whom they came into contact (see also Arai 2003). As other studies have similarly found, young mothers in particular were keen to demonstrate their role as a 'good mother', which in turn has implications for their potentially conflicting role as a student or worker (Kidger 2004, Graham and MacDermott 2005, Duncan 2007). At the same time, however, we also found that the young parents we interviewed saw parenthood as a source of inspiration for their future plans around education and employment. It is these two strands—becoming and being a young mother/father, and the tension between the roles of parent and worker—that we explore here.

6   continued
     levels of unemployment for men, has targeted these communities and families as potentially problematic (Anwar 2005, Peach 2005). A Home Office report in 2005 noted that 2/3 of Pakistani/Bangladeshi descent children lived in households with less than 60% of median income (ie below the poverty line) compared to 1/5 of the population as a whole (Home Office 2005).

Just a mum or dad: The experience of teenage parenting

The dominant picture that emerges from the media and from policy around teenage parenting is one where the pregnancy is unplanned and, by implication, unwanted. However, studies have shown that, whatever their age, only a minority of mothers actively 'plan' their pregnancy, in the sense of an active intention with their partner's agreement (Duncan 2007). The majority of expectant mothers are 'positively ambivalent'—that is, they do not actively plan pregnancy but are open to the idea of having a child and welcome this when it happens. There is a need then to distinguish between 'accidental' and 'unwanted' pregnancies, particularly in the discourse around teenage motherhood, which is generally conceptualised as a catastrophic accident (Arai 2003).

The young mothers we interviewed generally reflected this 'positive ambivalence'. Only one—Siobhan—experienced becoming a mother as a disruption to her life, which seemed to be related to subsequent difficulties with her parents who did not like her partner, John. Another, Maryam told us she had actively been trying for a child:

> It was planned because ... I had a miscarriage twice so I was really desperate for a baby.

Maryam, like Shamina, the other British Pakistani mother in our sample, was married to an older man and viewed childbirth as an expected and important part of her adult family life. The other young mothers saw their pregnancies as unplanned but not unwelcomed, what Nicole described as "a very happy accident". For them, the experience of motherhood more than compensated for the disruption to their previous lives; as Susie noted:

> I reflect back and think that if I had done my studying before I had a baby life would have been a bit different, but I don't think I'd change anything now. She's gorgeous. No, I couldn't send her back!

The two young fathers in the study expressed similar 'positive ambivalence', with Liam, who became a father at sixteen, claiming that he and his family were "over the moon", and that becoming a father was one of the key events in his life to date. Darren, who was eighteen when he became a father, told us, "It just happened ... [I was] shocked at first, then yes, happy about it now", although he acknowledged that, unlike Liam, his family "weren't happy".

As mentioned above, the young parents were acutely aware of the dominant stereotypes surrounding teenage pregnancies, particularly the role of the media. One young mother, Steffi pointed to the portrayal of figures like Vicky Pollard, the stereotypical 'feckless' young mother in the TV comedy series *Little Britain* as promoting these negative images:

> There's been speculation and people are getting pregnant now younger and younger aren't they, so there's something wrong with that. I mean Vicky Pollard, look how she's portrayed.

Susie noted that some people in her local community reflected these attitudes, assuming that she was:

> Another social statistic, another dull life. Some people have the wrong opinion and think you just have babies so you can stay home and screw the government but it's not like that—well, it isn't for me anyway.

Maryam also felt that:

> Some people think "oh she's too young", you know "how does she keep up with everything" ... They think they aren't responsible generally, but then again, they shouldn't give their opinion. They shouldn't say anything about anyone until you know them ... because everyone is different and you shouldn't be general in their appearance

Susie felt that these negative images had impacted on her experience of childcare professionals[7]:

> I think health visitors should be more open minded rather than judgemental ... they see you as just another statistic.

Although teenage mothers are at the forefront of social stigmatisation, the two young fathers we interviewed were also aware of the negative images of feckless fathers—as Liam put it "they just give the view that you are irresponsible".

7. See Arai 2003, and also David and Alldred, this volume

Although he did not feel that he had personally experienced problems from these images he, like the young mothers, felt that this did impact on the practitioners with whom they had contact—leading for example to being 'put' in unsuitable and unpleasant council estates.

However, although they were aware of these representations, and conscious of some of the potential consequences for how they were treated, the young parents we interviewed also pointed to a high level of local support and understanding, reinforcing the idea that there are alternative 'moral rationalities' based around locale, class and ethnicity. Susie, for example, acknowledged a change in attitudes towards young mothers:

> We're living in the twenty-first century … probably years and years ago it was seen as irresponsible and you didn't do it and were locked away.

Nowadays, she argued, teenage parenting was "a normal part of everyday life. I think everyone accepts it these days, thank God". Darren similarly told us that, in his neighbourhood, being a young father was not an unusual occurrence, "I've seen loads of young parents. It doesn't bother me … [We're viewed] as no different to anybody else".

Interestingly, Shamina felt that in her local, predominantly British Pakistani community, being a young (married) mother was viewed very positively, as part of the expected and valued role of becoming a wife and parent:

> I think our neighbourhood, they would actually proud of this … You know, I've got a child and I'm having a normal married life.

Although the issue of marriage is a crucial one here, Shamina points to the unexceptional, mundane condition of young parenthood in her local community:

> Now you see that the majority are teenage mothers. Nearly everywhere you go you see that a lot of people are around about the age of nineteen to twenty or eighteen, and they've got babies. Some of them have even two children at that age.

Far from the social stigmatisation popularly associated with teenage parenthood, the young parents we interviewed were able to draw upon broad and varied networks of support in managing their new roles and responsibilities, particularly on informal networks of family and friends. This contests the dominant policy picture of absent fathers and teenage mothers as isolated and cast out from wider structures of support, struggling to manage in terms of time, money and emotional resources. Rather, the young mothers and fathers in our study were enmeshed in multiple networks of support, which often substituted or supplemented for more formal social provisions, particularly around financing and childcare, as well as providing valuable emotional support. These networks were of crucial significance in facilitating their aspirations around education and work (discussed below).

Unlike the too common conflation of young motherhood with single motherhood, for the majority of the young women we interviewed (five out of the six), their partner and baby-father were still very much an active presence and source of support, particularly in providing financial stability and some basic childcare[8]. Maryam told us that her husband, "Financially … supports me and my baby" and spends whatever free time he has with their child, while Shamina reported that her husband:

> Helps me in financial ways and he helps me, like if I'm tired and I can't look after the baby then he'll make her sleep for me.

Steffi similarly described her partner as a "provider" and said that he helped "amuse" their son. Liam and Darren also saw their role as being primarily financial but also enjoyed being actively involved with their children's care. Liam thus spoke of how much pleasure he obtained from taking his son to the park, and both he and Darren spoke of how their future plans depended upon their role as a father. Darren, for example, said that "[Things are] promising in my work and I'm just looking forward to my son growing up", while Liam told us of his aspirations, "[I want to be] a businessman, a homeowner, [have] a happy family". The young fathers we interviewed spoke of being "just a father", "no different to anybody else" (Darren), and of the importance of being financially supportive and independent. Indeed, rather than the feckless fathers beloved of media and policy outrage, the young fathers we spoke to were committed to a traditional role of the father as breadwinner/provider.

---

8. In 2001 60% of teenage mothers were defined as 'single' (i.e. bringing up a child without a co-resident partner), although it seems likely that many more would be 'living apart together' (ie with a non-resident partner). See chapter one.

The young parents in our research also drew upon wider circles of family and friends as an important source of emotional and financial support and guidance, around both childrearing and education and work. Shamina, Maryam and Steffi lived in extended family households in which their parents and siblings were an integral part of the parenting process. Shamina told us that her sisters-in-law were crucial in providing a trusted source of childcare, "I know there are a lot of people to look after her and they will look after her really well", something that remains an issue for all mothers, of whatever age (see Duncan et al. 2003). Steffi's parents babysat every weekend while she went out with her partner and friends, as did Nicole's parents every other weekend, while Susie reported that "My mum's always there for advice and hands-on babysitting when I need her". Although friends were not generally as sought after for primary care support, they were seen as crucial in providing broader forms of advice and emotional support, particularly around career advice. In contrast, formal sources of social support (outside of financial and housing requirements) played a secondary role, due partly to financial constraints (around childcare) or problems of inadequate provision. Susie for example stated that the provision for young mothers where she lived was insufficient:

> There are a few young mums who've gone off the rails ... and not had the services and backup they felt they could.

In addition, several of the interviewees, both mothers and fathers, noted that council housing policies had often positioned them away from their informal networks of support, creating a situation of isolation reinforced by lack of adequate transport facilities and finances. Indeed, it sometimes seemed that the policy responses to teenage parents often worked towards creating negative experiences and consequences for young parenthood rather than alleviating them. Siobhan for example stated that in relation to housing, "We didn't have any choice, it was just what came up at that time and we had to have it" and she described her neighbourhood as "dirty" Susie noted that she had been placed by the council on an estate where there were other young single mothers, because "The council assumed it would be suitable for a young mum", but that the area was unsafe for bringing up a young child: "It's a bit rough ... you walk about and you see syringes and cider bottles In contrast the young mothers who had stayed in their local neighbourhood near family and friends had a more positive experience. Steffi noted that her area, where she had lived since the age of nine was "Brilliant ... there are parks, schools, crèches. There's playgroups", while Shamina described her neighbourhood as:

> A nice friendly area. There's a lot of young children the same age as my daughter, so by the time she grows up to about four or five years-old there'll be quite a lot of kids about her age to play with.

One of the most striking themes that emerged from our study was the continuity of experience of the young parents we interviewed with mothers and fathers more generally. With the exception of Maryam, who told us her mother felt she was too immature to have a baby, all the others described themselves as "just a mum" like any other. Shamina told us:

> It doesn't really matter if you are young or old ... it doesn't really matter about age, but your life does change, it does get really busy.

What was more important for the young mothers in our study was their competence as mothers, which had nothing to do with age:

> [Older people might have] stereotypical views about teenage parents ... but I don't think there is a problem as long as you look after your child.
>   (Nicole).

However, it might be possible to infer that their awareness of being a young mother led to a determination amongst our interviewees to demonstrate their competence as mothers, particularly to their own parents/mothers. Maryam, for example, responded to her mother's criticism of her immaturity by asserting her independence and capability as a mother:

> You shouldn't depend on anyone because your children are your responsibility,

While Susie pointed to the advantages of being a younger mother, of "hav[ing] more time with her being young and active".

Indeed, all our interviewees, both mothers and fathers, spoke of parenting as giving them a sense of adult responsibility and self worth, independence and maturity. Susie thus described the birth of her child as "beneficial in terms of a growth experience", while Maryam stated simply that becoming a mother was "the best thing that ever happened to me".

Mother/father or worker? Young parents and the work/life balance

As discussed previously, policy and popular/media concerns often focus on the economic 'costs' of young parenthood. These costs are expressed in both in terms of the 'burden on the welfare state' supposedly posed by teenage mothers and the spectre of their poverty, again supposedly caused by the disruption of young parenting to the education and employment trajectory posited as the normative route to social inclusion and success. This position remains the dominant one in policy, where a key objective of the Teenage Pregnancy Unit is to increase the participation in education, employment or training (EET), despite evidence that giving birth at a young age has little consequence for whether or not mothers are disadvantaged (Arai 2003, Duncan 2007, Hawkes, chapter four), and data that suggests that over half of all mothers of pre-school children have paid (usually part-time) work (ONS 2005). This policy assumes that young mothers, in particular, are deliberately 'opting out' from EET and from broader social participation through childbirth. However, as we argue above, and as reflected in the views of the young parents in our study, the picture is not so clear cut. On the one hand, young mothers feel torn between their obligations as a mother, together with the need to demonstrate being a 'good mother' by spending time with her child, compared to the need to be financially independent. On the other hand, both young mothers and young fathers stressed the importance of achieving in terms of education and employment as part of their role as parents and spoke of the inspiration they derived from this role to do better—again like mothers in general (see Duncan et al. 2003).

As we have already seen above, the young mothers in our study did not view pregnancy as an interruption to their life trajectories, or as a disruption of their education and career pathways. All but one had gained GCSEs and Nicole also had a vocational qualification. They had comparatively little experience of employment, although both Nicole and Steffi had a short period of working in the service sector prior to having their children. Shamina, who had worked for a week after having her child providing holiday relief for a friend who worked in a shop, spoke of the difficulties of combining work with childcare responsibilities:

It was really tiring. Well, because that work was really hard work, you would have to stand for about twelve hours, and when you came home your feet would be killing you, and then you have to try and look after the baby.

Shamina's experience speaks to the practical difficulties of combining paid work with childcare, but also to the often restricted employment opportunities open to working-class young women, mothers or not, which is not fully recognised in policy exhortations about the value of work. Within our small sample, all of the young mothers were currently full-time carers, although they had given consideration to the balance of work and family in the future. As with other, older mothers, this varied, with some seeing themselves as primarily mothers and homebuilders, some seeing themselves primarily as workers with motherhood separate to this, and others hoping to integrate the two, seeing financial independence as part of their role as a 'good mother' (Duncan and Edwards 1999, Duncan et al. 2003). Thus Shamina and Maryam, the two British Pakistani young mothers, focused more on their role as mothers and wives, with Shamina in particular planning to focus on her family life. Maryam was more ambivalent, struggling between the responsibility she felt for caring for her child—"at the end of the day he's my child and my responsibility" and the feeling that she would like to strengthen her educational qualifications in the future. Similarly Nicole told us that she wanted both to stay at home to "spend time and focus" on her son, but also to provide for him financially "instead of depending on benefits". She said that having a child had made her "more determined to get a job", for herself and her son, but also:

To show that you can have a child in your teens and also have a successful career.

The remaining mothers, Siobhan, Steffi and Susie laid more emphasis on their role as paid workers and had more immediate defined plans to either return to education or training in order to gain further qualifications to better their job prospects. Susie stated:

I'm looking forward to going back to college and I'm looking to enrol next semester in September when college starts again ... I need to get on in life so that means I need to go back to college and get some qualifications

… For my own self respect I want to go back to studying. I want to put something back into society … It's going to be very, very difficult, but I'm determined. I can't just stay at home every day looking after her [daughter]. She's growing up and she's going to be off, so I have got to look into the future for my own self worth.

For Susie, as for the other young mothers, the tension was balancing their own career aspirations with those of being a mother, which sometimes led to ambivalence or conflict with others. She noted that her although her parents had been supportive during and after her pregnancy, they had been:

A little disappointed because they had visions of me going on to [further] education and possibly having a full-time career.

Steffi told us that her parents were supportive of her plans to return to college, to train as a nail technician, but that:

My mum, she thinks I should stay at home with [my son] until he's full-time at school

Whereas Steffi herself felt:

I can't do that … I'm going to college with my friend, she's wanting to do the same thing.

By contrast, Siobhan's family shared her opinion about returning to work:

Well, my mum and sister think I should, perhaps I should go out and get a job and stuff.

These concerns point to the important role that wider networks of support play in deciding *whether* and *when* a young mother should re-enter EET. The issue of timing is a crucial one, with most stressing the importance of their children being 'ready' for their mothers to go out to work. All the young mothers in our study spoke of the importance of a period at home with their child to lay a foundation between them, when mother and child could bond and the children could settle. As Maryam put it:

Well, I think when your baby is really small, like from nought to one years of age, I think the baby would need more attention because they'd be small ... I would like to study as well, in law, do some sort of course and get some sort of experience later on. So I would let him [her son] get a bit mature, grow, before I do something I would like to do ... I'll just wait till my baby is a bit more mature.

For some of the mothers, this was linked too to their own sense of being ready and able to study or work. Steffi remarked:

It's important to stay at home for a certain length of time to get the bonding and everything, but when you're ready to go back to work and college and things, then that's fine. You've just got to be ready, haven't you? ... Now he's getting older and I'm getting bored I want to do something.

The length of this foundational period varied widely in the minds of these mothers—of those young mothers who were planning to enter education or training in the near future, Siobhan, Steffi and Susie's children were aged nine months, three years and two years respectively. For others, who were more ambivalent about combining motherhood and work, such as Maryam, the period extended indeterminately into the future. However, an important point to emphasise is that being young mothers was not seen as a permanent disruption to their plans, and that most of the young women in our study were taking a pathway that they would have traversed anyway.

For the young fathers in the study, for whom the gendered expectations were around their role as breadwinners, the issue of work/life balance was less ambivalent. Both spoke of their responsibility for providing financially for their families as a basic requirement of their role as fathers—when Darren was asked about whether fathers should work to support their children, he stated "I do that anyway", while Liam said that having a child had taught him "to hold down a job". Liam had no formal qualifications but was employed fulltime in the building trade, while Darren had gained GCSEs and a vocational qualification and was working as a management trainee. For both, their primary role was as a worker, although this was inextricably linked to their views of their familial position. This gendered division of labour was also reflected in the attitudes of the young mothers we spoke to who, with the exception of Susie, were all with the fathers of their children, all of whom (except Siobhan's partner) were primary financial providers. The tension for young fathers, as with fathers more generally, was perhaps on the constraints this placed on their wider involvement with their children (Lewis 2000). Several of the young mothers mentioned their partner's long working hours, with Maryam's comments about her husband's situation providing a good reflection:

> He supports me, yes, he helps me like when I'm doing something ... But mainly he's at work, you see. He goes in the morning about half nine and then comes about half seven or after half seven, whichever time ... He hardly gets to see him [their son]. He only has one day off a week ... Generally I think that he works and obviously when he comes back from work I have no right to say to him "get up and do this for him", because I've been at home. OK, I do the housework, but then again I'm at home.

Conclusion: Revaluing teenage parenthood

While the 'teenage mother/father' moral panic seems set to continue for the foreseeable future, and carries with it a set of highly specific gendered and classed social, economic and moral discourses, our research suggests that the picture is not so clear cut. The media, politicians and policy makers perpetuate an often misleading and stigmatising portrait of young parents as irresponsible, ignorant and underachieving, and point to the experience of teenage parenting as an unmitigated disaster and a barrier to full economic and social inclusion. However, the young parents in our study, as in other qualitative research, strongly challenge this portrait in a number of significant ways.

First, and contesting the idea of young parenthood as a disaster, the young mothers and fathers we spoke to spoke of their positive experience and the ways in which having children had given them a sense of responsibility and adult status. Second, while they faced many struggles, these were often linked to problems of wider social disadvantage, and they themselves strongly challenged the idea that these were related to their position as *young* parents. Rather, they saw themselves as facing the same problems and joys as any parents—as being "just a mum (or dad)".

Third, they resisted being characterised solely as a teenage mother or father and saw themselves as having multiple roles and identities, as individuals, partners, workers, students. Fourth, while they were aware of the broader social stigma of being young parents, their own experience was mainly one of family and community support; they were enmeshed in complex informal networks of family and friends—not only contesting the idea of social isolation and marginalisation put forward in policy but suggesting too the importance of alternative community norms and mores. Indeed, where our interviewees spoke of social isolation, this was often a direct result of policies towards teenage parents, such as housing policy, rather than being inherent in their position as young parents in and of itself. Fifth, rather than being outside of, and opposed to, the model of worker-parent-citizen that forms the basis of New Labour policy on social inclusion, most of the young parents in our study were keen to pursue education, training and employment in the future, or were already so engaged. There was no evidence that having a child had permanently disrupted their planned pathways into work or family life, although as individuals they did articulate different balances between these two spheres of activity. Moreover, most saw their economic participation in the labour market as an integral part of their parental responsibilities, although there was undoubted tension for the young mothers between this and how they saw their role as primary caregivers, and many spoke of their desire for a 'foundational' period at home to bond with their child.

Our study suggests strongly, then, that there is an urgent need to re-evaluate—and revalue—the role that teenage parents can and do play, both as parents and as part of the broader society in which we all live. Rather than viewing teenage parents as a problem and an economic and social burden, our research suggests that young mothers and fathers not only view parenthood as a valuable role in society in and of itself but also see it as a pathway into forms of economic and social participation through education and employment. In this, importantly, they are much like most other mothers and fathers which, indeed, is how they see themselves. As Shamina told us, "I think a mother is a mother, it doesn't matter if you're a teenaged mother or an older aged mother … having a baby or child in your life, your life does change".

References

Alam, M. Y. and Husband, C. (2006) *British Pakistani Men from Bradford*, York: JRF.

Alexander, C. (2007) Cohesive Identities: the distance between meaning and understanding, in M. Wetherell, M. LaFleche and R. Berkeley (eds) *Identity, Ethnic Diversity and Community Cohesion*, London: Sage.

Alexander, C., Duncan, S. and Edwards, R. (2007) *Listening to Young Mothers and Fathers. Research findings on the experiences of teenage mothers and fathers*, Bradford Upfront/Social Science and Humanities, University of Bradford.

Anwar, M. (2005) Muslims in Britain: Issues, Policy and Practice, in T. Abbas (ed) *Muslim Britain: Communities under Pressure*, London: Zed Press.

Arai, L. (2003) Low expectations, sexual attitudes and knowledge: explaining teenage pregnancy and fertility in English communities. Insights from qualitative research, *Sociological Review*, 521(2): 199-217.

Bell, J., Clisby, S., Craig, G., Measor, L., Petrie, S. and Stanley, N. (2004) *Living on the Edge: Sexual behaviour and young parenthood in seaside and rural areas, Department of Health*.

DCSF (Department Children, Schools and Families) (2007) *Teenage Parents: the Next Steps*, Nottingham, DCSF.

Duncan, S. (2005) Mothering, Class and Rationality, *Sociological Review*, 53(1): 49-76.

Duncan, S. (2007) What's the problem with teenage parents? And what's the problem with policy?, *Critical Social Policy*, 27(3): 307-334.

Duncan, S. and Edwards, R. (1999) *Lone Mothers, Paid Work and Gendered Moral Rationalities*, London: Macmillan.

Duncan, S., Edwards, R., Reynolds, T. and Alldred P. (2003) Motherhood, paid work, and partnering: values and theories, *Work, Employment and Society*, 17(2): 309-30.

Duncan, S., Edwards, R., Alldred P. and Reynolds, T. (2004) Mothers and childcare: policies, values and theories, *Children and Society*, 18(4): 245-65.

Edwards, R. (2004) Present and absent in troubling ways: families and social capital debates, *Sociological Review*, 52(1): 1-21.

Edwards, R. and Alexander, C (forthcoming) Researching with Peer/Community Researchers: ambivalences and tensions, in M. Williams, (ed) *Handbook of Qualitative Research*, London: Sage.

Goldsmith QC, Lord (2008) *Citizenship: our common bond*, (www.justice.gov.uk).

Graham H. and McDermott, E (2006) Qualitative research and the evidence base of policy: insights from studies of teenage mothers in the UK, *Journal of Social Policy*, 35(1): 21-37.

HM Government (2005) *Youth Matters*, (www.everychildmatters.gov.uk).

Home Office (2005) *Improving Opportunity, Strengthening Society*, London: Race, Cohesion, Equality and Faith Directorate.

Kidger, J. (2004) Including young mothers: limitations to New Labour's strategy for supporting teenage parents, *Critical Social Policy*, 24(3): 291-311.

Murray, C. (1990) *The Emerging British Underclass*, London: Institute of Economic Affairs.

Office for National Statistics (ONS)(2005) *2005 Social Trends*, Basingstoke: Palgrave.

Peach, C. (2005) Muslims in the UK, in T. Abbas (ed) *Muslim Britain: Communities under Pressure*, London: Zed Press.

Quinton, D. Pollock, S. and Golding, J (2002) *The Transition to Fatherhood in Young Men*, Regard, www.regard.ac.uk, ESRC.

Rolfe, A (2005) 'There's helping and there's hindering': young mothers, support and control, in M. Barry (ed) *Youth Policy and Social Inclusion*, London: Routledge.

SmithBattle, L. (2000) The vulnerabilities of teenage mothering: challenging prevailing assumptions, *Advanced Nursing Science*, 23(1): 29-40.

Social Exclusion Unit (SEU) (1999) *Teenage Pregnancy*. Cm 4342, London, HMSO.

TPU (Teenage Pregnancy Unit) (2000) *Implementation of the Teenage Pregnancy Strategy*, Progress Report, London: Teenage Pregnancy Unit/Department of Health.

Thompson, R. (2000) Dream on: the logic of sexual practice, *Journal of Youth Studies*, 3(4): 407-27.

UNICEF (2003) *Teenage Births in Rich Nations*, Innocenti Report Card No. 3, Paris.

Wilson, H. and Huntington, A. (2006) Deviant (m)others: the construction of teenage motherhood in contemporary discourse, *Journal of Social Policy*, 35(1): 59-76.

Chapter 8

Young mothers from 'minoritised' backgrounds: Shakira, Lorna and Charlene

Jenny Owen, Gina Higginbottom, Mavis Kirkham, Nigel Mathers and Peter Marsh

Interviewer: how would you describe yourself, in terms of your background?

Shakira: crap (laughs).

Interviewer: I mean in terms of your ethnic group, perhaps?

Shakira: ethnic group?

Interviewer: your identity, perhaps?

Shakira: I don't know, it's not been so bad, I have got friends and you know, I like being Asian, I like being ethnic.

Interviewer: is that how you would describe yourself?

Shakira: I don't know how I would describe myself, I'll pass ... I don't know what you mean, I can't really describe myself ... Yeah, I have lived in England all my life, my mum died when I was five of cancer, I have got asthma, I have got a little girl, I am a lone parent, her dad is in prison, and I think that is how I would describe myself.

Interviewer: Right OK. In terms of your religion?

Shakira: I am Muslim.

(Shakira, aged 18, living in West Yorkshire).

Introduction

There has been very little explicit debate about ethnicity in recent research and policy in the UK, in connection with teenage parenthood (as noted by McDermott and Graham, 2005). While some studies have reported higher-than-average rates of teenage pregnancy and parenthood among certain minority ethnic communities in the UK (Robson and Berthoud, 2003), these patterns have usually been acknowledged briefly, rather than becoming the focus of debate or investigation. Whether in UK government policy documents, in media coverage or in academic research studies, the most familiar image of the 'teenage parent' remains the young, working-class woman (Arai, 2003), whose white British ethnic identity attracts no direct comment. In some recent media contexts, the key image has been the young 'chav mum' caricatured in television comedy and tabloid news reports (Tyler, 2008).

In this chapter, we explore a number of themes in the findings from a two-year qualitative study, carried out in two cities and three London boroughs between 2002 and 2004[1]. The study was commissioned specifically to investigate the views and experiences of young parents from minority ethnic backgrounds in England, as part of a wider programme of policy-oriented research funded by the Department of Health and the Teenage Pregnancy Unit. Two parallel studies in the same programme were commissioned to investigate other themes related to sexual health, contraception and ethnicity.[2]

We interviewed many young mothers, as well as a smaller number of young fathers and grandmothers; we also interviewed staff and service managers working with young parents in a range of support services. In earlier articles, we have presented broad summaries both of young minority ethnic parents' own perspectives and those of support service staff. In fact, we found many areas of convergence between the two (Higginbottom et al., 2006; Owen et al., 2008), particularly in their challenges to the negative picture of teenage parenthood that has dominated recent UK policy discourses. The overwhelming message was that a national policy based on the view of 'teenage parenthood' as a problem in itself failed to reflect both staff and young parents' views and experiences, and

1   The project was entitled An Exploration of the Teenage Parenting Experiences of Young People of Bangladeshi, African Caribbean, Pakistani and Dual Ethnic Origin in England, and the Principal Investigator was Dr Gina Higginbottom, then a Senior Lecturer at the School of Nursing and Midwifery at the University of Sheffield.

    We gratefully acknowledge the support of the Teenage Pregnancy Unit and the Department of Health Policy Research Programme in the UK, who funded the study. The authors would also like to thank all the participants who gave their time for interviews between 2002 and 2004, in Sheffield, Bradford and the London boroughs of Lambeth, Lewisham and Southwark. We also thank the other members of the research team: Matthew Griffin, Iqlak Khan, Ayesha Charles and Zolesha Browne. The views expressed here are those of the authors and not necessarily those of the Department of Health or the Teenage Pregnancy Unit.

2   Including the study discussed in this chapter, three out of nine projects in this programme focused topics related to ethnicity. In addition to the study described here, the briefings relating to the two others can be found at: www.everychildmatters.gov.uk/resources-and-practice/RS00037/
    ('Protective and Risk Factors for Early Sexual Activity and Contraception Use among Black and Minority Ethnic Adolescents in East London')
and www.everychildmatters.gov.uk/resources-and-practice/RS00038/
(Exploring the Attitudes and Behaviours of Bangladeshi, Indian and Jamaican Young People to Reproductive and Sexual Health). [Last accessed on 27.3.09]

tended to focus attention and resources on pregnancy prevention much more than on providing effective support services. References to racism, in health and other support services, were rare; in contrast, young parents (and some staff) gave many examples of hostile or ambivalent attitudes expressed in relation to a young parent's age.

Staff also made it clear that appropriate monitoring data was not available to show whether or not patterns of inequality were present in the design and delivery of support services, in relation to ethnicity: this is an area still in need of further research. We did find examples in which teachers, youth workers, health visitors and other professionals acted as 'street-level bureaucrats' (Lipsky, 1980); their actions sometimes mitigated the stigmatising effects of dominant policy discourses about teenage parenthood, offering flexible, affirming forms of support and recognition instead (see also, for example, Cooke and Owen, 2006; Fisher and Owen, 2008). Finally, in terms of underlining the importance of poverty in shaping young parents' experiences, the findings from our study have many parallels with other qualitative studies of teenage pregnancy and parenthood over the last two decades, including those discussed elsewhere in this volume.

However, when writing up these findings, we knew that our initial analyses had not explored in depth the ways in which ethnic identification may inter-relate with gendered and classed patterns in young mothers' lives. In this chapter, therefore, we consider these 'intersections' (Brah and Phoenix, 2003), by revisiting the narratives of three young women in some depth. In order to retain the coherence of each narrative, we present each young woman's account in its own right, rather than grouping findings by theme. Nevertheless, while these are very personal stories, each has also been chosen because it illustrates important aspects of the wider study findings; as part of each account, and in our concluding comments, we make a number of links with these broader interpretations. First, we set the scene with a short discussion of relevant perspectives in recent research.

Ethnicity, identity and 'early' parenthood

The approach we take in this chapter is based on a view of ethnicity as part of social identity, as situational (Mason, 2003) and as shaped through the twin processes of group identification and social categorisation by others: 'ethnicity depends on ascription from both sides of the boundary' (Jenkins, 1997: 22). Individuals may choose to emphasise or to play down specific factors, as circumstances shift; identifying as 'black British' may loom large in one context, for example, while a sense of being of Indian or African-Caribbean descent, or of Muslim faith, may be more prominent in another. These dynamic processes of identification are, by definition, hard to capture through formal monitoring processes. The short interview extract from Shakira, above, underlines some of the complexities in play here. Her initial response to the interviewer's use of the term 'ethnic group' is good-humoured, while also anticipating that the interviewer (who was also of South Asian origin) may expect her to associate a minority ethnic background with problems of one kind or another: *"it's not been so bad ... I like being Asian, I like being ethnic ..."* Having made this statement, her follow-up response transcends any ethnic or other formal category, and instead draws together various strands in her life story: bereavement, poor health, sole responsibility for a daughter and (when asked directly) being of Muslim faith.

In writing about a project whose starting-point was a focus on minority ethnic young parents, we also need to note the shifts that have taken place in political and academic discourses about 'race' and ethnicity. Alexander (2002) argues that the 'triumph of ethnicity', as the preferred term, alongside an increasing emphasis on culture, 'difference' and diversity, have been associated with a tendency to talk less and less about racism and inequality. She also identifies a polarisation in the ways in which 'African Caribbean and 'Asian' identities are constructed, in many areas of UK academic and political discourse:

> Where black/African-Caribbean identities have become defined as fluid, fragmented negotiated and creative, Asian identities have been defined—in opposition—as static, bounded, internally homogeneous and externally impenetrable ... The dilemmas of these two versions of 'difference' are most clearly apparent in relation to youth: where African-Caribbean youth cultures are seen as moving outwards, into mainstream cultures, transforming and transgressing ideas of integral British cultural identity, Asian youth cultures, if acknowledged any existence outside the black hole of 'community' identity, are seen as mysterious, incomprehensible to 'outsiders' and exclusive ... African-Caribbeans once had 'race', they now have 'difference'; Asians *still* have (too much) culture, but with the additional weight of a stifling demand for authenticity.
>
> (Alexander, 2002:557-8).

In fact, recent research and policy documents related to teenage motherhood give us a very limited purchase on debates about the intersection between ethnicity, class and other factors in relation to identity. We suggest that there are three sets of themes, in recent academic and policy-related research, which have a bearing. First, there is the body of applied research and related practitioner guidance which has underpinned UK policy on teenage pregnancy and parenthood since the publication of the 1999 Social Exclusion Unit report (SEU, 1999). This has focused particularly on identifying 'risk factors' in relation to teenage pregnancy, arguing that teenage parenthood is both a cause and an effect of poverty and social exclusion. For example, a 2002 resource pack about working with 'diverse communities' (Department of Health, 2002) encouraged practitioners to pay attention to diverse 'cultural and religious norms and beliefs', within minority ethnic groups as well as between them; there were also clear references to the impact of racism and discrimination, supported by extensive illustrations and examples from discussions with young people. Nevertheless, despite these efforts to avoid simplistic generalisations, the resource pack still illustrates the ways in which identity and culture tend to be problematised only in relation to 'minoritised' groups—the 'other' in relation to a white majority norm. The document's list of sections on working with specific groups—from Travellers to British-born Chinese—rather reinforces this impression, especially as familiar stereotypes are reproduced rather than discussed critically, in several places. For example, the need to address low individual self-esteem is the point of departure in the section about African-Caribbean young people; in contrast, the section on South Asian communities opens with reference to the importance of 'collective structures where family and community have greater significance than the individual' (Department of Health, 2002:30).

In 2006, the Department for Education and Skills issued new guidance to local authorities and health services, on continued implementation of the national Teenage Pregnancy Strategy. In connection with 'risk factors' related to family and social circumstances, this noted above-average rates of teenage parenthood among some minority ethnic communities. This point was picked up briefly in the national press, which in turn prompted a call from the Commission for Racial Equality for sensitivity and for consultation with 'local community groups'. [3] The later *Next Steps* document (Teenage Pregnancy Unit, 2007: 9)

---

3. The Times July 21, 2006. 'Black girls to be the targets of plan to cut teen pregnancy'. Daily Telegraph, 25 July 2006. 'CRE raises concerns about teenage pregnancy targets'

included an early statement about rates of teenage motherhood and ethnicity, in the context of guidance about support services for young parents:

> The vast majority of mothers aged under 19 are white British although in local authorities with large black and minority ethnic populations the picture is different, with less than 60% of mothers in London classified as 'white British' and less than a third in six London Boroughs. However, the *likelihood* of teenage motherhood is higher among young women of 'Mixed white and Caribbean', 'Other black', 'black Caribbean' and 'white British' ethnicity. All Asian groups have a lower than average incidence of teenage motherhood.

Following this, however, there was no further discussion of ethnicity; the significance of the early references to prevalence rates remained unclear, both at a general level and in relation to recommendations concerning support services for young parents.

Turning to academic research, Berthoud (2001a) has produced quantitative analyses of trends in teenage parenthood in relation to ethnicity, using data from the Labour Force Survey. He found that white and Caribbean teenage birth rates remained stable from the mid-1970s to the late 1990s: on average, thirty young white women in every thousand became a mother between the ages of fifteen and nineteen, while forty-one young Caribbean women did so. In contrast, the rates among young Indian, Pakistani and Bangladeshi women all fell markedly: to seven per thousand among Indian women, thirty among Pakistani women and fifty-three among Bangladeshi women. The diversity in these figures point to the crucial importance of unpicking the category 'Asian' in policy discourses. However, it is worth noting too that the overwhelming majority of teenage births, among all South Asian mothers, took place within marriage.

In later research, Berthoud and colleagues (2004) compared outcomes for adult women who had had children as teenagers and those who had not, matched in socioeconomic terms. They found that the long-term consequences of a teenage birth were less marked than previously reported, both in research and in government policy documents. As Phoenix (1991) had found thirteen years earlier, poverty and deprivation emerged as more significant than the timing of parenthood. In their analyses concerning ethnicity, they found that the social and economic penalties for early motherhood were strongest among young white women. Among young minority ethnic women, the 'age effect' (e.g. in terms of the prospects of living in a working family) varied according to background, but was less marked in all cases, and was non-existent for Pakistani and Bangladeshi women. They concluded:

> when early fertility is the norm in a minority community, it does not lead to any further disadvantage beyond that experienced by the ethnic group as a whole.
>
> (Robson and Berthoud, 2003: 1).

In terms of the wider context for these observations, Jayaweera et al. (2007:8) note that the average age of first motherhood, among all ethnic groups, is rising; however, it is still lower for Pakistani and Bangladeshi women (the early twenties) than for others (the mid to late twenties). Average family size is also slightly larger for Pakistani and Bangladeshi mothers than for other ethnic groups, and rates of employment for women are lower.

A second but much smaller body of research, has considered the 'racialisation' of teenage parenting identities. As these studies come from contexts that are radically different from the UK, their relevance is mainly in raising questions for exploration, rather than suggesting conclusions. In North America, both Geronimus (2003) and Horowitz (1995) have argued that young African American parents are stigmatised in specific ways, for example through disproportionate representation in both policy and research initiatives that focus on them as undeserving welfare dependents.

Challenging this view, Geronimus found that 'fertility timing norms' varied to reflect local family forms and economic constraints: in African American neighbourhoods where incomes were low, life-expectancy below average but social networks strong, 'early' childbearing had advantages (2003:885). Some US data also showed African American teenage mothers having lower rates of low birth weight babies and infant mortality than older mothers, and incurring lower rather than higher costs to public services (Hotz et al., 1996). Geronimus' original analysis has been supported by more recent research showing a decrease in teenage births among African American women, in parallel with increased economic well-being (Colen et al., 2006).

Geronimus' central argument is that the stigmatisation of young parents contributes to wider processes of surveillance and social control, and that the element of racialisation in public discourses performs a specific disciplinary role in promoting conformity among white middle-class youth. In the very different context of South Africa, Macleod and Durrheim (2002) also found evidence of racialisation in their analysis of policy and research publications. Drawing on Phoenix's earlier work (1993), they found that racialised notions of 'culture' and 'tradition' were deployed in policy and research documents related to young black African mothers, while psychological interpretations were deployed to explain young white motherhood:

> culture, tradition and socio-economic status are basically absent in the documents with 'white' only participants. Instead, these studies focus on the psychological experience of pregnancy and motherhood ...
>
> (MacLeod and Durrheim, 2002: 784)

This brings us to the third area of relevant research, which concerns UK studies focusing on transitions to motherhood, and on parental identities. Ann Phoenix's work remains the most directly relevant. Her study of young mothers (1991) discussed ethnicity, noting both some important differences between the UK and the USA, and the difficulties involved in distinguishing between factors related to 'race' and those related to class. Phoenix concluded that comparisons between ethnic groups were not appropriate within her sample; her main finding was that poverty, rather than age, was the dominant factor in the experiences of young mothers and their children. As indicated above, a later article explored issues of racialisation in connection with teenage motherhood, with particular reference to the ways in which notions of 'culture' are selectively deployed (Phoenix, 1993). Tracey Reynolds' in-depth study of Caribbean mothers' perspectives has challenged pathologising representations of Caribbean motherhood in the UK, including pejorative images of the young 'babymother' and of lone motherhood more generally. Critiques have also been developed of the ways in which South Asian family forms and practices have been stereotyped, for example through assumptions that young women are the passive victims or beneficiaries of extended family networks, rather than exercising agency in relation to marriage and fertility (Majumdar, 2007).

In terms of research related to parental identities, the ongoing study of 'the making of modern motherhood' (Thomson et al., 2008:18) makes some reference to ethnic identity, but in very limited terms. The authors acknowledge that 'ethnicity, sexuality and disability were important factors in shaping the situation of mothering, as was relationship status, locality and the proximity of family networks ...' They conclude, however, that 'age is the master category through which normative notions of mothering are constituted, with a powerful discourse of efficient biographical planning incorporating social class, and mediating differences of sexuality, ethnicity and disability'. We return to this point in our concluding discussion below.

We now turn to our own study, and to an in-depth discussion of the transition to parenthood as described by three young women: Shakira, Lorna and Charlene.

About the study

As indicated above, the study was commissioned to explore the perspectives of young minority ethnic parents—an area seen as under-researched, in the context of the UK Teenage Pregnancy Unit policy research programme. We identified three locations with contrasting demographic profiles: two London boroughs with large populations of African Caribbean origin, and of dual or multiple heritage; Bradford, with a large and internally diverse South Asian population; and Sheffield, in which a range of minority ethnic communities represent roughly the national average in relation to the UK population. We interviewed seventy-nine young mothers of African Caribbean, dual or multiple ethnic origin and Muslim faith; the latter were of Bangladeshi, Pakistani, Somali and Yemeni origin. Most were born in England. Participants were invited to self-assign ethnicity, and to describe their religious affiliation (if any). Almost half the main study sample was made up of young people of dual or multiple ethnic origin. As indicated in Table 1, the young parents included one cohort aged nineteen or under, and a second cohort aged twenty or over, who had become pregnant at nineteen or under. We conducted focus groups initially, in order to identify themes for further exploration in long, semi-structured individual interviews.

Table 1

Staff	Grand-mothers	Young mothers aged up to 19		Young mothers aged 20-23		Young fathers
41	10	45 individual interviews (16 African Caribbean, 19 multiple or dual ethnic origin; 10 of Muslim faith—of Pakistani origin (3), Bangladeshi (4), Yemeni (1) and Somali (2) origin).	3 audio diaries	19 (Focus group participants)	15 individual interviews	6 individual interviews

Our initial analysis drew on the 'Framework' approach (Ritchie and Spencer, 1994). Researchers identified emerging themes from transcripts; these were refined in discussion, and transcripts were coded independently and compared by three team members. Team members then produced draft interpretations for discussion; these focused particularly on young parents' experiences of the transition to parenthood and any support services accessed. Later we revisited the individual interview data, and focused in more depth on personal histories and accounts of social and family relationships. This chapter draws on that second phase of analysis. The accounts below have been chosen to illustrate the range of experiences in our sample of young mothers, exploring in particular their accounts of their family relationships and locality contexts, including any references to ethnic identification and to racism. Each woman's detailed reflections are introduced with a short overview. Pseudonyms are used in all cases, and some details that might have made individuals identifiable have been omitted.

Three young women, three stories

Shakira: 'I met her Dad, and had a baby, and got married ...'

When interviewed in 2003, Shakira was eighteen; she was living with her eighteen month old daughter Maya, in a flat rented through a short-term rehousing scheme. She and her husband Mahroof, aged twenty two, had been married for two and a half years (since she left home at sixteen). Shakira was living alone with Maya, because Mahroof had recently started serving a prison sentence for public order offences associated with the Bradford riots[4]

Shakira's parents were both born in Pakistan; as young adults, they married and settled in Bradford, where Shakira, her younger sister and four younger brothers all grew up. As indicated in the earlier extract, Shakira's mother died when she was five. After some years as a mill worker, her father had developed a small business; ten years after his first wife's death, he remarried. Relationships in the family then became strained, with episodes of violence. For Shakira, this was the context for leaving the family home:

---

4. The 'Bradford riots' took place in July 2001, in a context in which far-right, racist groups had begun to establish a public presence in neighbourhoods with ethnically mixed populations, in various towns in Northern England. For a discussion of these events, their context and the later government report, see for example Alexander (2004)

I had problems at home ... Because my dad remarried, I got two stepsisters ... I was the oldest girl, so in like in Muslim tradition you have to do the housework and look after the others ... I was fairly bright, I had good target grades; it was the commitment, it was doing the work, and at that time because I was having problems ... I got to the point where I couldn't be bothered and I decided to leave home ... He [father] didn't know, I just left one day and I never went back home ... My family were really right rough and tumble ... Very violent.

Shakira continues, explaining how she thinks her life might have been different if her mother had not died young:

I wouldn't have had Maya [daughter] ... it's weird, it's just life isn't it, you know, I met her dad, and had a baby, and got married ... I would have married someone anyway, wouldn't I; obviously I married her dad, and I am sort of settled with him now forever, but yeah, I would have stayed at home and studied and I would probably have got an arranged marriage.

These reflections lead to more explicit comments about the ways in which the loss of a mother, gendered divisions of labour and competing interpretations of Pakistani and Muslim norms and values became intertwined, as Shakira grew up:

I didn't have a mum ... it was all males really, so I didn't have anyone to talk to ... no one cared if I did my homework, they just cared if they had clean clothes ... it was just up to me: if I thought right, I need to get this portfolio done I would sit and do it at night ... I wanted to do German as a GCSE, but my dad was saying no, do health and social care ... so I ended up doing health and social care.

Shakira sees notions of 'Muslim tradition' as important, but also as variable across generations and open to debate; in this, she is completely representative of the other young Muslim mothers in the study sample. The sense of 'being Pakistani' becomes the focus of some tension; values and traditions related to gender roles and to family practices are seen as being shaped and reinforced in response to perceived trends and problems in the majority white population.

While she uses the shorthand of 'westernisation' when comparing herself with older Pakistanis, this is framed in terms that recognise personal transitions as complex, both to describe and to enact:

> I have lived here all my life so ... I go out to work, but we never got encouragement because that isn't the way really, old traditions ... people get it wrong, Muslim religion says that women have got to cover their bodies ... but they don't say stuff like women can't work. ... my mum got married at sixteen and ... never worked, my dad always went out to work in the mills ... [he] got his own business, and he probably would let me work for him but ... people think it's wrong if your daughter goes out to work.
>
> I think a lot of white people's families are breaking up and ... our parents want us to be different ... it's all about respect, so we are supposed to stay at home, and ... to then get married at a fairly young age ... All right, I still wear Asian clothes and stuff like that, but I am still a bit westernised because I went to school you know, so because I want to go out to work, I have got different views ... they want us to be like what they think Pakistanis should do. We want to be Pakistani, yeah, eat halal or whatever, but we have still got this westernised bit haven't we?

Shakira left school halfway through her final GCSE year, having gained a GNVQ in Health and Social Care and a BTEC award. Some of her teachers had offered flexible, outreach support in the final year, but this had not been enough to enable her to take her final exams. By 2003 she was claiming benefits, and working two mornings a week in a local café. Her thoughts on her own future, and her daughter's future, reflect a complex set of negotiations. First, there is the sense of having to 'prove oneself', both as a good parent and a competent adult, that recurs in many young mothers' accounts of their experiences (McDermott and Graham, op. cit.):

> I have done a mentoring course through Bradford University ... IT courses ... I don't want to go into full- time ... obviously it's my little girl, isn't it, so I have got to look after her until she's a bit older ... Hopefully one day I will go back ... full-time and go to college ... I always feel underestimated, because I have got nothing on paper ... because I

have to fend for myself ... I am going to show people that I can get qualifications.

Second, Shakira describes a contrast between her own experience and the experience of other women in her extended family networks. She is well aware that a Muslim extended family network can be supportive, and can be an arena in which women exercise agency (Majumdar, 2007):

[My husband's] younger sister, she is still not married and she is twenty-two, but she has got loads of confidence, she has always had that support to get her grades, to get new jobs you know ... she is really happy, even though she will have to go to Pakistan and get married ... she is happy with what she has achieved ... But my dad was more stubborn ... so I wasn't allowed to go out and I wasn't allowed to ring friends and she can, she has got a mobile.

Third, despite the difficulties in her own circumstances, Shakira's relationships both with her in-laws and her husband show an active, continuing process of negotiation and compromise. She has distanced herself from the conventional daughter-in-law role, forfeiting some degrees of support in the process:

When he went to prison I was going to move in with his mum and dad ... [but] I knew that I would have to cook and clean all the time, and ... get up when they get up ... go to bed when they go to bed ... His mum won't do it [babysitting] ... she won't even do the two mornings now that I work ... The only day she would look after her is on a Saturday ... It makes me feel awful in a way, because I don't see my family, and that is like the only family she [daughter] has got.

In this respect, Shakira's comments are completely consistent with those of the other young Muslim mothers in the study sample. Her circumstances are particular, but in seeking a compromise between her own aspirations and family expectations, she reflects a broader picture in which most of the young Muslim mothers described their own aspirations as differing from those of their parents (Jayaweera et al., 2007; Basit, 2002). As part of this, Shakira still wants to look after her younger sister, in the absence of their mother. But continuing conflict with their father means that they can only see each other in secret:

I always looked after her … I try to give her that support now, I say you better stay on at school … But … I feel that she is not getting that support now, because I am not at home.

Finally, she continues to maintain a close relationship with her husband. He is her ally, the focus of good memories and of plans for the future, when the couple hope to renovate and move into a terraced house of their own. Before going into prison, he had become very involved in Maya's care, after Shakira suffered a serious asthma attack:

Everything we did [during pregnancy], he looked after me, he did with me … I had a baby very young and I didn't have a mum … I was breastfeeding for two months and there was only her dad there and what is he supposed to do … it was a shock … I had a big asthma attack. After I had that, her dad like used to support me, he used to bath her, he used to make the bottles … and take over looking after her … when she was on the bottle he started to get up in the night … and I still maintain that link with her dad even though he is prison, we write to each other, we go and see him … so he gives me a lot of support … he says 'when I come out I will have a better job and I will take Maya to Morrisons every week and you can stay at home' … he already sees ways to make his life better.

However, Shakira's husband and his family are also the likely obstacles to her future plans. She would like to go to university and qualify as a counsellor or social worker, working with young women. Her husband's family includes two uncles who are policemen and an aunt who is a university lecturer: there are good precedents for entering higher education and a professional career But she anticipates opposition, and sees her own control over her fertility as an additional factor in potential negotiations over future options:

I would like to go to college … he [husband] doesn't want me to because he says … his family won't see it as right. So I am not allowed to go to college until he gets out … I am married to him, so how can I do wrong by him … but then like when he comes out … if I say I want to go to college and if he says no, then I will say I want another baby … So in a way obviously I can always make that decision, and it's me who's going to have the baby.

The balancing of options, here, in terms of fertility and educational or career aspirations was a common theme in the study findings, in relation to mothers from all backgrounds. Here, Shakira continues to look ahead as a young, Muslim woman who expects to combine marriage and motherhood with education, a degree of autonomy and a chance to make good the emotional losses she had experienced as a teenager:

> Because of her dad as well, I don't think I would let her wear English clothes because we are Muslims ... we can't say we are not Muslims now ... I would bring her up to read the Koran ... I would make sure that we don't eat non-halal ... But I would still influence her to ... know more than what I did ... I think it's important that they [children] like get educated and they are shown love as well as education, especially when they get to twelve, thirteen ... if it was up to me, I wouldn't let my daughter have an arranged marriage.

Overall, Shakira's interview focuses almost entirely on her relationships with her husband and family, as the dominant features in her experience of pregnancy and parenthood. In this respect, too, her account is very similar to those of the other Muslim mothers in the sample. The recurring thread is her own assertion of personal autonomy, as a young woman, alongside a continued sense of living in a wider Muslim and British Asian community, albeit with a sense of challenging the ways in which gender roles are constructed in some sections of that community. She acknowledges negative public perceptions of young mothers, based on age, but only mentions these in passing.

The contacts Shakira describes with public agencies such as schools and hospitals have all been positive. Her one reference to racism is in connection with housing: with her temporary tenancy due to end, she needs a longer-term solution until Mahroof's release from prison, and expects that she will face hostility if she is housed on a local estate:

> It's really hard ... all the council properties are on an estate, so obviously you would get racism, because they mostly are white ... why put me on a council estate where I am going to get abuse?

The presence of racism is taken for granted, here: Shakira wants support in avoiding its damaging effects, but considers it inevitable among her potential neighbours. In contrast, there is no mention of racism in connection with education, health services or employment opportunities. This is broadly in line with the views from other young Muslim mothers, with one exception: one young woman had felt that her hospital midwife had treated her much less attentively than she treated white patients, on the basis of ethnicity rather than age.

Shakira's interview concludes with some reflections on the turning-point represented by parenthood:

> After I had Maya, it made me more like I want to grab life more ... I have got more determination, because I have got no one to rely on ... when I see my little girl smile, I always want her to have a better life ... I don't want my daughter to grow up ... thinking 'my mum has lived off income support all these years', because I know that I can do it. All it takes is getting some qualifications.

Lorna: 'Me and him have just grown, it's our way of life now. We don't fret, we just have to do it ... if you have got family that support you, it's easy'

Lorna was born and brought up in Sheffield, and described herself as black British, with grandparents of Scottish and Jamaican origin. She became pregnant when she was sixteen, three months after she started going out with her boyfriend Al, then aged fifteen. She left school halfway through her final year, without taking her GCSE exams. When interviewed in 2003, Lorna was living in a council house with Al and their son Samuel. She and Al got the tenancy while she was still pregnant; her grandfather and other family members helped the couple to clean, repair and decorate the house. It lacked central heating and Lorna later blamed its damp condition for her son's chronic asthma and eczema. Following her complaints, the council installed heating and made other improvements.

Lorna and Al have stayed together: she described herself as "lucky" in this respect, observing that "the majority of young Dads don't stop around". In contrast with Shakira, Lorna describes a context of unambiguous support and affirmation from her own and her boyfriend's social and family networks. There are sisters and cousins with babies; there are grandmothers who acknowledge the difficulties of managing on little money, but who have done so successfully themselves as young parents. Lorna was hoping to add to her family soon, and then to return to employment. She envisaged a period of part-time work in her boyfriend's father's business, but hoped eventually to return to part-time study while working, and then to qualify and work full-time as a nurse.

For Lorna, pregnancy was not planned but nor was it a surprise:

> Me and my friend were talking about having a baby, because we used to work together … we were saying we wanted kids, we didn't want to go to college … I wanted to be a young mum because my mum and her mum … they were young mums. Then coincidentally, we both got pregnant.

However, this was a shock to her boyfriend. Lorna, conscious of a family context in which support was readily available, and termination disapproved of on religious grounds, emphasised the centrality of women in taking on family responsibilities:

> He was fifteen and I was sixteen … it was like hard for him at first, he didn't want it … I said "I don't really need you as a dad … I have got support here, my mum will support me … later on when you are about twenty or twenty-one, if you want to come back and say 'yeah I'm your dad', you can do that." … My family are Catholic, and abortions, they don't do that. I'm not a practising Catholic, I don't really go to church; but for everyone else to know that … I didn't want to do it. My mum has got five brothers, three sisters … some of them would have … said 'well, if you don't want him, I will have him'.

In the event, Lorna explains Al's decision to 'stop around' in terms of their joint sense of a strong relationship based on interdependence and easily-shared family networks:

> He would stop at my house or I would stop at his … he dumped all his friends for me … they never see him, because he is always with me'

Lorna's expectations about family support were realistic:

> Oh I had loads of support [laughs] my family wouldn't leave me alone … my cousin, she was always around, because she just had a girl … Mum was very supportive when I was pregnant, moneywise, getting me up on my feet … and his [i.e. the baby's] dad … at least he stuck around;

normal dads don't ... My grandad put me a new wooden window sill, he stuck the doors on ... My half-sister from my dad's side, she had a baby my age. I was thinking of all the down points, how am I going to afford it ... but she was saying 'it's not all like the way they put it out to you as if it's hard, because it isn't really, as long as you have got a head on your shoulders.

Lorna had initially dropped a hint to her mother, by leaving books about pregnancy in a drawer where they would be noticed: she knew the reaction would be surprise but also excitement. In contrast, she described her father as a much more marginal and mistrusted figure:

I only knew him from when I was like thirteen ... when I was younger my mum and dad weren't together ... whatever he has got to say, it's not going to bother me ... But I still went and told him ... he was just like 'oh, it's hard', but I didn't really take any notice.

However, cautionary messages are not rejected when they come from a trusted female figure, Al's mother. Her initial reservations are seen as a legitimate point of view, and the context is a transition to acceptance and affirmation:

She was like, not being negative ... she was saying how hard it is ... but me and him have just grown, it's our way of life now ... we don't fret, we just have to do it. So she was just showing the other point of view ... because they were young when they had him [boyfriend] ... And now they say that I remind her of her and he reminds him of his dad.

It is in the public domain of benefits claims, education and—as with Shakira —housing options that sources of stress and pressure are evident. Being under eighteen makes it difficult to negotiate the separate but interdependent processes of claiming housing and welfare benefits, for example, and family support is essential in coping with this (Mitchell et al., 2006):

You have to get Jobseekers Allowance but when I applied for that, they said I'm not allowed to get it ... The housing said I've got to apply for some benefits and no one wants to give me none ... it's not straightforward, if you are pregnant ... sometimes when my money was supposed to come through, it didn't … and then I would have to phone … I would be without money for a week … My family are all right, they lent it me.

Lorna's descriptions of her encounters with housing and benefits services include a sense of outrage about the way in which she feels she is being positioned as an undeserving 'welfare subject', rather than as someone with legitimate needs:

> I'm in some trampy office where crackheads are, I felt ill … It's like they treated me the same as everyone else, like some druggie … I'm pregnant, but they didn't treat me with any sympathy.

Later, her experience when Samuel is hospitalised leaves her feeling that she is being dismissed as 'too young' to be a competent, caring mother:

> [Samuel] had really bad eczema … I was in the hospital, and they were treating me like a little kid … my mum stopped there the first two nights, and they were fine with her … but I stopped there … after that, and they were horrible to me … the park is only across the road … and I said 'can I take him across there?' and they were like 'no …', so my son was stuck in this cubicle … nothing for him to look at … they must have thought because I was a kid, I don't know … That was my worst experience. I am a mum, do you know what I mean? I want to be treated like a mother, not some little kid.

Like Shakira—and like a number of other study participants—Lorna identifies social housing as an area in which racism is an issue. She feels that she and her partner are being categorised by the neighbours in their predominantly white area, as 'black' and suspect:

> My next door neighbour, I have never seen her curtains on the washing line or her bed sheets … my windows get cleaned every week; I never see a window cleaner round her house and her windows are loppy … They were giving me funny looks, when my settee come … all noseying out of the window … Al's dad has got a shop, he is making money … One of the neighbours across the street said someone's cracked on that he's

dealing ... Just because he's black, he's drug dealing because he's in and out of the house.

Lorna comments about local mother and baby groups also emphasise the importance of feeling accepted, and feeling part of a network of peers. She compares the local, mainly white groups with a local African-Caribbean centre:

I was approached by a load of mother and baby things. At first I didn't want to bother with them, but I thought why not ... [But] the people weren't on my kind of level, do you know what I mean? It's like 'The Centre', for instance, that's all just black people ... and that was a place that I could settle in, where people were on my kind of level.

When talking about the housing and benefits offices, and about hospital care, Lorna did not identify racism as a factor; the tensions were about being 'too young'. However, as Lorna's account continues, issues of age and ethnicity converge; there is a clear thread of memory and observation about being categorised and sometimes treated differently as a black girl. Her memories of moving from one secondary school to another are dominated by being seen as black, loud and in trouble:

I left the Catholic school because my head of year was really against blacks ... I am not that person, I might be loud but it doesn't mean that whatever goes off I know everything about it ...

When she eventually became pregnant in her last year, she felt that the school's main priority was to get her out of circulation; this was framed in health and safety terms, which she rejected as dishonest:

Because you are pregnant, it's like you get put with the bad kids ... go over there and do your work elsewhere, where you are not going to be in danger of having other people knocking into you ... I remember what they tried to do was 'if you do this, this and this and go there we will let you work in a dance school ... and get experience in like teaching and helping out' ... but I said there is no dance school that's open through the daytime. That's the way I caught them out, it seems a bit funny to me that they tried all this to get me out ... they are obviously going to categorise me and stereotype me ... and that is what they did.

Refusing to be located 'with the dunces', Lorna left without completing her GCSEs. Looking back, she emphasises the same determination, and sense of a positive turning-point that Shakira describes:

Before ... I would spend money on clubbing, I would smoke weed ... you didn't do anything positive with yourself, you just do what other teenagers do, what they categorise us [as] ... And now I am matured, do you know what I mean? You start talking to people more on a level ... like adults, in a positive way ... I look after myself, but [my son] is still the main priority.

Lorna's own sense of agency revolves around having a family and then moving into her preferred career. Like Shakira, although in a very different context, she is also negotiating her way forward with her partner and his family. She is prepared to defer some of her own aspirations, if this makes it possible to combine motherhood with a flexible and supportive family context:

I wanted a job, I wanted to go to college but I wanted kids ... I want a big family ... I went for a job interview a couple of months ago, to do with ... nursing homes, but at the same time do a NVQ ... to be a nurse. And that's what I wanted to do, but he [her partner] didn't want me to work. He said there is no point having a kid and then getting a job and then the year after you are going to have another kid, you may as well get your kids out of the way ... he wants me to work in the shop, it's a family business and I said fair enough ... when I'm about 30 or 40 ... I think that will be the best time to have a career ... I can do a nursing course.

Charlene: 'I've made arrangements with my Mum ...'

Charlene grew up in South London, living with her mother and younger brother. She described herself as African Caribbean. She was just seventeen when she became pregnant in 2002. This was a shock, and in contrast with Shakira and Lorna, Charlene had no expectations of staying with this boyfriend; she described the relationship as a short-lived response to having experienced a physical attack that left her feeling vulnerable. Neither her friends nor her family thought that the couple should stay together. When interviewed in 2003, Charlene had recently moved out of her mother's house and into a council flat with her daughter Sophie, aged just over a year-old. Charlene was beginning to explore options for employment and work-based training, but she found this frustrating: she had had to give up the opportunity of training as a web page designer, for instance, because she was not eligible for any funding for the course. She was also in a new and more supportive relationship. However, despite these new beginnings, things were not going as she had hoped. As in Lorna's story, strong and dependable older women are central figures for Charlene. Unlike Lorna or Shakira, however, Charlene was not finding it easy to adapt to motherhood.

Charlene found out about her pregnancy a week before she was due to start a dance course at college:

> [My] ex-boyfriend, he was using condoms. So I was like 'How did this
> …?' I … went to clinic and the woman … just assumed I was going to get
> rid of her. I was in a state of shock and the woman was like 'yeah, you're
> pregnant', handing me the abortion papers … I just signed … I didn't see
> him [boyfriend] for about two months, didn't tell my mum. My mum
> knew, she was like 'you're pregnant' and I was like 'no!' … Then … the
> day I was supposed to have the abortion, my mum just started kicking
> up a fuss … she goes to me, "are you pregnant?" I goes "yeah". And my
> brother goes "see, I told you!" … My mum was like, "what do you want to
> do?" And I was like, "I want to keep it", proper crying like a baby … My
> mum was heavy, but she helped me. She didn't change my mind; it was
> the first time I had a choice basically … The next day, she hadn't met my
> boyfriend yet … I was like 'mum, he hasn't got a job, he can't read, what
> do I have to tell him for?' … Mum said, "well … he has a right to know; if
> you don't phone, I'll phone". I phoned him and he was like … "what you
> telling me for?" … my mum didn't like him from then … The only thing
> that's good from him is the child that he brought in, she's pretty.

Like Lorna—although without the Catholic context—Charlene felt that she could not go through with having an abortion. She was aware of people commenting on her age, but also aware of the protection available from her own mother:

> Everybody was like 'hmm look at that baby having a baby!' kind of thing ... mum was like 'she's eighteen, what are you looking at? Turn your head'. So basically people were like quite negative. Well not everybody ... Some people were really nice.

Charlene describes enjoying the early days of being home with her baby. But practical demands soon make themselves felt:

> When she came home it was like, I was celebrating ... you can work around her, because she's sleeping most of the time ... But as she got older, she started to move and pull things down and want more ... it got hard. Especially if you're doing it on your own ... you budget your money for that week ... By the time you've done, you're broke.

As Charlene continues, it's clear that emotional issues are as important as practical ones. Coping alone is hard, but accepting help—for example, from her new partner —feels overwhelming:

> I really like to do things on my own; even when I was unpacking today, and my boyfriend's like helping me ... I was like, 'sit down downstairs and leave me alone, I'm tired, I want to do this by myself, go away'. He was like, 'you don't have to shout' ... If boys start doing too much it's like they're taking over ... I suppose I'd be happy that when I go out, obviously he'd be glad to take her ... I suppose it wouldn't be so hard to get her stuff, but then on the other hand I don't know how I'd be ... Because I have got a nasty attitude ... he usually runs out, he usually just looks at me like he wants to cry and I feel bad.

Later in the interview, it becomes clear that things have reached breaking-point, and Sophie is going to live with Charlene's mother from now on:

> I've made arrangements with my mum ... Sophie's going to live at my mum's for like two years ... so I can sort myself out. 'Cos I left school early, so I haven't got no qualifications ... I need to decide what I want to

do … I'm pointing towards either a paramedic or retail manager. Retail manager means that I have to go to college; I don't want to go back to college. I'm not into the school environment, I wasn't good at school … I'm not the person I expected I would be, basically. Right, I accept that I'm a mum, I've adapted to that. But … part of the reason why my mum is going to take the baby is because when I'm with my baby I try and do ten things at once … I've got to shout at her to stop pulling down the TV and I've got to clean the floor, and I've got to fold up the clothes and I've got to cook her dinner all at the same time. I can't breathe. In my mind I feel like I'm in this little box and I just go mad, I can't take it. It's what I expected it to be: I know kids are stressful … [but] I can't adapt to it as well as I thought I would.

Charlene wants employment, and she wants to escape from the low-paid, casual options that are available to someone without formal qualifications. She has had some involvement with the local Sure Start programme, but dismisses this as offering opportunities to 'make friends' with other young mothers, when what she wants is financial independence:

I've got enough friends, I want a job and I want to work and I want some childcare … at the end of the day we don't want to be sitting in college, we want to be earning some money to pay the rent and put some money in the gas and food in the fridge … get qualified, and work at the same time … proper wages, for doing a job.

For now, Charlene's mother has laid down strict boundaries: she will remain 'Nana' for Sophie, and will not replace Charlene as 'mum'; however, she will be the main carer and there will be a strict routine. Charlene's boyfriend's mother has also offered some practical help:

[I'm] not going to see her every day … my mum says I'm not allowed. She says it will mess up her routine, 'cos I let her do whatever … at first … I was like 'I can't do that' … And then I thought about it, and my boyfriend was like 'no, you can't do that!', and I was like 'yeah but I can sort myself out then' … He was like 'well, my mum did that to me' … he just carried on like his mum just left him on his gran's doorstep … I goes, 'she left you with your gran to help you,' cos at the end of the day you're sitting there with your sporty Nike top, Nike shirt ... You got the latest phone, the biggest room in the house ... His mum's really nice ... she had him at my age, she was seventeen ... yesterday she said "I'm going to buy you a washing machine" ... I want one, but ... you feel funny because it's your boyfriend's mum ... She says, "like you, I didn't have no qualifications ... at the end of the day, the quicker you can get where you need to be, the quicker you can take her [the baby] back".

Like Lorna, Charlene finds advice easier to accept from a woman, and one who has been a young mother herself, than from a father or a boyfriend. In this respect, her experiences are similar to those of most of the young women in our study, and to those reported in other studies (Mitchell et al., 2006). The interview ends with a very positive assertion of the value of motherhood, and of relationships of solidarity between Charlene, her own mother and her boyfriend's mother. This is not a racialised picture of problematic, lone motherhood, but one in which relationships of mutual support between younger and older women can be depended on, and underpin the patterns of aspiration and of high levels of economic activity that now characterise African Caribbean motherhood in the UK (Reynolds, 2006; Dale et al., 2005). Unlike Lorna, Charlene does not reflect on her ethnic identity explicitly, and in this she is similar to many other London-based participants in our study, who defined themselves as black British or African Caribbean. Most commented on feeling visible (and criticised) primarily as *young* mothers. This may reflect the fact that most were living in neighbourhoods with extensive and well-established black social networks, where—as Robson et al. (2003) suggest—teenage parenthood was not unusual and attracted no additional material disadvantage, relative to peers and neighbours. However, an alternative interpretation is simply that their strength of feeling about age-based stigmatisation outweighed other concerns, during the interview process.

Lastly, Charlene also stands for the small minority of mothers in our study, across ethnic groups, who talked openly about having substantial difficulties with the emotional transition to motherhood, and who articulate something very complex in relation to the resilience described by McDermott and Graham (2005) and others. In challenging negative constructions of teenage motherhood, it can become difficult to acknowledge difficult experiences; in that sense, her account needs clear recognition, within the overall picture. In Charlene's final comments, there is a degree of resignation:

I suppose I'll get a bit upset, but you get what I'm saying ... I only have to get up there and say I want to see my baby. So I suppose I'll just get on with it.

Concluding discussion

The three narratives presented above illustrate the broader findings in our study in their main features, and they also show strong parallels with the experiences of young white mothers. For example, Shakira, Lorna and Charlene all position themselves as the coping figures described by McDermott and Graham (2005): good, responsible and respectable mothers, differentiated from the 'undeserving' drug-users Lorna refers to in the housing office, or the nosey neighbours with 'loppy windows'. Even Charlene, who has temporarily handed over the care of her daughter to her own mother, has done this in the name of providing a better home in the long-term, following her boyfriend's mother's example. All three have experienced pregnancy and parenthood as a 'critical moment' (Thomson et al., 2002), when risks and future pathways can be reappraised: while Shakira and Lorna see themselves as positively 'grabbing life more', in response, for Charlene there are difficulties and painful new levels of self-awareness.

As Phoenix commented in 1991, many of the experiences of these young mothers are also 'strikingly unremarkable': like older mothers, they are proud of their children; they aim to put them first; and they encounter familiar dilemmas in reconciling 'care' commitments with making a living and reaching accommodations with partners and other family members. As Mitchell and Green noted in their study (2006) of young mothers in North-East England, late modern times have not eroded kinship ties as comprehensively as some would claim, particularly between young mothers and their own mothers. For Lorna and Charlene, 'Mum' is pivotal in providing practical and emotional support, within family and locality networks; in this respect, their experience illustrates patterns documented both in our wider findings, and in other studies with young white mothers and with the increasing numbers of grandmothers who are being drawn into childcare responsibilities in later life. Shakira—who has no mother to call on—underlines the importance of these points, in the ways in which the absence of a mother echoes through her account of 'fending for myself'; neither husband nor in-laws can fill this gap. These are clearly gendered kinship patterns: fathers and grandfathers can be powerful patriarchal figures, either exercising emotional and material control, sometimes through physical violence and coercion (Shakira), or offering access to employment and other resources (Lorna). On the other hand, for many of the young women in our study, partners (within marriage or not), were more ambiguous and sometimes marginal figures. Many young women commented on their own sense of exercising choice and control over their presence, at an everyday level, and over their own fertility. Nevertheless, partners can still influence young mothers' decisions, for example in terms of deferring career aspirations, as Shakira and Lorna both illustrate.

Our analysis of these three accounts, and of the wider study of which they form a part, suggests that 'intersections' between class, gender and ethnicity take different shapes in the private domains of personal and family relationships, compared to the public (or at least, semi-public) domains of school, college, the street or the labour ward. In terms of social class, almost all of the study participants came from contexts we can broadly define as working-class, for example in terms of housing options (social housing or private rented accommodation) and of the unskilled or semi-skilled manual occupations pursued by themselves and by family members. All lived in neighbourhoods with above-average levels of deprivation. A limitation of the study is that we recruited young parents partly through contacts with health and welfare agencies, and so may have under-represented young parents with lower levels of need for, and contact with, these agencies. Overall, experiences of relative poverty, poor job opportunities and poor educational experiences form the backdrop, for all three young women and for their peers in the study as a whole: almost all commented on wanting to 'do better' for their own children, as an explicit response to this (cf. McDermott and Graham, 2005).

With reference to the private domain, the young mothers in the study talk about gendered patterns a great deal, sometimes but not always in connection with ethnic identification and allied social or family norms and expectations. Reflecting the patterns described in large-scale studies (Berthoud, 2001b; Jayaweera, 2007), most young mothers prioritised staying at home, either full- or part-time, while their children were young; young Muslim women were least likely to be employed outside the home, while Charlene's determination to achieve financial independence illustrates a wider picture in relation to motherhood and employment among African-Caribbean women (Berthoud, 2001b; Dale et al., 2005). The personal circumstances are diverse, but the common thread is the sense of renegotiating relationships with partners, family members and social networks, as young women experience pregnancy, childbirth and parenthood. Shakira, for example, was not the only young Muslim to live separately from the extended family, while trying to retain contact: two other young Muslim women in the study described significant tensions in family relationships, and one had experienced sustained conflict and eventual marital separation. Age is only mentioned as an issue in these family contexts by a small minority in the overall study, who had experienced critical comments from family members about their parenting capacity.

In contrast, in more public settings, age—the sense of being seen and sometimes addressed or described explicitly as 'too young' for parenthood—consistently emerges as the overwhelming factor in young mothers' accounts of being stigmatised and treated differently from other mothers. The most frequent examples given were in hospital settings, similar to the experience described by Lorna, whereas community-based health services were commonly described as non-judgmental and supportive. There were also examples similar to Charlene's, of critical looks or comments on the street. While these were not prominent issues for Shakira, they were mentioned by some other young Muslim mothers in the sample. In that sense, with reference to contexts such as health care and a 'public' parental identity, we did find age to be the 'master category through which normative notions of mothering are constituted … mediating differences of sexuality, ethnicity and disability' (Thomson et al., op. cit.).

With the study as a whole, references to racism and ethnic identification occurred, but were much less prominent than discussions of age or gender. The key examples, in relation to racism, concerned three areas: social housing, hospital care and secondary school. References to housing options commonly showed the impact of years of white dominance, so that for a young, minority ethnic mother or couple, the offer of social housing could represent isolation and vulnerability to hostile or stigmatising reactions from neighbours. With reference to hospital doctors and midwives, those young mothers who had felt looked down upon or ignored sometimes saw this as a combination of racism and reactions to their youth; however, youth was the factor commented on consistently. In terms of secondary schools, responses were mixed: there was a strong contrast between young women like Lorna, with her experience of racist attitudes, and Shakira, who had experienced support and recognition. The low numbers of Muslim young women in our study sample make it impossible to make claims about whether or not young Muslim women experienced racist attitudes at school as commonly as young women from other ethnic backgrounds.

To conclude, then, these personal accounts underline the need to acknowledge the variable ways in which ethnic identification may inter-relate with class, gender and age, within experiences of teenage parenthood. This adds further weight to the general argument that 'teenage parents' should not be described as a homogenous group: a major flaw in recent and current UK social policy. Our study has not shown evidence of the 'racialisation' of young mothers' identities, either alongside or within class-based public 'chav mum' discourses. While there is evidence from other sources of racialising processes in relation to social policy and welfare provision, (for example Cochrane et al., 2001), those are not the dominant features in the young mothers' accounts we have discussed here. At the level of teenage pregnancy policy initiatives, and of representations of these in the media, 'race' is also an occasional reference point—not a routine one. But to date, young minority ethnic parents—fathers as well as mothers—have only been marginally and intermittently visible, either in research or in public policy. Through broader processes of consultation, partnership with youth networks and prioritisation of research resources, the way needs to be opened for their own, active contributions to further explorations of the themes raised here.

References

Alcock, C., Payne, S. and Sullivan, M., (2000) *Introducing Social Policy,* Edinburgh, Pearson Education.

Alexander, C., (2002) Beyond Black: Rethinking the Colour/Culture Divide, *Ethnic and Racial Studies,* 25(4):552-571.

Alexander, C., (2004) Imagining the Asian gang: ethnicity, masculinity and youth after 'the riots', *Critical Social Policy,* 24(4), 526-549.

Arai, L., (2003) Low Expectations, sexual attitudes and knowledge: Explaining teenage pregnancy and fertility in English communities: Insights from qualitative research. *Sociological Review,* 51(2): 199-217.

Basit, T. N., (2002) 'I'd hate to be just a housewife': career aspirations of British Muslim Girls. *British Journal of Guidance and Counselling,* 24: 227-242.

Berrington, A, Diamond, I., Ingham, R. and Stevenson, J. with Borgoni, R., Cobos Hernandez, I. and Smith, P.W.F., (2005) *Consequences of Teenage Parenthood: Pathways which minimise the long-term negative impacts of teenage childbearing; final report.* Southampton, University of Southampton.

Berthoud, R., (2001a) Teenage births to ethnic minority women. *Population Trends,* 104, Summer 2001.

Berthoud, R., (2001b) Family Formation in multi-cultural Britain: three patterns of diversity. Institute for Social and Economic Research, University of Essex. www.iser.essex.ac.uk/publications/working-papers/iser/2000-34.pdf (last accessed 31.3.09).

Berthoud, R., Ermisch, J., Francesconi, M., Liao, T., Pevalin, D., Robson, K., (2004) Long-term Consequences of Teenage births for Parents and their Children. Teenage

Pregnancy Unit, March 2004.www.everychildmatters.gov.uk/resources-and-practice/ RS00034/ (last accessed 27.3.09).

Brah, A. and Phoenix, A., (2004) Ain't I a Woman? Revisiting Intersectionality, *Journal of International Women's Studies,* 5(3): 75-86.

Cochrane, A., Clarke, J. and Gewirtz, S., (2001) *Comparing welfare states,* London, Sage.

Colen, G. C., Geronimus, A. T. and Phipps, M. G., (2006) Getting a piece of the pie? The economic boom of the 1990s and declining teen birth rates in the United States, *Social Science and Medicine* 63: 1531-1545.

Cooke, J. M., and Owen, J., (2007) A place of my own? Teenage parents' experience of housing and housing-related support', *Children and Society,* 21: 56-68.

Dale, A., Lindley, J. and Dex, S., (2005) *A life-course perspective on ethnic differences in women's economic activity in Britain,* CCSR Working Paper 2005-08, Centre for Census and Survey Research, University of Manchester.

Department of Health, (2002) *Diverse Communities: Identity and Teenage Pregnancy,* London, Department of Health.

Fisher, P. and Owen, J., (2008) Empowering interventions in health and social care: recognition through 'ecologies of practice', *Social Science and Medicine,* 67(12): 2063-2071.

Geronimus, A. T., (2003) Damned if you do: culture, identity, privilege, and teenage childbearing in the United States, *Social Science and Medicine,* 57: 881—893.

Higginbottom, G., Mathers, N., Marsh, P., Kirkham, M., Owen, J. and Serrant-Green, L., (2006) Young people of minority ethnic origin in England and early parenthood: views from young parents and service providers, *Social Science and Medicine,* 63: 858-870.

Hotz, V. J., McElroy, S. W. and Sanders, S. G., (1996) The costs and consequences of teenage childbearing for mothers, *Chicago Policy Review* Fall, 64: 55-94.

Jayaweera, H., Hockley, C., Redshaw, M. and Quigley, M., (2007) *Demographic and socio-economic characteristics of ethnic minority mothers in England: Millenium Cohort Study first survey,* University of Oxford.

Jenkins, R., (1997). *Rethinking Ethnicity: Arguments and Explorations,* London, Sage.

Lipsky, M., (1980) *Street-level Bureaucracy: Dilemmas of the Individual in Public Services,* New York, Russell Sage Foundation.

Low, N., (2002) *Briefing paper on the sexual health of young people from Black and minority ethnic groups,* London, Teenage Pregnancy Unit.

Majumdar, A., (2007) Researching South Asian Women's Experiences of Marriage: Resisting Stereotypes, *Feminism and Psychology,*17: 316-322.

Mason, D., (2000). *Race and Ethnicity in Modern Britain,* Oxford: Oxford University Press.

McDermott, E. and Graham, H., (2005) Resilient young mothering: social inequalities, late modernity and the 'problem' of 'teenage' motherhood, *Journal of Youth Studies,* 8(1): 59-79.

Mitchell, W. and Green, E., (2006) 'I don't know what I'd do without our Mam' motherhood, identity and support networks, *The Sociological Review* 50(1): 2-22.

Owen, J., Higginbottom, G., Mathers, N., Kirkham, M. and Marsh, P., (2008) Ethnicity, Policy and Teenage Parenthood: findings from a qualitative study, *Social Policy and Society,* 7 (3).

Phoenix, A., (1991). *Young Mothers?* Cambridge, Polity Press.

Ritchie, J. and Spencer, L., (1994). Qualitative data analysis for applied policy research, in A. Bryman and R. G. Burgess (eds.), *Analyzing Qualitative Data*, London, Routledge.

Reynolds, T., (2006) Caribbean *Mothers: Identity and experience in the UK*, London: the Tufnell Press.

Robson, K. and Berthoud, R., (2003). *Early Motherhood and Disadvantage: A Comparison Between Ethnic Groups*, ISER working paper 2003-29, Colchester: Institute for Social and Economic Research, University of Essex.

Teenage Pregnancy Unit, (2007) *Next Steps*, London, Department for Children, Schools and Families.

Thomson, R., Bell, R., Holland, J., Henderson, S., McGrellis, S. and Sharpe, S., (2002) Critical Moments: Choice, Chance and Opportunity in Young People's Narratives of Transition, *Sociology* 36(2): 335-354.

Thomson, R. (2008) *The Making of Modern Motherhood: Memories, Representations, Practices: Full Research Report ESRC End of Award Report, RES-148-25-0057*, Swindon: ESRC.

Tyler, I., (2008) 'Chav mum chav scum': class disgust in contemporary Britain. *Feminist Media Studies*, 8(1): 17-34).

Chapter 9

Conclusion: Hazard warning

Rosalind Edwards, Simon Duncan and Claire Alexander

Policy formulation and popular depictions have it that teenage parenthood is a personal hazard that young people need to avoid, or else ruin their own lives and those of their children. These representations also demonise young motherhood and fatherhood as a hazard for society as a whole, comprising both a symptom and a cause of current and future social and moral breakdown. Yet the contributions to this book challenge this way of thinking about young parenthood, as personal and social hazards, and present quite a different story of teenage mothers' and fathers' experiences. Readers of this collection will note several recurring motifs across the contributions. Notably, it seems that teenage pregnancy is not necessarily the result of ignorance about contraception and sexual health, or of low expectations on the part of young people about the choices and opportunities available to them. And it seems that teenage parenthood is not necessarily a disaster for young women's and men's outcomes and life chances, and indeed can sometimes improve them.

In chapter two, Miriam David and Pam Alldred survey teenage pregnancy and PSHE in schools. They discuss the disjuncture between the assumptions behind education, employment and training initiatives and the value that young mothers place on parenting and fulfilling their responsibilities, including through future economic provisioning of their family. Indeed, the in-depth considerations of the everyday worlds of young parents in the chapters of this book reveal a number of complex and encouraging processes at work. In chapter three, for example, Jan Macvarish and Jenny Billings discuss how the teenage mothers in their study made moral and thoughtful decisions about contraception, proceeding with their pregnancy, and engagement with health and welfare services. Rather than suffering 'broken' family circumstances, they were often embedded in networks of support, and were optimistic that parenthood would shift them onto a positive life trajectory. This is followed by Denise Hawkes' overview of circumstances and outcomes in chapter four. Hawkes shows that it is not young birth in itself that is the source of problems for teenage mothers and their children, but disadvantaged life circumstances prior to and continuing after the birth of their child. In chapters five and six, Eleanor Formby and colleagues, and Anne McNulty, each explore three generations of young mothers, with Formby and colleagues looking at young parents in different age cohorts and McNulty focusing on young mothers down the generations in particular families. Both of these chapters point to the importance of social and temporal context and norms in understandings and experiences, illustrating the shift from normalcy towards negative conceptualisation of young parenthood that has occurred over recent decades. Formby and colleagues focus on the positive desire to be a good parent across the generational cohorts, and the importance of support from family and community. McNulty challenges ideas about intergenerational transmission of low aspirations, and shows how each generation of young mothers in a family wanted their daughters to achieve in education and employment, as did the daughters themselves, alongside the centrality of motherhood in all their lives. Our own research findings, in chapter seven, are that teenage parents saw themselves unexceptionally as 'just a mother or a father' like any other, and were motivated to achieve well in education and employment so as to provide a stable future for their children, while at the same time they lived in communities where family and parenting was placed centrally as a form of local inclusion and social participation. Our research points to the role of ethnicity as well as class in shaping expectations around motherhood, and this is developed more strongly in the next chapter. Young minority ethnic mothers' transition to motherhood is given in-depth attention by Jenny Owen and colleagues in chapter eight, showing the complexity of their understandings and experiences. They reveal the strengths that these young mothers draw on to deal with double-faceted prejudice—based on age and race/ethnicity—and their determination to make something of their own and their children's lives. Overall then, the chapters warn against conceptions of teenage parenthood as a hazard rather than warning against the hazards of young motherhood and fatherhood.

It is easy enough then, to answer a question about why some young people become a teenage mother or father. In contrast to the ignorance, fecklessness and hazardous consequences reiterated in policy and media, it is clear that young parenthood can make sense and be valued within particular class and ethnic local cultural contexts and their accompanying social constitutions of opportunity and constraint, and can even provide an impetus for teenage mothers and fathers to strive to provide a better life for their children.

But there are other sorts of questions associated with teenage parenthood in Britain that are not so easy to answer. These turn the telescope around to gaze on those who usually judge and pronounce remedial sentence on young people who become mothers and fathers—policy shapers and makers. Another recurring issue that readers of this collection will have noticed, astutely, is that the British social policy context seems to be unaffected by the messages that teenage parenthood is not an inevitable hazard to well-being for young women and men, or for society as a whole. In this final chapter we consider why this yawning gap between research evidence and policy responses exists. Why is it that New Labour policy makers are fixated on teenage pregnancy as a personal and collective disaster in the first place, and perceive teenage parents as people who both have problems and are problems? And following on that, why is it that they ignore research evidence to the contrary? And then why do they continue to pursue remedies that address teenage parenthood as an individual and social hazard in need of eradication?

Why the fixation on teenage parenthood?

Teenage mothers and fathers have a great deal of emphasis placed on them as symbolic of the state of society. This is accompanied by a focus on reduction targets that serve as a totemic marker of effective policymaking. The 'problem' of young parenthood is subject to the same series of factors that give impetus to other sorts of situations undergoing the shift from being—in C. Wright Mills' famous formulation—a 'personal trouble' to a 'public issue'. As Mills pointed out (1959), not all aspects of people's behaviour or circumstances are considered issues that create social anxieties, and demand policy intervention or regulation. Social concerns do not emerge on their own—they do not thrust themselves to public attention because of troubling qualities that are inherent in and of themselves. Nonetheless, it is in the constitution of an issue as a public rather than private matter that it should appear to be 'naturally' or 'obviously' the source of negative consequences for society. Understanding of the condition is subject to a dominant orthodoxy and there is a consensus about the penalties for society should action not be taken. This process can—as seems to be happening for teenage parenting—ignore much of the evidence about the phenomenon or situation that is problematised in this way. How does this happen?

There is a range of factors that mean that people feel that 'something must be done' about a condition, and then turn to social policy as a means to effect a solution. First, and crucially, there must be widespread knowledge about the situation, not only through research but also through media publicity. Second, the meaning of the situation needs to shift away from being thought of as infrequent, personal, socially harmless or unremarkable, and to become a cause for public concern. Third, the people who are suffering from and/or creating the anxiety are usually of a social standing that means either they have the power to put their own concerns on the public agenda, and/or they are easily typified as falling into a deserving group in need of social justice, or (importantly for our concerns) a defective group threatening social order. Fourth, the situation is seen as impairing the functioning of social and economic systems, or even a form of challenge to social order and stability. In these ways knowledge, meaning and social positioning combine to produce a situation whereby politicians and the public are receptive to the condition being seen as a difficulty that society needs to deal with—or bear the consequences. Finally, and importantly, policymakers need to have an idea of how to solve the supposed problem, and to regard implementing this solution as feasible. They need to feel that they understand the causes of the situation, and can and want to make the required resources available for the solution. (See Groenemeyer 2007; Spector and Kitsuse 2000, for discussions of the emergence and characteristics of social problems.)

We consider these various drivers in the understanding of what constitutes a social problem in relation to the particular issue of teenage parents below (see also chapters three and four on the construction of the problem). Before we do so however, we point to a more specific undergirding of the construction of young motherhood and fatherhood as an individual and social hazard, and New Labour's fixation with this situation—the social construction of childhood in contemporary society and its moral overtones. A key theme of the construction of childhood is its separateness from adult responsibilities and activities (Hockey and James 1993; Jenks 1996; James et al. 1998; Moss et al. 2000), underpinned by idealisations of their naturalness, vulnerability, immaturity and in particular innocence: '[The child's] purity is that of ignorance. The innocent do not sin because they do not know how to' (Archard 1993: 37). A good example is the characterisation of children as 'a sacred trust' in a report by the 'Good Childhood Inquiry', initiated by a major children's charity (Layard and Dunn 2009: 12). Childhood also involves dependency—a categorical state that has been extended with the raising of the school leaving age, and apparent in New Labour's extension of the category of 'problem' teenage parent from under-sixteens to under-eighteens. Further, teenagers sit uneasily on the boundary between childhood and adulthood, between innocence and (original) sin, especially for young women. David and Alldred's description of the pregnant teenage body in school in chapter two illustrates this disjuncture. Referring to a recent case of under-sixteen parenthood given media prominence (discussed in chapter one), the current Leader of the Opposition regretted that: '... these kids have lost the innocence, the fun, the spontaneity that childhood is all about ... When girls and boys become parents before their time it reveals problems deep in society' (Cameron 2009, unpaginated). In obviously having sex, impregnating and becoming pregnant, and in taking on the 'adult' responsibilities of parenthood before they have shaken the immaturity of childhood from their shoes, young mothers and fathers destabilise conceptions of the social and generational order that see a fundamental, essential boundary between the states of being of childhood and adulthood.

This destabilisation is so significant because children are also idealised as the ultimate source of the meaning of life (Beck and Beck-Gernsheim 1995; Walkover 1992), and images of childhood and the rearing of children are linked to the economic and moral destiny of the nation. Modernity strives to control the future through children in the context of a declining belief in the ability of other mechanisms to determine the nation's trajectory, notably a lack of faith in the possibilities of economic control (Prout 2000) (though rational economistic assumptions persist as we discuss below). Children are regarded as the nation's future and if they are deficient in some way then the prospect is grim. As the Good Childhood Enquiry report has it, 'Unless we care properly for our children, we shall never build a better world' (Layard and Dunn 2009: 12). Teenage parents thus present a double jeopardy for the future of the nation. They are (almost) children who have disrupted the regulation represented by the boundaries of adulthood and childhood, embodying the breakdown of social order and the nation's moral turpitude. Further, on top of this, young parents are producing children who they cannot possibly care for adequately and rear to be the responsible citizens of the future since they themselves fall outside of the boundary of mature, self-regulating rational behaviour (another issue we return to below). Hence the popular characterisation of teenage mothers and fathers as 'children having children' (e.g. Daguerre and Nativel 2006). Indeed, as we discuss in chapter one, policymakers often pose Britain as 'lagging behind' other European countries in reducing the number of teenage conceptions and young mothers, and making 'social progress' in this respect. Young parenting is not part—and may even be an antithesis—of New Labour's modernisation agenda for a high-skilled, fast-adapting globalised post-industrial nation (Arai

2009; Carabine 2007). From this perspective, the state has a responsibility to intervene to rescue society.

The threat from which society needs rescuing, though, is understood implicitly to come from a particular group of young people rather than teenagers in general—working-class young women whose supposedly out-of-control sexuality has historically concerned the ruling classes as having a dangerous potential for social disorder and dilution of national moral and physical vigour (Finch 1993). Stereotypes of such young women as poor and ignorant, dysfunctional and immoral, engaging in casual sex and churning out babies who they cannot care for adequately and do not care about in order to gain access to welfare benefits and council housing, often underlie concerns about teenage pregnancy and parenting.

The identification of teenage parents as hazardous to the collective future is bolstered by wider concerns about parenting in general. Parents are seen as fostering and transmitting crucial values and behaviour for their children that determine the public good, with advice and guidance remedying 'poor' parenting, through imposition if necessary, for society's sake (Edwards and Gilles 2004). New Labour's fixation on young motherhood and fatherhood is thus driven by an interest in the fate of the nation. And guiding the nation towards positive destinies, and avoiding negative fates, is what politicians think they should be doing.

The associations between adult-child boundaries and social order, and between children and the nation's future, provides fertile soil in which anxieties about teenage parenting can grow—despite the fact that in reality teenage parenthood is only a minor numerical and consequential problem if it is any sort of social problem at all. These associations around social order and national future are an implicit, taken-for-granted or even sub-conscious starting point for the political and policy agenda around teenage parenting, and for the sense of moral panic that infuses media scare stories about young mothers and fathers. Yet commentators often point to the media, especially tabloid newspapers, as the major reason why policy makers regard teenage pregnancy as a personal and collective disaster. A focus on moral panic discourses emphasises the sway that certain sectors of the media and right wing commentators have on policymaking (see for example Arai 2009). Unusual, extreme stories are often held up as indicative of a moral decline that policy needs to deal with. In chapter one, for example, we note the recent example (spring 2009) of the furore over a thirteen year-old boy fathering a child with a fifteen year-old girl. This resonates with a case given equal media prominence around a decade previously (1999) concerning a fourteen year-old boy and twelve year-old girl (though involving a more traditional gendered age difference), which bolstered the Child Support Agency's strategy of ensuring young fathers took financial responsibility (SEU 1999: 11.2). The media presentation of the 2009 upward 'blip' in teenage pregnancy, in an otherwise consistent downward trend, as evidence of 'soaring' rates, also noted in chapter one, provides another example.

It is not these extreme stories though that 'cause' policymakers to develop policies to address teenage parenthood (Duncan 2007). Indeed, while the media informs public understanding and the policy agenda, it is equally the case that governments and the political agenda influence the media (Franklin 1999). Further, in addition to the 'knowledge' about the social and moral hazard of teenage parents disseminated through the popular media, academic research studies also provide policymakers with information about the causes and consequences of young parenthood, and thus with policy direction for where and how to intervene, regulate and prevent the undesirable. The only puzzle is that research evidence does not necessarily reveal a picture of individual and social hazard.

Why is the research evidence ignored in policy-making?

The mounting, recurrent research evidence in this book and elsewhere demonstrates that young parenthood can make sense and be positive, or at any rate is not an inevitable catastrophe for either society or for the young parents and their children. Why does this reality make barely a dent on the carapace of constructions of teenage parenthood as the alarming fate promulgated in reports by the government's Teenage Pregnancy Unit, Social Exclusion Unit, Department for Children, Schools and Families, and so on? So powerful are popular conceptions of ignorance or fecklessness, and the official orthodoxy about individual and social hazard, that virtually no public agencies or grass roots organisations lobby to present an alternative understanding on behalf of young parents and support their interests. Indeed, the dominance of particular discourses around teenage parenting is often identified as an explanation for why the more positive outcomes for teenage mothers and fathers are ignored or discounted, or their experiences are reinterpreted in line with the policy orthodoxy about individual and social hazard.

We have already noted the idea that certain sections of the media promulgate a sensationalist discursive image of young mothers and fathers in discussing why current social policy has a fixation with teenage parents. The proclivity of policy makers to favour quantitative over qualitative evidence, as providing rigorous and superior foundations for social policy development, is another consideration in commentators' explanations for why policymakers seem to overlook contrary evidence to the prevailing construction of teenage parenthood as an individual and social hazard. Government pays attention to large numbers. But statistics, it is argued, provide a misleading picture because they cannot capture why becoming a young parent might be a sensible course of action and affirming experience, while the qualitative data that demonstrates this possibility is left aside as unreliable (Wilson and Huntington 2005). But is this unequivocally the case? The Teenage Pregnancy Unit review and strategy documents do indeed privilege statistics. But equally uncomfortable results from quantitative studies that challenge the orthodox position on teenage parenthood as hazardous, such as the analysis by Hawkes in chapter two of this volume, are left aside.

The way that New Labour's social exclusion policy paradigm closes down on any other understanding of social inclusion—except for their own interpretation of social participation and belonging as achieved through paid work and formal (occupational and educational) social mobility—forms yet another explanation put forward for the negative evaluation of teenage parenthood that drives social policy (Graham and McDermott 2005). New Labour's pronouncements about welfare dependency being the characteristic trait and root of social exclusion are a fundamental part of policy understanding of the causes and consequences of teenage parenthood, and teenage pregnancy and parenting has become firmly associated with social exclusion in the policy world (Arai 2009; Levitas 1998; Williams 2004). Becoming a mother or father, and parenting as a valued family and community activity, is not regarded as social inclusion in this paradigm. Bringing up children and other caring activities do not feature as socially useful, and it is no coincidence that these are activities that are predominantly carried out by women. Rather it is employment, the 'breadwinning' activity associated with men, that is posed as securing independence and entry to mainstream society and its values, in contrast to dependency and the perpetuation of dysfunctional norms associated with social exclusion. Yet even in terms of this limited and gendered political and policy model of social inclusion, it is clear from the research in this volume (and see also Hoise 2007) that becoming a mother or father can provide some young people with the impetus to achieve educationally and in employment. This evidence of young parents' social inclusion in the dominant political terms, however, has not registered on the policymaking radar.

Media panics, some of the quantitative social science, and New Labour social exclusion explanations all resonate with aspects of New Labour's teenage parenting strategy. But we would argue that there are also deeper assumptions about the foundations of human action and the way the social world works that also play their part in why policy understanding of personal and social hazard holds sway and mounting evidence to the contrary is ignored.

Discursive constructions of young mothers and fathers as feckless and failing are underpinned and given purchase in New Labour policy through neo-liberal ideas about individual choice and rationality. As we have argued in relation to a range of family policy issues (lone motherhood: Duncan and Edwards 1999; cohabitation: Barlow et al. 2005), this outlook on social life understands choice as driven by the rational economic impetus to maximise personal benefit. Policy makers assume that the foundation of people's behaviour is individualistic cost-benefit decision-making. The strength of New Labour belief in the efficacy of this model is demonstrated in the Secretary of State for Work and Pension's commissioning of an economics professor to review welfare reforms. The Gregg Review (2008) recommended the extension of conditionality (the principle that entitlement to benefits should be dependent on satisfying certain conditions) so that virtually no-one can claim non-employment-based benefits without actively pursuing the rationally approved choice of demonstrating that they are attempting to overcome the 'barriers' that prevent them from taking up paid work. In line with economic rationality, the plan is that those who do not will be severely sanctioned through benefit cuts. Having a child is thus reduced to a 'barrier' to taking up paid work in this formulation, and while perhaps those with established careers might be allowed some 'time out' to have a child, becoming a young parent just seems totally irrational in this view. Such ideas are divorced from the social circumstances that structure freedom and choice (Brannen and Nielson 2005). They are also some distance away from the everyday worlds of young mothers and fathers explored in this volume, where becoming a parent can be a rational choice in the social context of family, community and locality, and hands-on parenting regarded morally as more valuable than employment.

Indeed, ideas about what is 'rational' are integrally linked to what is held to be socially acceptable, which in turn is regarded as a universal 'common sense' applicable in all contexts, rather than being rooted in the specific perspectives of a particular classed and gendered group of people who have the ability to judge others and place them as outside of rationality. Thus policy makers' reliance on economic rationality criteria to understand human behaviour and shape policy then leads to morally dysfunctional assessments of actions that are motivated by alternative foundations. Economic rationality is not only understood as a motivation by policy shapers and makers, but becomes understood as a legitimate motivation. Economic rationality thus takes on a moral authority. If an action cannot be understood as economically rational, then it is not morally defensible—albeit it is discussed politically in terms of the 'hazard' language of risk and harm rather then explicitly in terms of values.

In the case of teenage mothers and fathers, they are envisaged as ignorant, immoral or both because they have deviated from the cost-benefit calculative, future-oriented planned pathway of life. The very fact that they have impregnated or become pregnant is proof that young people are not acting rationally in their own best interests. In other words, 'The sin that modern teen mothers commit is not the sin of desire, but the sin of not *planning and rationally choosing* their future' (SmithBattle 2000: 30, original emphasis). A social and emotional gap, then, exists between the understandings, experiences and actions of young mothers and fathers, and those of the policy makers who formulate the policies that attempt to channel their lives and decisions. On the latter side, are those who, personally and professionally, have invested in and prioritised education, training and career development over parenthood as their planned route into autonomous adulthood (Duncan 2007). In their gaze are those who, in their terms, have behaved recklessly by, firstly, becoming pregnant, secondly, proceeding to have the child, and thirdly, assumedly depending on public assistance in order to bring the child up.

Thus a monochrome stereotype of teenage parents is embedded in policy thinking that is at odds with the complex reality of young mothers' and fathers' understandings and motivations, and yet is unequivocally accepted as an accurate portrayal. Teenage mothers and fathers are not an homogeneous or unified population who occupy the same social positions and social relations, acting in a similar way for similar reasons. Furthermore, their age may not be the main issue at all. As the contributions to this collection and other studies have revealed, it is often being a member of a particular class and ethnic group, located in a particular neighbourhood, that provides the substantive context for certain actions and their meaning. Issues of social location articulate with each other in complex ways, however. A cohabiting white teenage mother living on a peripheral housing estate in a northern city and a young married Asian mother in owner-occupied housing in the same city, for example, will have quite different understandings and experiences, and yet as chapter five indicates, they can still share some similarities of outlook and aspiration. Debates about teenage parents though tend implicitly to assume white working-classness. In contrast, young black mothers, for example, may be subsumed into broader assumptions and arguments about pathological black family structures and the prevalence of single mother households (chapter six and also Reynolds 2002, 2005), while young married Asian mothers can be encompassed within preconceptions about arranged marriage and patriarchal control (Majumdar 2007). For black and minority ethnic young mothers then, one unilluminating and negative categorical stereotype is often replaced with others.

Research that challenges the 'hazard consensus' that we have described, such as that reported in this book, may not even be acknowledged by policy makers (Brannen 1986; Stone et al. 2001). The conclusions of all the contributions to this book—that current policy is misconceived, and that policy attention should be focused on another aspect of the issue—do not seem to have registered with those who develop and implement policy. This lack of attention can be understood as proceeding through the social role of 'epistemic communities' in recognising—or not recognising —research as relevant (see discussion in Cleaver and Franks 2008). The term epistemic community refers to a network of professionals or policymakers with a shared set of normative, analytical and causal beliefs, with an agreed and shared knowledge base and a common set of interests. This collective framing of the terms of understanding is often self-reinforcing. Parameters of preferred policy models and narratives of cause and effect are set, to the exclusion of other ideas and information, even if those other data are more representative of everyday reality. The impetus is to retain these dominant and agreed conceptions in developing (further) policies, protecting them not only from critical scrutiny but from recognition of the existence of challenging alternative scenarios of understanding and intervention. Researchers working outside of these favoured models, with messages that are thus at odds with current policy directions, are unlikely to be heard and considered relevant. Rather, others who speak in the 'right' epistemic language will stand out from amongst the broad range of 'stakeholders' that government heeds in formulating policy goals and initiatives.

The chosen paradigm of the epistemic community that makes and shapes social policy, as we have elaborated, is economic rationality. Peter Taylor-Gooby (2008) has argued New Labour's embrace of the market as part of its 'Third Way' welfare policy modernisation agenda is supported by 'new managerialist' ideas. New managerialism is characterised by practices such as targets, performance indicators and audits. Setting targets and putting auditing mechanisms in place are regarded as the way to get a grip on situations identified as socially hazardous, and ensure they are addressed in the approved way. Great significance and confidence are placed in cost-effectiveness and quantifiable outcomes as part of welfare reform and on strategies that emphasis the logic of individual rational choice. New managerialist ideas resonate strongly with the economic rationality approach we have identified as infusing policy and practice on teenage parenting. Further, and importantly for our consideration of policy constructions and responses to teenage parenting, Taylor-Gooby poses the new managerialism of modernist welfare reform as a response to family and other changes in contemporary society that destabilise previously taken-for-granted social categories and hierarchies. In our view, one such change is the challenge to the social construction of adult-child boundaries represented by young motherhood and fatherhood, resulting in welfare reform that is infused with fears for the moral destiny of the nation—all of which is invested in the government fixation with teenage pregnancy, as we discussed above.

Conclusion: Avoiding Hazards

Rather than teenage mothers and fathers creating troubles for society, it seems that policy responses and service provision cause hazards for them. Given the reasons that we have rehearsed above on why policymakers ignore evidence from research that challenges the orthodox view of ignorant and reckless young parents, then policies aimed at this social group tend to be misdirected in their aims, inappropriate in their implementation, and unhelpful in their outcomes. Some of the recurrent examples in the chapter contributions to this collection are the way that public housing allocation policies can place teenage mothers in accommodation in areas that are far away from the support of their family and friends, and the deficiencies of the schooling and employment experiences and opportunities available to them. The weight of policy expectations and service targets addressing teenage pregnancy and parenting that seek to 're-educate' individual aspirations and sense of contribution to society away from motherhood, and towards employment, compounds this unsupportive context. Indeed, while being a mother or father can make good sense for particular groups of young people in the social circumstances in which they live, while young mothers and fathers can value and experience parenthood positively, and while they can feel motivated to improve their lives on this basis, policies addressing teenage parents assume the very opposite. As we have argued above, policy making is infused with concerns about the moral and social order of the nation and its modernised future, and is based on gendered and classed stereotypes, and on assumptions about individualised rationality that prioritise the economic over care.

On coming to power in 1997, New Labour committed itself to pursue evidence-based policymaking. This was part of its concern with welfare policy modernisation, involving an emphasis on policy making as a skill (Bochel and Duncan 2007). The underlying principle of evidence-based policymaking is that decision-making based on the facts of a situation and latest research findings provides for better policymaking, as opposed to ideological dogma, media furore, prejudice or assumption. As the Cabinet Office has put it:

> [Government] must produce policies that really deal with problems, that are forward-looking and shaped by evidence rather than a response to short-term pressures; that tackle causes not symptoms (Cabinet Office 1999: paragraph 2.2).

Reports by the government's Teenage Pregnancy Unit, Social Exclusion Unit, Department for Children, Schools and Families, and Teenage Pregnancy Strategy Unit, that recurrently paint such a personal and collective hazardous picture of young parenthood for policymaking to address, assert that they are based on evidence. As this book show all too well, claims that policies addressing teenage pregnancy are built on comprehensive evidence ring hollow, and even are misleading.

Merely tinkering with social policies and provisions around teenage parenthood, so that more appropriate support is provided, will probably not be sufficient to remedy this situation and insert more real 'evidence' into policy. This is because of the multitude of unacknowledged assumptions underpinning the fixation on young parents in the first place, and the misattributions informing policies that attempt to 'deal' with teenage mothers and fathers, and prevent young people becoming individual and social hazards. Rather, the evidence from the contributions to this collection point towards the need for policy to start from another place altogether. The mould of the epistemic community of policymaking with respect to young parents needs smashing. Recognition of the value of parenthood in itself, both for the individual mothers and fathers concerned—of whatever age and partnership status, as well as collectively for society as a whole—is an important starting point (for example, Williams 2004). A balance between care, education and employment is a necessity for all parents, rather than the positioning of children as 'barriers' to the uptake of paid work and the imposition of conditionality. A focus on improving and providing good quality education, training and employment opportunities for people who live in declining labour markets, especially for young people, and on regenerating disadvantaged neighbourhoods is another important building block. It is clear that a long timescale will be required in order to generate and embed such a shift in knowledge and perception at a policy level. In the meantime, the contributors to this collection and other researchers into teenage parenthood will continue to build up the alternative, grounded formulations of young motherhood and fatherhood that are needed for such an epistemic shift.

References

Arai, L. (2009) *Teenage Pregnancy: The Making and Unmaking of a Problem*, Bristol: Policy Press.

Archard, D. (1993) *Children, Rights and Childhood*, London: Routledge.

Barlow, A., Duncan, S., James, G. and Park, A. (2005) *Cohabitation, Marriage and the Law: Social Change and Legal Reform in the 21st Century*, Oxford: Hart.

Beck, U. and Beck-Gernsheim, E. (1995) *The Normal Chaos of Love*, Cambridge: Polity Press.

Bochel, H. and Duncan, S. (eds) (2007) *Making Policy in Theory and Practice*, Bristol: Policy Press.

Brannen, J. and Nielson, A. (2005) 'Individualisation, choice and structure: a discussion of current trends in sociological analysis', *Sociological Review* 53: 412-429.

Brannen, P. (1986) 'Research and social policy: political, organizational and cultural constraints', in F. Heller (ed.) *The Use and Abuse of Social Science*, London: Sage.

Cabinet Office (1999) *Modernising Government* White Paper CM4310, London: The Stationery Office.

Cameron, D. (2009) 'I looked in his eyes ... it was so sad', *The Sun*: www.thesun.co.uk/sol/homepage/news/article2237957.ece?, accessed 14.2.09.

Carabine, J. (2007) 'New Labour's Teenage Pregnancy Strategy', *Cultural Studies* 21(6): 952-973.

Cleaver, F. and Franks, T. (2008) 'Distilling or diluting? Negotiating the water research-policy interface', *Water Alternatives* 1(1): 157-176.

Daguerre, D. and Nativel, C. (2006) *When Children Become Parents: Welfare State Responses to Teenage Pregnancy*, Bristol: The Policy Press.

Duncan, S. (2007) 'What's the problem with teenage parents? And what's the problem with policy?', *Critical Social Policy* 27(3): 307-334.

Duncan, S. and Edwards, R. (1999) *Lone Mothers, Paid Work and Gendered Moral Rationalities*, Basingstoke: Macmillan.

Edwards, R. and Gillies, V. (2007) Support in parenting: values and consensus concerning who to turn to, *Journal of Social Policy* 33(4): 627-647.

Finch, L. (1993) *The Classing Gaze: Sexuality, Class and Surveillance*, St. Leonards, Australia: Allen and Unwin.

Franklin, B. (ed.) (1999) *Social Policy, The Media and Misrepresentation*, London: Routledge.

Graham, H. and McDermott, E. (2005) Qualitative research and the evidence base of policy: insights from studies of teenage mothers in the UK, *Journal of Social Policy* 35(1): 21-37.

Gregg Review (2008) *Realising Potential: A Vision for Personalised Conditionality and Support*, London: Department for Work and Pensions.

Groenemeyer, A. (2007) Social problems, concept and perspectives, in G. Ritzer (ed.) *Blackwell Encylopaedia of Sociology*, Wiley-Blackwell.

Hockey, J. and James, A. (1993) *Growing Up and Growing Old: Ageing and Dependency in the Life Course*, London: Sage.

Hosie, A.C.S. (2007) "I hated everything about school": an examination of the relationship between dislike of school, teenage pregnancy and educational disengagement, *Social Policy and Society* 6(3): 333-347.

James, A., Jenks, C. and Prout, A. (1998) *Theorising Childhood*, Cambridge: Polity Press.

Jenks, C. (1996) *Childhood*, London: Routledge.

Layard, R. and Dunn, J. (2009) *A Good Childhood: Searching for Values in a Competitive Age*, London: Penguin Books.

Levitas, R. (1998) *The Inclusive Society? Social Exclusion and New Labour*, London: Macmillan.

Majumdar, A. (2007) Researching South Asian women's experiences of marriage: resisting stereotypes through an exploration of 'space' and 'embodiment, *Feminism and Psychology* 17(3): 316-322.

Mills, C.W. (1959) *The Sociological Imagination*, Oxford: Oxford University Press.

Moss, P., Dillon, J. and Statham, J. (2000) The 'child in need' and 'the rich child' discourses, constructions and practice, *Critical Social Policy* 20(2): 233-254.

Prout, A. (2000) Children's participation: Control and self-realisation in British late modernity, *Children and Society* 14(4): 304-315.

Reynolds, T. (2002) Analysing the Black family, in A. Carling, S. Duncan and R. Edwards (eds) *Analysing Families: Morality and Rationality in Policy and Practice*, London: Routledge.

Reynolds, T. (2005) *Caribbean Mothers: Identity and Experience in the UK*, London: the Tufnell Press.

Social Exclusion Unit (1999) *Teenage Pregnancy*, Cm. 4342, London: HMSO.

Spector, M. and Kitsuse, J.I. (2000) *Constructing Social Problems*, New Brunswick, NJ: Transaction Publishers.

Stone, D. with Maxwell, S. and Keating, M. (2001) *Bridging Research and Policy*, Centre for the Study of Globalisation and Regionalisation Working Paper, University of Warwick.

Taylor-Gooby, P. (2008) *Reframing Social Citizenship*, Oxford: Oxford University Press.

Walkover, B.C. (1992) The family as an overwrought object of desire, in G.C. Rosenwald and R. Ochberg (eds) *Storied Lives: The Cultural Politics of Self-Understanding*, New Haven: Yale University Press.

Williams, F. (2004) *Rethinking Families*, London: Calouste Gulbenkian Foundation.

Wilson, H. and Huntington, A. (2005) Deviant mothers: the construction of teenage motherhood in contemporary discourse, *Journal of Social Policy* 35(1): 59-76.

Notes on Contributors

Pam Alldred is based in the Centre for Youth Work Studies, Brunel University, and teaches youth workers and education practitioners. Since the publication of *Get Real About Sex: The politics and practice of sex education* (Open University Press 2007, with M David) her research has focused on local practitioners' views of the Teenage Pregnancy Strategy; youth work approaches and inter-professional working on sexuality issues; school exclusion and 'pupil behaviour management'; and on LGBT equalities. Pam has contributed to several book collectives which look critically at methodology, psychology and researching childhood. She is also a member of the Feminist Review Collective and Feminist Review Trust

Dr. Claire Alexander is a Reader in Sociology at the London School of Economics. Her research interests are in the area of race, ethnicity, masculinity and youth identities, particularly in relation to ethnography. Her main publications include *The Art of Being Black* (OUP 1996) and *The Asian Gang* (Berg 2000). She is co-editor of *Beyond Difference* (Ethnic and Racial Studies July 2002), and *Making Race Matter: Bodies, Space and Identity* (Palgrave 2005) and editor of *Writing Race: Ethnography and Difference* (Ethnic and Racial Studies, May 2006). She is co-director, with Dr Joya Chatterji, of an AHRC funded research project (2006-2009) on 'The Bengal Diaspora: Bengali Settlers in South Asia and Britain'.

Jenny Billings is Deputy Director and Senior Research Fellow in the Centre for Health Service Studies, University of Kent. She researches and teaches in health and social care, with a special interest in vulnerable groups and mixed methodology. Jenny's special skills lie in managing and co-ordinating methodologically challenging projects that focus on providing evidence for practice. Her research has led to sustainable service developments, particularly in the field of teenage pregnancy. She is increasingly becoming involved with European research and has funding through a number of EU Framework and Interreg Programmes, focusing on teenage pregnancy, families and children and older people. She is also a methods research advisor for the EU Framework Programme.

Miriam E. David, AcSS, FRSA is Professor of Sociology of Education and Associate Director (Higher Education) of the ESRC's Teaching and Learning Research Programme at the Institute of Education University of London. She has a wide research experience on social diversity, gender and inequalities in education, including lifelong learning and higher education, and has published widely in these areas. She is chair of the Council of the Academy of Social Sciences (AcSS), a member of the ESRC's Research Grants Board and the Governing Council of Society for Research in Higher Education (SRHE). She is co-editor (with Philip Davies) of *21ˢᵗ Century Society journal of the Academy of Social Sciences* and an executive editor of *British Journal of Sociology of Education*. Her most recent publications include *Get Real About Sex: the politics* *and practice of sex education* (2007 with Pam Alldred, London: McGraw Hill/Open University Press), *Degrees of Choice: Social Class, Race and Gender in Higher Education* (2005, with Diane Reay and Stephen Ball, Stoke-on-Trent: Trentham Books).

Simon Duncan is Professor of Comparative Social Policy at the University of Bradford. He has research expertise in the 'new family'; motherhood, employment and work-life balance; the geography of family formations; and comparative gender inequality in welfare states. He is currently working on the nature of 'Living Apart Together' and on personal life in Britain and Sweden in the 1950s. Recent publications include *Analysing Families: Morality and Rationality in Policy and Practice* (2004 ed. with A Carling and R Edwards), *Cohabitation, Marriage and the Law: Social Change and Legal Reform in the 21ˢᵗ Century* (2005 with A Barlow, G James, A Park), 'Individualisation versus the geography of new families' (*21st Century Society*, 2006 with D Smith), 'Actualising the 'democratic family'? Swedish policy rhetoric versus family practices' *Social Politics* (2008 with J. Ahlberg and C. Roman) and 'New families? Tradition and change in partnering and relationships' in Park, A. et al. (eds.) *British Social Attitudes: the 24ᵗʰ Report*, London: Sage (2008 with Miranda Phillips).

Rosalind Edwards is Professor in Social Policy and Director of the Families and Social Capital Research Group at London South Bank University. Her main research interests are family lives and family policy, and she is currently working on a qualitative longitudinal archiving study of children's sibling and friend relationships as part of the Timescapes consortium, and a comparative feasibility study exploring qualitative secondary analysis of family and parenting across sources and timeframes. Recent publications include: *Sibling Identity and Relationships: Sisters and Brothers* (with L. Hadfield, H. Lucey and M. Mauthner, Routledge, 2006); and *Assessing Social Capital: Concept, Policy and Practice* (ed. with J. Franklin and J. Holland, Cambridge Scholars Press, 2007). *Researching Families and Communities: Social and Generational Change* (ed., Routledge, 2008). She is founding and co-editor of the *International Journal of Social Research Methodology* (with J. Brannen).

Eleanor Formby, Senior Research Fellow at Sheffield Hallam University, is a sociologist with over ten years experience in qualitative research. She has presented research findings at national and international conferences, and written research reports for different funding bodies, including a variety of local authorities and Primary Care Trusts. Her areas of expertise include sexual health, teenage pregnancy/parenthood, and lesbian, gay and bisexual health and well-being.

Denise Hawkes is a Lecturer in Economic Sociology in the Department of International Business and Economics at the University of Greenwich, and a Research Associate in the Centre of Longitudinal Studies at the Institute of Education, University of London. Her work focuses on the use and application of twin and longitudinal data in understanding the effects of family background and individual characteristics on educational achievement, income, employment and early motherhood. She has published in a wide range of academic journals including the *American Economic Review*, the *Journal of the Royal Statistical Society Series A* and the *Journal of Social Policy*.

Dr Gina Marie Awoko Higginbottom holds a Tier II Canada Research Chair in Ethnicity and Health, and is Associate Professor in the Faculty of Nursing, at the University of Alberta. Formerly she was Principal Research Fellow in the Centre for Health and Social Research at Sheffield Hallam University, England. Prior to this she worked as a Senior Lecturer and Research Fellow at the University of Sheffield for 11 years in the School of Nursing and ScHARR in the Faculty of Medicine following twenty years clinical experience as a nurse, midwife and health visitor in a number of different care settings. Gina is affiliated Associate Professor of Nursing at the Karolinska Institute, Stockholm, Sweden and visiting Professor at Sheffield Hallam University. She is Assistant Editor of Ethnicity and Health journal and co-chair of the IIQM 9th Advances in Qualitative Methods conference. She has worked with many different communities as research partners e.g. African Caribbean, Pakistani, Bangladeshi and Somali communities. Gina is founder and convener of CRESH (*Collaborative Research in Ethnicity Social Care and Health*) a network of researchers, educators, community groups and associations, policy makers and other key stakeholders with an interest in ethnicity

Dr Julia Hirst is a Senior Lecturer in Sociology, Research Leader on 'Sexualities, Health and Youth' and faculty lead on public health at Sheffield Hallam University. She has worked with young people throughout her professional life on issues of sexualities, identities, learning about sex and transitions to adulthood, with numerous publications in this field.

Mavis Kirkham is Emeritus Professor of Midwifery at Sheffield Hallam University and holds honorary professorial positions at the University of Huddersfield and the University of Technology, Sydney. She has worked continuously as a midwife researcher and a clinical midwife for over thirty years.

Dr Jan Macvarish is a researcher and lecturer at the University of Kent. Her interests lie in the sociology of interpersonal relationships, parenting, family life, sex and intimacy. Her doctoral thesis (2007), entitled 'The New Single Woman: Contextualising Individual Choice', explored the construction of contemporary singleness through qualitative interviewing of single, childless women and cultural analysis of the new 'culture of singleness'. Her subsequent work on teenage pregnancy and parenthood has incorporated an engagement with social policy into her broader interest in questions of risk culture, re-moralisation and individualisation. Her involvement in the ESRC seminar series, 'Changing Parenting Culture', has allowed her to contextualise teenage parenthood within a broader understanding of contemporary parenting culture.

Dr Ann McNulty is based in the Sociology area of the School of Geography, Politics and Sociology, Newcastle University, as Research Associate working on an ESRC funded project in sexuality, equality and local governance. Ann worked with young people as a modern languages teacher in the 1980s and then moved into the area of community development, working as Coordinator of Northern Initiative on Women and Eating to 1996, and as Coordinator of Northumberland Young People's Health Project. She job-shared the Newcastle and North Tyneside Teenage Pregnancy Coordinator post while working part-time as a Research Associate at Newcastle University, and since 2006 has been Coordinator of Newcastle Health and Race Equality Forum. Her publications include *Young People, Sexuality and Relationships*, Newcastle University (2002, with Diane Richardson) and *Evaluation of Gateshead Secondary Schools' Sex Education Programme*, Northumbria University Primary Care Development Centre (2004 with Hilary Snowdon).

Professor Nigel Mathers is Chair of General Practice and Unit Director, Academic Unit of Primary Medical Care, University of Sheffield. Nigel has conducted research about the doctor-patient relationship and medically unexplained symptoms (somatisation); educational innovations in multi-disciplinary, practice-based education; substance misuse; postnatal depression; clinical trials in general practice; and transcultural primary care research.

Professor Peter Marsh is Professor of Child and Family Welfare, Department of Sociological Studies, University of Sheffield. Peter's research focuses on policy and practice in child welfare services.

Dr Jenny Owen is a sociologist, and a Senior Lecturer in the Public Health section of the School of Health and Related Research, University of Sheffield. She also is a member of the multidisciplinary Centre for the Study of Childhood and Youth at the University. In addition to research on teenage parenthood, she has recently completed work, with colleagues, on two qualitative studies about family forms and food practices. One examined fathers' perspectives on food and care in the family; the other has analysed the models of family and parenting reflected in recent UK public health interventions about diet.

Lightning Source UK Ltd.
Milton Keynes UK
14 July 2010

156995UK00001B/117/P

9 781872 767086